Book 1

Language Arts

Lesson Guide

Book Staff and Contributors

Kristen Kinney   *Senior Content Specialist*
Alane Gernon-Paulsen   *Content Specialist*
Anna Day   *Senior Instructional Designer*
Miriam Greenwald, Cheryl Howard, Michelle Iwaszuk, Amy Rauen   *Instructional Designers*
Karen Ingebretsen, Jill Tunick   *Text Editors*
Suzanne Montazer   *Creative Director, Print and ePublishing*
Sasha Blanton   *Senior Print Visual Designer*
Carol Leigh   *Print Visual Designer*
Stephanie Williams   *Cover Designer*
Amy Eward   *Senior Manager, Writers*
Susan Raley   *Manager, Editors*
Seth Herz   *Director, Program Management Grades K–8*

Maria Szalay   *Senior Vice President for Product Development*
John Holdren   *Senior Vice President for Content and Curriculum*
David Pelizzari   *Vice President, Content and Curriculum*
Kim Barcas   *Vice President, Creative*
Laura Seuschek   *Vice President, Instructional Design and Evaluation & Research*
Aaron Hall   *Vice President, Program Management*

Lisa Dimaio Iekel   *Production Manager*
John Agnone   *Director of Publications*

About K12 Inc.

K12 Inc. (NYSE: LRN) drives innovation and advances the quality of education by delivering state-of-the-art digital learning platforms and technology to students and school districts around the world. K12 is a company of educators offering its online and blended curriculum to charter schools, public school districts, private schools, and directly to families. More information can be found at K12.com.

978-1-60153-141-4

Printed by LSC Communications, Willard, OH, USA, May 2019.

Contents

Language Skills

Colors, Body Parts, and Poems

Body Parts, Jobs, and Poems

Families, Friends, and Poems

Communities, Friends, and Poems

Colors, Shapes, and Poems

Kitchens, Food, and Poems

Animals, Subjects, and Poems

Music, Reading, and Poems

Travel, Comparison, and Poems

Literature & Comprehension

Good Choices

Get Moving

House and Home

Three Fairy Tales

Dig Deep

Peter Rabbit

Among Animals

Helping Hands

K¹² Language Arts Blue

General Program Overview and Structure

The K¹² Language Arts Blue program lays a strong foundation for beginning readers and writers. A well-balanced Language Arts program provides instruction on getting words off the page (reading) as well as on the page (writing). According to the National Reading Panel, a comprehensive reading program covers phonemic awareness, phonics, fluency, vocabulary, and text comprehension—all of which are covered in the following four programs:

Program	Daily Lesson Time (approximate)	Online/Offline
K¹² Language Arts PhonicsWorks	50 minutes	30 minutes offline/ 20 minutes online
Big Ideas		

- Readers must understand that print carries meaning and there is a connection between letters and sounds.
- Fluent readers blend sounds represented by letters into words.
- Breaking words into syllables helps us read and spell unfamiliar words.
- Good readers practice reading grade-level text with fluency.
- Reading sight words helps young readers read complete sentences and short stories.

Program	Daily Lesson Time (approximate)	Online/Offline
K¹² Language Arts Language Skills	30 minutes	15 minutes offline/ 15 minutes online
Big Ideas		

- Vocabulary words are words we need to know in order to communicate and understand.
- A *speaking vocabulary* includes the words we know and can use when speaking.
- A *reading vocabulary* includes the words we know and can read with understanding.
- A *listening vocabulary* includes the words we know and understand when we hear them.
- A *writing vocabulary* includes the words we know and understand when we write.
- The more we read, the more our vocabulary grows.
- Early learners acquire vocabulary through active exposure (by talking and listening, being read to, and receiving explicit instruction).

Program	Daily Lesson Time (approximate)	Online/Offline
K[12] Language Arts Literature & Comprehension	30 minutes	All offline

Big Ideas

- Comprehension is the reason for reading.
- Comprehension entails having and knowing a purpose for reading.
- Comprehension entails actively thinking about what is being read.
- Comprehension requires the reader to self-monitor understanding.
- Comprehension requires the reader to self-correct errors made while reading by using a wide variety of strategies.
- Comprehension requires an understanding of story structure.
- Comprehension entails asking and answering questions about the text.
- Comprehension strategies can be taught through explicit instruction.
- Connecting new information to previously learned information facilitates comprehension.
- Readers who visualize, or form mental pictures, when they read have better recall of text than those who do not.
- Reading strategies are conscious plans that readers apply and adapt to make sense of text.
- An understanding of physical presentation (headings, subheads, graphics, and other features) facilitates comprehension.
- Comprehension entails an understanding of the organizational patterns of text.
- Comprehension is enhanced when information is presented through more than one learning modality; learning modalities are visual (seeing), auditory (hearing), and kinesthetic (touching).
- Verbalizing their thoughts while modeling a reading strategy allows students to see what occurs in an effective reader's head; it makes visible the normally hidden process of comprehending text.
- Self-questioning improves comprehension and ensures that reading is an interactive process.
- Rereading texts helps students improve memory, listening skills, and comprehension.

Program	Daily Lesson Time (approximate)	Online/Offline
K[12] Language Arts Blue Handwriting	10 minutes	All offline

Big Ideas

- Instruction in posture, pencil grip, and letter formation improves students' handwriting skills.
- Proper modeling of letter formation is imperative for developing handwriting skills.
- Students who have formal instruction in handwriting are more engaged in composition writing.

The PhonicsWorks, Language Skills, Literature & Comprehension, and Handwriting programs are independent courses that work together to give students a complete, well-balanced education in Language Arts. Some programs try to fit these four major components into one large "supercourse" that requires all students to move at the same pace through a very structured and ultimately confusing or limited program. By having students complete PhonicsWorks independently of Literature & Comprehension, K[12] ensures they do not develop and reinforce misconceptions about letter–sound knowledge. Keeping Language Skills separate from Literature & Comprehension allows students to increase their speaking vocabularies and listening vocabularies while developing their comprehension skills, rather than mastering one at the expense of another.

Suggested Order of Lessons

K[12] highly recommends that students complete the Language Arts lessons in the following order:

1. PhonicsWorks

2. Language Skills

3. Literature & Comprehension

4. Handwriting

A key aspect of K[12] courses is the flexibility they offer students. Doing things that work best for them is vital to students' mastery. If students benefit from completing the Handwriting lesson first thing in the morning and closing the day with Literature & Comprehension, that is acceptable.

How to Work Through a Lesson

Types of Activities

The K[12] Language Arts programs contain both offline and online activities as well as assessments.

Offline Activities   Offline activities take place away from the computer and are described in detail in the lesson plans within the Lesson Guide. During offline activities, you will work closely with students. (**Safety note:** When students are working with scissors, please supervise them to make sure they use their scissors safely and stay seated.)

Online Activities   Online activities take place at the computer. At first, you may need to help students learn how to navigate and use the online activities. You may also need to provide support when activities cover new or challenging content. Eventually students will complete online activities with minimal support from you.

Assessments   Students will complete online assessments, called Unit Checkpoints, in the Language Skills program. Because these assessments are all online, the computer will score them for you. You do not need to enter assessment scores in the Online School.

Where to Begin?

There is more than one way to begin a lesson; either way will get you where you need to go.

Beginning Online   If you begin from the online lesson, the lesson screens will walk you through what you need to do, including gathering materials and moving offline if necessary. If the lesson begins with online activities, students will need to come to the computer and complete them. If the lesson begins with offline activities, gather the materials listed and begin the activities described in the lesson plan with students when you're ready.

Beginning Offline   You may choose to begin a lesson by first checking the lesson plan for the day in the Lesson Guide. The table on the first page of the lesson plan will indicate whether the lesson begins with online or offline activities. If the lesson begins with online activities, students will need to move to the computer and complete them. If the lesson begins with offline activities, gather the materials listed and begin the activities described in the lesson plan with students when you're ready.

After you've completed a unit or two in a particular course, you'll be familiar with the pattern of the units and lessons and you'll know exactly where and how to begin.

How to Use This Book

The *K¹² Language Arts Lesson Guide* contains overviews for the Language Skills, Literature & Comprehension, and Handwriting programs and lesson plans for the Language Skills and Literature & Comprehension programs. Lesson plans for the PhonicsWorks program appears in a separate book.

The overviews on the following pages provide information on instructional philosophies, program content, and structure.

Each lesson plan gives you detailed instructions for completing the lesson. The first page of each lesson plan contains some or all of the following elements, depending on the program and lesson. (The sample on this page is from a Literature & Comprehension lesson.)

Program Name
This banner identifies the section of the book. Each program has its own banner color, so you can easily flip to a section if you know the color.

Lesson Title
The title indicates the lesson topic.

Unit Overview
The first lesson of each unit describes the content covered in the unit.

Lesson Overview Table
This table provides an overview of the lesson's activities, their approximate times, and whether they take place offline or online.

Advance Preparation
This section calls out what you need to prepare before beginning the lesson.

Big Ideas
These points are the major organizing ideas in Language Arts students will work toward.

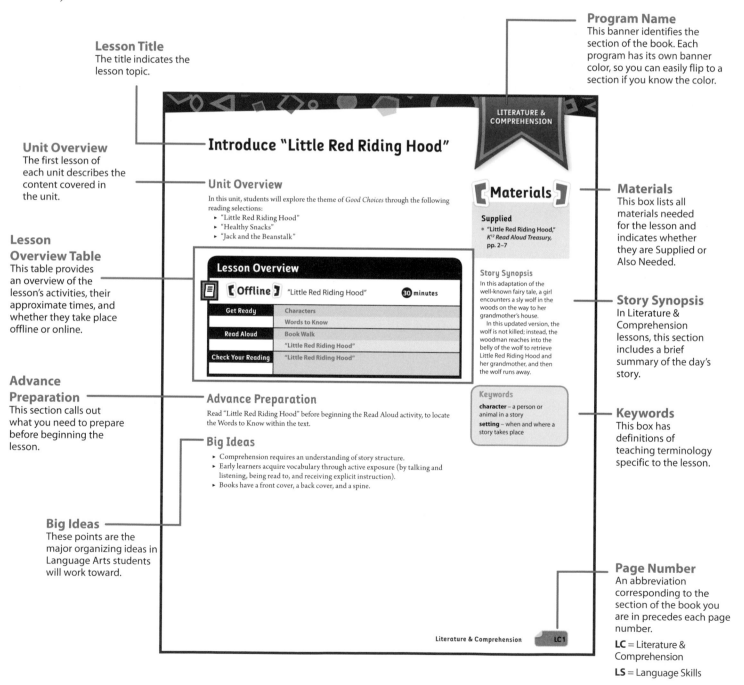

Introduce "Little Red Riding Hood"

LITERATURE & COMPREHENSION

Unit Overview
In this unit, students will explore the theme of *Good Choices* through the following reading selections:
- "Little Red Riding Hood"
- "Healthy Snacks"
- "Jack and the Beanstalk"

Lesson Overview

Offline	"Little Red Riding Hood"	30 minutes
Get Ready	Characters	
	Words to Know	
Read Aloud	Book Walk	
	"Little Red Riding Hood"	
Check Your Reading	"Little Red Riding Hood"	

Advance Preparation
Read "Little Red Riding Hood" before beginning the Read Aloud activity, to locate the Words to Know within the text.

Big Ideas
- Comprehension requires an understanding of story structure.
- Early learners acquire vocabulary through active exposure (by talking and listening, being read to, and receiving explicit instruction).
- Books have a front cover, a back cover, and a spine.

Materials

Supplied
- "Little Red Riding Hood," *K¹² Read Aloud Treasury*, pp. 2–7

Story Synopsis
In this adaptation of the well-known fairy tale, a girl encounters a sly wolf in the woods on the way to her grandmother's house.
In this updated version, the wolf is not killed; instead, the woodman reaches into the belly of the wolf to retrieve Little Red Riding Hood and her grandmother, and then the wolf runs away.

Keywords
character – a person or animal in a story
setting – when and where a story takes place

Materials
This box lists all materials needed for the lesson and indicates whether they are Supplied or Also Needed.

Story Synopsis
In Literature & Comprehension lessons, this section includes a brief summary of the day's story.

Keywords
This box has definitions of teaching terminology specific to the lesson.

Page Number
An abbreviation corresponding to the section of the book you are in precedes each page number.

LC = Literature & Comprehension

LS = Language Skills

Literature & Comprehension — LC 1

My Accomplishments Chart

Research shows that rewarding students for quality work can increase their motivation. To help you reward students, you will receive a My Accomplishments chart and sticker sheet for use throughout the Language Arts program. This chart gives students a tangible record of their progress and accomplishments throughout the Language Skills, Literature & Comprehension, and PhonicsWorks programs. Help students proudly display and share their accomplishments with others by placing the chart somewhere visible, such as on the refrigerator or wall.

Throughout the online lessons, look for the reward icon 🎀, which indicates when and where students should place a sticker on the chart. Encourage students to set goals and watch their stickers accumulate. Praise them to help them understand the connection between their own growing skill set and the My Accomplishments chart. By the end of all programs, students should have filled up the entire chart.

For specific information about how to use the chart in each program, see the My Accomplishments Chart section in the following individual program overviews.

▶

Student Portfolios

As students progress through each program, K[12] recommends keeping a student portfolio as a record of their progress. Students will write in the *K[12] Language Arts Activity Book* and *K[12] All About Me*, so place the Activity Book pages and the entire *K[12] All About Me* in the portfolio (a simple folder, large envelope, or three-ring binder would work) along with handwriting samples. Look back through the portfolio monthly and at the end of the program with students and celebrate their progress and achievements.

K¹² Language Arts PhonicsWorks Program Overview

K¹² provides the PhonicsWorks materials separately from the Language Arts materials, so you will not find PhonicsWorks lesson plans or activity book pages in the *K¹² Language Arts Lesson Guide* or the *K¹² Language Arts Activity Book*. Please refer to the PhonicsWorks Kit for all phonics materials.

K¹² Language Arts Language Skills Program Overview

Program Philosophy

The K¹² Language Arts Language Skills program guides students through vocabulary, early composition work (here, called All About Me), and poetry.

Vocabulary

What Is It?   People have various types of vocabulary. We have *speaking vocabulary* (words we use proficiently when talking with others), *listening vocabulary* (words we understand well when hearing others speak), *reading vocabulary* (words we can decode and comprehend), and *writing vocabulary* (words we can spell and comprehend). Students typically have larger speaking vocabularies than listening, reading, and writing vocabularies. National Reading Panel research shows that students learn most vocabulary indirectly (through daily speaking and listening in the home, listening to stories, reading stories, and so on), but some vocabulary must be learned directly (through instruction on specific words, meanings, and proper uses).

Why We Do It   Vocabulary includes the words we need to know in order to communicate. To write or read something, we must have a strong vocabulary so we can communicate effectively. Students with a strong and varied vocabulary have an easier time comprehending and composing written material. Researchers Margaret McKeown and Isabel Beck concluded that robust vocabulary instruction involving active learning, prior knowledge, and frequent encounters with vocabulary words is more powerful and effective.

The Vocabulary component of the K¹² Language Skills program gives students direct instruction on word meanings through a wide variety of words grouped in conceptually related sets, such as colors or jobs. You will introduce the words in each word set to students offline. They will then spend time online reviewing and practicing the words.

All About Me

What Is It?   The All About Me activities in the K[12] Language Skills program are designed to help students develop basic composition skills, including brainstorming, drafting, writing, revising, and publishing, in a developmentally and age-appropriate manner. Each All About Me activity is offline and most span two lessons. Each activity includes guiding discussion questions to help students develop a habit of talking through ideas to brainstorm about a topic.

You will do most of the basic writing for students, who will then illustrate sentences based on the discussion and written sentences. Some students may benefit from or truly enjoy doing the small amount of required writing on their own. In those cases, K[12] encourages you to simply help them spell the words properly.

Most of students' work involves illustrating a topic in K[12] *All About Me*. If time allows, students should begin their drawing typically on the first day, immediately following the discussion time. Typicaly on the second day, students should spend most of their time completing their illustration and adding supporting details.

Why We Do It   As you do when assigning a written composition, encourage students to review their work and add more details to their picture. Developing this habit helps students get used to revising their writing, which becomes increasingly important in subsequent grades. In the All About Me activities, they share their illustration with others. Whether they show their work to 1 person or 20 people, students should use complete sentences and a wide variety of vocabulary. This simple task lays the groundwork for sharing written compositions and public speaking activities in subsequent grades.

Poetry

What Is It?   The Poetry activities in the K[12] Language Skills program are all offline and use one of three sources for the poems: K[12] *Read Aloud Treasury, The Rooster Crows,* and *Tomie DePaolo's Rhyme Time.* Traditional nursery rhymes from Mother Goose, songs, and classic poems from Dorothy Aldis, Robert Louis Stevenson, and Christina Rosseti round out the Poetry lessons. The Lesson Guide gives you a plan for discussing the poems and their language, rhythm, and rhyme.

Why We Do It   The K[12] Language Skills program includes Poetry for two main reasons. First poetry is a fun and engaging way to expose students to a wider variety of language they may not hear in a traditional literature or phonics program. Second poetry's rhythm and rhyming nature make it easy to memorize and repeat—thereby providing opportunities for public speaking practice.

Overview of Language Skills Lessons

Materials

The following books are supplied for the Language Skills program:

K¹² Language Arts Lesson Guide

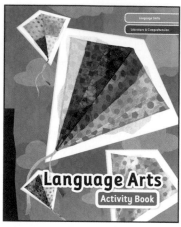

K¹² Language Arts Activity Book

K¹² All About Me

K¹² Read Aloud Treasury

The Rooster Crows and *Tomie DePaolo's Rhyme Time* are also supplied.

(Keep in mind that students will write in and tear pages out of the Activity Book and *K¹² All About Me*; you may want to store loose Activity Book pages in a three-ring binder. Remember to build students' portfolios with completed work from these books.)

You will also need the following general materials to complete the Activity Book pages and optional flash card activities:

▶ 3½ x 5-inch index cards
▶ crayons or colored pencils
▶ scissors (**Safety note:** When students are working with scissors, please supervise them to make sure they use their scissors safely and stay seated.)
▶ glue stick

Lesson Structure

The K[12] Language Skills program consists of 18 ten-day units that follow a set, repeated pattern. In each unit, students rotate through Vocabulary, All About Me, and Poetry lessons. The following chart is an overview of how lessons are organized in each unit.

Day	Offline (15 minutes)	Online (15 minutes)
1	Vocabulary: Introduce Word Set 1 Create Flash Cards (optional)	Skills Update (except first unit) Learn: Introduce Word Set 1
2	All About Me	Practice: Word Set 1
3	Poetry	Practice: Word Set 1
4	Vocabulary: Introduce Word Set 2 Create Flash Cards (optional)	Skills Update (except first unit) Learn: Introduce Word Set 2
5	All About Me	Practice: Word Set 2
6	Poetry	Practice: Word Set 2
7	Vocabulary: Introduce Word Set 3 Create Flash Cards (optional)	Skills Update (except first unit) Learn: Introduce Word Set 3
8	All About Me	Practice: Word Set 3
9	Poetry	Unit Review
10	Unit Checkpoint (Online—30 minutes)	

Lesson Activities

Lesson plans in the Language Skills section of this Lesson Guide include detailed descriptions or instructions for each activity. Language Skills lesson plans include the following elements:

Activity Description

This text describes what will happen in the activity. For offline activities, it provides step-by-step instructions. Look for words in bold, like **Say**, which highlight actions you should take. Answers to questions you ask students are shown in pink.

Program Name

This banner identifies the section of the book.

LANGUAGE SKILLS

 [Online] 🕐 minutes

Students will work online **independently** to complete an activity on Vocabulary words. Help students locate the online activity, and provide support as needed.

Practice ·····································

Community Words

Students will practice the community words *mailbox, neighborhood, street, car, fence, road, sidewalk,* and *sign.*

Offline Alternative

No computer access? At any time, you can print a list of the unit Vocabulary words and their definitions from the online lesson. Use this list to review the words with students offline. In addition, if students made their own flash cards, these can be used for offline review.

Objectives
- Increase oral vocabulary.
- Increase reading vocabulary.
- Increase concept vocabulary.

Offline Alternative

If you will be away from the computer, this offline activity is an alternative for the online activity. (However, K12 recommends completing the online activity whenever possible.)

Objectives

These learning goals indicate what students should be able to do as a result of the lesson.

Language Skills activity types include the following:

- **Vocabulary (Offline)**   You will introduce students to one of three sets of words covered in the unit. In addition, as an optional activity, encourage students who are reading and writing and who would benefit from the use of flash cards to write each vocabulary word on an index card and to write their own definition of that word on the back of the card. Students may study the cards during the course of the unit.
- **All About Me (Offline)**   Students will work with you to complete an All About Me activity designed to engage them in drawing, writing, and oral language.
- **Poetry (Offline)**   Students will work with you to explore a wide variety of poems, rhymes, and songs. Encourage students to repeat the poems, songs, and rhymes often. If they are assigned an Activity Book page, have them practice reciting the poem while coloring the page. Give students opportunities to recite poems from memory while standing erect and enunciating clearly. These small tasks provide a solid foundation for future public speaking activities.
- **Skills Update (Online)**   The first day of each unit (after the first unit) contains a Skills Update. Students will refresh their knowledge of vocabulary words from previous units with this online assessment.
- **Learn (Online)**   Students will become more familiar with one of three sets of words covered in the unit. The activity typically focuses on each word to give students a strong grounding in that word.
- **Practice (Online)**   Students will review and practice one of three sets of words covered in the unit. This activity reinforces the meaning and use of the words and focuses on any vocabulary skills particular to the word set being studied, such as sorting or using context clues.
- **Unit Review (Online)**   Students will work independently to review all vocabulary words from the unit in preparation for the Unit Checkpoint. They do the review by playing the online Boat Adventure game.
- **Unit Checkpoint (Online)**   Students will work independently to complete an online Unit Checkpoint. This assessment covers all vocabulary words from the unit.

My Accomplishments Chart

Rewards in Language Skills are tied to completing Unit Checkpoints. Each time students score 80 percent or higher on a Unit Checkpoint, have them add a sticker for that unit to the My Accomplishments chart. If students score lower than 80 percent, review each Checkpoint exercise with them and work with them to correct any exercises they missed. Although students may retake the Unit Checkpoint anytime, K¹² recommends that they wait until the next day.

K¹² Language Arts Literature & Comprehension Program Overview

Program Philosophy

The K¹² Language Arts Literature & Comprehension program includes four effective, instructional approaches to reading: Read Aloud, Shared Reading, Guided Reading, and Independent Reading. Each approach contributes to students' skill level and ability to apply specific reading strategies.

Read Aloud

What Is It? A proficient reader (in this case, you) reads aloud to students carefully selected texts from various genres. The texts have features that lend themselves to modeling what good readers do.

Why We Do It Reading aloud engages students in an enjoyable experience that promotes a love of reading. It is an opportunity to share quality literature that is too challenging for students to read independently. Listening to stories helps students build vocabulary knowledge and develop a sense of story structure. While reading aloud, you will model the following behaviors for students: fluent, expressive reading; what good readers think about as they read; and how good readers use strategies to understand text.

Shared Reading

What Is It? In Shared Reading, students join in reading text while guided by a proficient reader (in this case, you). Shared Reading is introduced in K¹² Language Arts Green.

Guided Reading

What Is It? In Guided Reading, students read books specifically selected to challenge them and give them problem-solving opportunities. They become familiar with each new book through instruction that supports and enables them to read the text themselves. Guided Reading is introduced in K¹² Language Arts Green.

Independent Reading

What Is It? When they do Independent Reading, students often choose their own books from a wide range of reading materials and read on their own for an extended block of time. During Independent Reading, they need to read books at a level just right for them, called their *independent level*. Independent Reading is introduced in K¹² Language Arts Orange.

Overview of Literature & Comprehension Lessons

Materials

The following books and nonfiction magazines are supplied for the
Literature & Comprehension program:

K¹² Language Arts Lesson Guide

K¹² Language Arts Activity Book

K¹² Read Aloud Treasury

**K¹² World: Taking Care of
Ourselves and Our Earth**

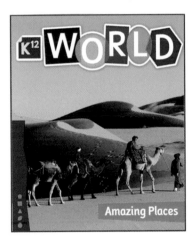

**K¹² World:
Amazing Places**

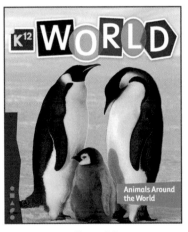

**K¹² World:
Animals Around the World**

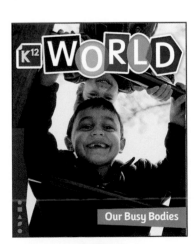

**K¹² World:
Our Busy Bodies**

The following trade books are also supplied:

- *A Chair for My Mother*
- *Mike Mulligan and His Steam Shovel*
- *Caps for Sale*
- *Make Way for Ducklings*
- *A Story, A Story*
- *Tikki Tikki Tembo*
- *The Complete Adventures of Peter Rabbit*
- *The Snowy Day*

(Keep in mind that students will write in and tear pages out of the Activity Book; you may want to store loose Activity Book pages in a three-ring binder. Remember to build students' portfolios with completed Activity Book pages.)

You will also need the following general materials to complete Activity Book pages:

- crayons or colored pencils
- scissors (**Safety note:** When students are working with scissors, please supervise them to make sure they use their scissors safely and stay seated.)
- glue stick

Lesson Structure

The K¹² Literature & Comprehension program consists of 23 entirely offline units with reading selections from the *K¹² Read Aloud Treasury*, nonfiction magazines, and trade books. The daily 30-minute lessons build in a sequence designed to meet new readers' needs and are developmentally appropriate for a kindergarten reader's growing comprehension abilities. The following chart is an overview of how most lessons, which follow a three-day pattern, are organized for each reading selection.

Day	Offline (15 minutes)
1	**Get Ready** **Read Aloud** **Check Your Reading**
2	**Get Ready** **Read Aloud** **Check Your Reading** **Reading for Meaning**
3	**Get Ready** **Reading for Meaning** **Making Connections** **Beyond the Lesson (optional)**

Research on reading comprehension indicates that rereading improves memory and accuracy in comprehension. As such, each reading selection is read aloud to students in two consecutive lessons—first in the Introduce lesson and again in the Explore lesson. Typically the first reading focuses on the story, Words to Know, and comprehension, while the second reading focuses on the story, a specific feature of the text, and additional, deeper comprehension. Some students may benefit from a third reading of the text. In the Review lesson, the schedule includes time for **Reread or Retell**. Many students will have improved performance on the Reading for Meaning and/or Making Connections activities because of this third and final rereading.

Lesson Activities

Lesson plans in the Literature & Comprehension section of this Lesson Guide include detailed descriptions or instructions for each activity. Literature & Comprehension lesson plans include the following elements:

Program Name
This banner identifies the section of the book.

Activity Description
This text describes what will happen in the activity. For offline activities, it provides step-by-step instructions. Look for words in bold, like **Say**, which highlight actions you should take. Answers to questions you ask students are shown in pink.

LITERATURE & COMPREHENSION

[Offline] **30** minutes

"Sleeping Beauty"
Work **together** with students to complete offline Get Ready, Read Aloud, Check Your Reading, and Reading for Meaning activities.

Get Ready

What Is a Fairy Tale?
Tell students that "Sleeping Beauty" is a fairy tale. A **fairy tale** is a folk story with magical parts, such as a fairy godmother who can turn a pumpkin into a carriage with her wand. Magical characters don't exist in real life. Tell students to listen for parts of the story that could not happen in real life.

Objectives
- Identify genre.
- Build vocabulary through listening, reading, and discussion.
- Use new vocabulary in written and spoken sentences.

Words to Know
Before reading "Sleeping Beauty,"

1. Have students say each word aloud.

2. Ask students if they know what each word means.

   ▸ If students know a word's meaning, have them define it and use it in a sentence.
   ▸ If students don't know a word's meaning, read them the definition and discuss the word with them.

canopy – a cover above a bed
feast – a large, fancy meal attended by many people
hedge – a thick row of bushes
passage – a long, thin space that you can use to get from one place to another
prick – to poke a small hole with something sharp like a pin
spindle – the round stick on a spinning wheel that holds and winds the thread

Objectives
These learning goals indicate what students should be able to do as a result of the lesson.

Literature & Comprehension activity types include the following:

- ▸ **Get Ready**   Every lesson begins with a Get Ready activity, which include detailed instructions on how to prepare students for the reading selection and lesson. You will provide instruction to help students understand the reading selection and develop knowledge of comprehension strategies. You will then complete steps for introducing Words to Know, which are words from the selection that students should become familiar with.

- ▸ **Read Aloud**   You will read aloud all texts in the Literature & Comprehension lessons to students. The Read Aloud activities begin with a Book Walk. This activity is a structured introduction to the reading selection that familiarizes students with the content, and helps them recall related background knowledge and make predictions. After the Book Walk, you will read the selection aloud, following any directions related to the lesson focus. For example, you may be asked to emphasize the Words to Know, or you may be directed to pause at certain points in the selection and ask students to make predictions. K^{12} recommends that you preview the questions you will ask students before reading the selection.

- ▸ **Check Your Reading**   You will ask students to demonstrate general comprehension of the reading selection by retelling what happens and answering basic comprehension questions. In most cases, answers to Check Your Reading questions are stated directly in the reading selection.

- ▸ **Reading for Meaning**   You will work with students to develop a deeper understanding of the reading selection through Reading for Meaning activities. The main focus of these activities is comprehension strategies and analysis of the reading selection.

- ▸ **Making Connections**   Students will apply information and strategies learned from lessons to the reading selection. This activity often involves connecting the reading selection to students' lives and the larger world, often through Activity Book pages.

- ▸ **Beyond the Lesson (Optional)**   These activities are for students who have extra time and interest in exploring the reading selection further. These activities are *not required* and can be skipped.

My Accomplishments Chart

Rewards in the Literature & Comprehension program are tied to completing units. When students complete a unit, have them add a sticker for that unit to the My Accomplishments chart.

Reader's Choice Units

Throughout the K[12] Language Arts Literature & Comprehension program, Planning and Progress in the Online School will alert you to an approaching Reader's Choice Unit. These units are designed to give students an opportunity to self-select texts while fine-tuning their comprehension skills. Research indicates that providing opportunities for choice enhances performance and motivates early readers. Titles range from the classic to the contemporary and include fiction, folktales, and nonfiction.

In the six Reader's Choice Units spread across the program, you will have a bank of 18 texts to choose from. K[12] suggests you discuss the possible texts with students to guarantee that they will engage with texts that interest them. Like the regular Literature units, these Choice units are also three lessons each. There are two important differences:

1. **You will need to acquire these texts on your own, through a library or bookstore.** To help you choose a text for a Reader's Choice Unit, K[12] includes a brief synopsis of the story and information about grade and interest level.

2. Once you have selected the text, you will be prompted to *print* the accompanying lesson guide and activity pages. **You must print these pages because they are not provided in this Lesson Guide or the Activity Book.**

K¹² Language Arts Handwriting Program Overview

Philosophy

K¹² supplies handwriting practice workbooks for students in kindergarten through grade 3. It is important for students to practice at a pace that suits students' fine motor skills development.

Overview of Handwriting Lessons

Lesson Structure

The K¹² Handwriting program is entirely offline. In each lesson, you will work with students for 10 minutes. (You may want to set a timer for 10 minutes; many students enjoy handwriting, so it's easy to lose track of time and do too much in one day.)

Students should complete as many workbook pages as they can, picking up where they left off during the previous Handwriting lesson and continuing from there. They are not expected to complete a set number of pages during the 10-minute lessons. Be sure to monitor students' writing time so you can help them develop good letter formation habits.

Depending on students' pace, the workbook may take up to one full semester to complete. Move as fast or slowly as students need. When they have completed the workbook, have students practice their handwriting each day by writing words or sentences from Phonics, Literature and Comprehension, or All About Me activities. Alternately, students may choose to simply practice their handwriting by writing words or sentences of their own choosing.

K¹² Language Arts Blue Keywords

author – a writer

autobiography – the story of a person's life written by that person

biography – the story of a person's life written by another person

brainstorming – an early step in writing that helps a writer come up with as many ideas about a topic as possible

caption – writing under a picture that describes a picture

cause – the reason why something happens

character – a person or animal in a story

compare – to explain how two or more things are alike

comprehension – understanding

connection – a link readers make between themselves, information in text, and the world around them

context – the parts of a sentence or passage surrounding a word

context clue – a word or phrase in a text that helps you figure out the meaning of an unknown word

contrast – to explain how two or more things are different

detail – a piece of information in a text

dialogue – the words that characters say in a written work

draft – an early effort at a piece of writing; not the finished work

drama – another word for *play*

draw a conclusion – to make a decision about something not stated directly in a text by considering information provided and what you know from past experience

effect – the result of a cause

environmental print – words and symbols found in the world around us, such as those on signs, ads, and labels

fable – a story that teaches a lesson and may contain animal characters

fact – something that can be proven true

fairy tale – a folktale with magical elements

fantasy – a story with characters, settings, or other elements that could not really exist

fiction – make-believe stories

first-person point of view – the telling of a story by a character in that story, using pronouns such as *I*, *me*, and *we*

folktale – a story passed down through a culture for many years that may have human, animal, or magical characters

genre – a category for classifying literary works

glossary – a list of important terms and their meanings that is usually found in the back of a book

graphic organizer – a visual tool used to show relationships between key concepts; formats include webs, diagrams, and charts

illustration – a drawing

illustrator – the person who draws the pictures that go with a story

imagery – language that helps readers imagine how something looks, sounds, smells, feels, or tastes

infer – to use clues and what you already know to make a guess

inference – a guess you make using the clues in a text and what you already know

informational text – text written to explain and give information about a topic

legend – a story that is passed down for many years to teach the values of a culture; the story may or may not contain some true events or people

line – a row of words in a poem

listening vocabulary – the words you can hear and understand

literal level – a reference to text information that is directly stated

literal recall – the ability to describe information stated directly in a text

literature – made-up stories, true stories, poems, and plays

main idea – the most important idea in a paragraph or text

moral – the lesson of a story, particularly a fable

multiple-meaning word – a word that has more than one meaning

narrative – a text genre that tells a story; a narrative usually includes characters, setting, and plot

narrator – the teller of a story

nonfiction – writings about true things

plot – what happens in a story

point of view – the perspective a story is told from

predictable text – text written with rhyme, rhythm, and repetition

prediction – a guess about what might happen that is based on information in a story and what you already know

prior knowledge – things you already know from past experience

problem – an issue a character must solve in a story

realistic fiction – a made-up story that has no magical elements

retelling – using your own words to tell a story that you have listened to or read

rhyme – when two or more words have the same ending sounds; for example, *cat* and *hat* rhyme

rhythm – a pattern of accented and unaccented syllables; a distinctive beat

self-monitor – to notice if you do or do not understand what you are reading

sensory language – language that appeals to the five senses

sequence – order

setting – when and where a story takes place

solution – how a character solves a problem in a story

speaking vocabulary – the words you can say and use correctly

stanza – a group of lines in a poem

story events – the things that happen in a story; the plot

story structure elements – components of a story; they include character, setting, plot, problem, and solution

summarize – to tell the most important ideas or events of a text

summary – a short retelling that includes only the most important ideas or events of a text

supporting detail – a detail that gives more information about a main idea

table of contents – a list at the start of a book that gives the titles of the book's stories, poems, articles, chapters, or nonfiction pieces and the pages where they appear

text feature – part of a text that helps a reader locate information and determine what is most important; examples include the title, table of contents, headings, pictures, and glossary

theme – the author's message or big idea

tone – the author's feelings toward the subject and/or characters of a text

topic – the subject of a text

vocabulary – the words we know and use to communicate

Language Arts

Language Skills

Color Words (A)

Unit Overview

In this unit, students will

- ► Learn color and body parts vocabulary words.
- ► Complete the *All About Me* pages *Self-Portrait*, *My Hand*, and *My Foot*.
- ► Explore the poems "One, Two, Buckle My Shoe"; "I Eat My Peas with Honey"; and "Old Mother Hubbard."

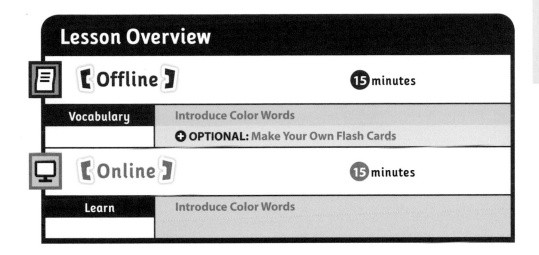

Lesson Overview

📄	**[Offline]**	**15** minutes
Vocabulary	Introduce Color Words	
	⊕ OPTIONAL: Make Your Own Flash Cards	
🖥️	**[Online]**	**15** minutes
Learn	Introduce Color Words	

[Materials]

Supplied
- There are no supplied materials to gather for this lesson.

Also Needed
- index cards (9) (optional)
- crayons (optional)

[Offline] **15** minutes

Work **together** with students to complete an offline Vocabulary activity.

 **Vocabulary** ••

Introduce Color Words

Introduce students to the following color words:

black	green	red
blue	orange	white
brown	purple	yellow

1. Walk around the room with students and identify objects with the listed colors.

2. Play a game to help students identify colors.

   - ► Pick a color from the list. Find one item that color in the room. Don't tell students what color or item you picked.
   - ► Say "I spy something [color that you chose]."
   - ► Let students guess which item you chose.
   - ► Repeat the process, but let students pick a color and choose an item, and you attempt to guess the item.
   - ► Continue the game as time allows.

 Objectives
- Increase oral vocabulary.

✚ OPTIONAL: Make Your Own Flash Cards

This activity is intended for students who have extra time and would benefit from practicing their vocabulary words with flash cards. Feel free to skip this activity.

Gather nine index cards and crayons. Have students create flash cards by writing each vocabulary word on the front of an index card and drawing a shape on the back in the corresponding color. For example, on the back of the card for *red*, students might draw a red circle.

TIP If students are not ready to read and write on their own, skip this optional activity.

 **[Online]** **15 minutes**

Students will work online **independently** to complete activities on Vocabulary words. Help students locate the online activities, and provide support as needed.

Learn ••

Introduce Color Words

Students will be introduced to the color words *red, orange, yellow, green, blue, purple, brown, black,* and *white*. Students will also learn that colors can be used to describe things.

Objectives
- Increase oral vocabulary.
- Increase reading vocabulary.
- Describe people, places, things, locations, actions, events, and/or feelings.

Self-Portrait and Color Words

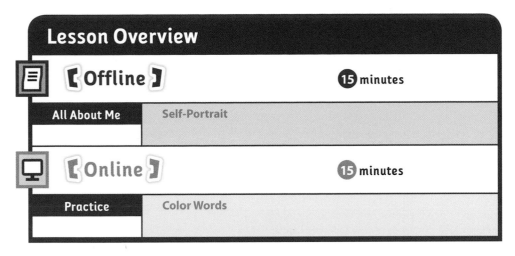

Lesson Overview

Offline		15 minutes
All About Me	Self-Portrait	
Online		15 minutes
Practice	Color Words	

Materials

Supplied
- *K¹² All About Me*, p. 1

Also Needed
- crayons

 **Offline** 15 minutes

Work **together** with students to complete an offline All About Me activity.

 All About Me ....

Self-Portrait

Students will begin drawing a self-portrait and practice writing their name. They will complete this page over two lessons.

1. Help students begin page 1 in *K¹² All About Me*.

2. Discuss with students the features of their head (hair color, eye color, nose, mouth, ears, and so on).

3. Have them begin drawing a self-portrait, focusing only on their head and face rather than their entire body.

4. Write students' first and last names on the top line provided, spelling aloud the names as you write them. Point out to students that you capitalize the first letter of each name.

5. Have students read aloud their first and last names, and practice writing them on the lower line. Make sure they capitalize only the first letter of their first and last names.

> **Objectives**
> - Read own first and last name.
> - Capitalize proper names.
> - Draw and label pictures.

 [Online] 15 minutes

Students will work online **independently** to complete activities on Vocabulary words. Help students locate the online activities, and provide support as needed.

Practice ···

Color Words

Students will practice the color words *red, orange, yellow, green, blue, purple, brown, black,* and *white*.

Offline Alternative

No computer access? At any time, you can print a list of the unit Vocabulary words and their definitions from the online lesson. Use this list to review the words with students offline. In addition, if students made their own flash cards, these can be used for offline review.

 Objectives
- Increase oral vocabulary.
- Increase concept vocabulary.

"One, Two, Buckle My Shoe" and Color Words

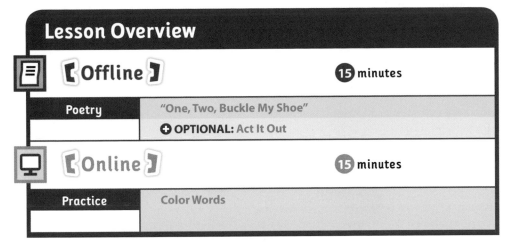

Lesson Overview

Offline 15 minutes

Poetry	"One, Two, Buckle My Shoe"
	⊕ **OPTIONAL: Act It Out**

Online 15 minutes

Practice	**Color Words**

Materials

Supplied
- *K¹² Read Aloud Treasury*, pp. 8–9

Also Needed
- paper, drawing
- crayons

Keywords
rhyme – when two or more words have the same ending sounds; for example, *cat* and *hat* rhyme

Offline 15 minutes

Work **together** with students to complete an offline Poetry activity.

Poetry ....

"One, Two, Buckle My Shoe"

It's time to read the poem "One, Two, Buckle My Shoe" from *K¹² Read Aloud Treasury*. When reading this poem, you'll teach about rhyming. Gather paper and crayons.

1. Explain that poetry is a type of writing. A piece of poetry is called a poem. Poems are made up of lines. The lines of a poem may **rhyme**, which means that their last words end with the same sound.
   Say: These lines rhyme: "Twinkle, twinkle, little star / How I wonder what you are."

2. Have students sit next to you so they can see the picture and words while you read the poem aloud. **Read aloud the entire poem**, and then ask:

   ▶ Which word from the poem rhymes with *four: shoe, door,* or *stick*? *door*
   ▶ What does the poem say to do after the numbers five and six? pick up sticks
   ▶ What is the highest number in the poem? twenty

3. Start to reread the poem, emphasizing the last word in each line. Stop after every other line.

   ▶ Do the last words of these two lines rhyme? Only the lines following "Fifteen, sixteen" and "Nineteen, twenty" do not rhyme. All others rhyme.

Objectives
- Listen to and discuss poetry.
- Respond to text through art, writing, and/or drama.
- Identify rhyme in poetry.

4. Have students draw a big, fat hen. You may need to tell them that a hen is a chicken.

   ▶ Which number rhymes with *hen*? *ten*

   Have students write the answer on their paper.

5. Tell students to say *hen* and *ten*, stressing the rhyming sounds.

✚ OPTIONAL: Act It Out

This activity is intended for students who have extra time and would benefit from acting out the poem. Feel free to skip this activity.

Have students act out the poem as you read. For instance, after you read line 2, students should pretend to buckle their shoes. After you read line 4, they should pretend to shut a door.

   **15 minutes**

Students will work online **independently** to complete activities on Vocabulary words. Help students locate the online activities, and provide support as needed.

Practice ●●●

Color Words

Students will practice the color words *red, orange, yellow, green, blue, purple, brown, black,* and *white.*

> **Objectives**
> • Increase oral vocabulary.
> • Increase concept vocabulary.

Offline Alternative

No computer access? At any time, you can print a list of the unit Vocabulary words and their definitions from the online lesson. Use this list to review the words with students offline. In addition, if students made their own flash cards, these can be used for offline review.

Body Part Words (A)

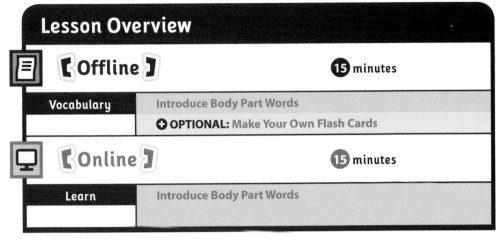

Lesson Overview

[Offline]   🕒 **15** minutes

Vocabulary	Introduce Body Part Words
	➕ OPTIONAL: Make Your Own Flash Cards

[Online]   🕒 **15** minutes

Learn	Introduce Body Part Words

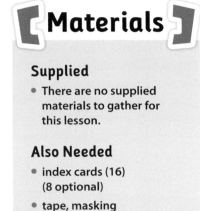

Materials

Supplied
- There are no supplied materials to gather for this lesson.

Also Needed
- index cards (16) (8 optional)
- tape, masking

Advance Preparation

Gather eight index cards. On the front of each card, draw a simple picture of one of the following words: *head, neck, shoulders, arm, leg, hips, chest,* and *feet.* (For *neck, shoulders, chest,* and *hips,* you can draw an outline of a body with an arrow pointing to the part you are identifying.)

[Offline]   🕒 **15** minutes

Work **together** with students to complete an offline Vocabulary activity.

Vocabulary

Introduce Body Part Words

Students will be introduced to the following body part words:

arm	feet	hips	neck
chest	head	leg	shoulders

1. Say each word and point to the corresponding part of your body.

2. Play a game to help students identify body parts.

   ▶ Gather the tape and the index cards you prepared.
   ▶ For each card, show students the picture, and then tape the card to your corresponding body part. Ask them to point to the body part and name it.

Objectives
- Increase oral vocabulary.

- ▸ Reverse roles: Remove the index cards and tape, shuffle the cards, and pass them to students. Have students look at each picture and then tape it to their corresponding body part.
- ▸ Say the words a final time with students.

⊕ OPTIONAL: Make Your Own Flash Cards

This activity is intended for students who have extra time and would benefit from practicing their vocabulary words with flash cards. Feel free to skip this activity.

Gather eight index cards. Have students create flash cards by writing each vocabulary word on the front of an index card and their own definition for each word on the back. Help students with spelling as necessary.

 **15 minutes**

Students will work online **independently** to complete activities on Vocabulary words. Help students locate the online activities, and provide support as needed.

Learn ....

Introduce Body Part Words

Students will be introduced to the body part words *head, neck, shoulders, arm, leg, hips, chest,* and *feet*.

Objectives
- Increase oral vocabulary.
- Increase reading vocabulary.
- Increase concept vocabulary.

Self-Portrait and Body Part Words

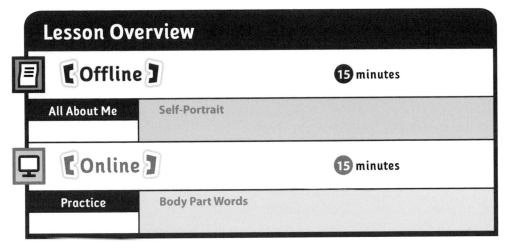

Lesson Overview

Offline		**15** minutes
All About Me	Self-Portrait	

Online		**15** minutes
Practice	Body Part Words	

Materials

Supplied
- *K¹² All About Me*, p. 1

Also Needed
- crayons

Offline **15** minutes

Work **together** with students to to complete an offline All About Me activity.

All About Me

Self-Portrait
Students will complete their self-portrait.

1. Help students complete their self-portrait on page 1 in *K¹² All About Me*.

2. Remind students to focus on only their head and face in their portrait, rather than their entire body. If necessary, encourage them to add more details to their picture.

3. Ask students to describe their drawing. Encourage them to use color words in their descriptions. Answers to questions may vary.

   ▸ What color is your hair?
   ▸ What color are your eyes?

Objectives
- Draw and label pictures.

 **minutes**

Students will work online **independently** to complete activities on Vocabulary words. Help students locate the online activities, and provide support as needed.

Practice

Body Part Words

Students will practice the body part words *head, neck, shoulders, arm, leg, hips, chest,* and *feet*.

Offline Alternative

No computer access? At any time, you can print a list of the unit Vocabulary words and their definitions from the online lesson. Use this list to review the words with students offline. In addition, if students made their own flash cards, these can be used for offline review.

 Objectives

- Increase oral vocabulary.
- Increase concept vocabulary.
- Use new vocabulary in written and spoken sentences.

"I Eat My Peas with Honey" and Body Part Words

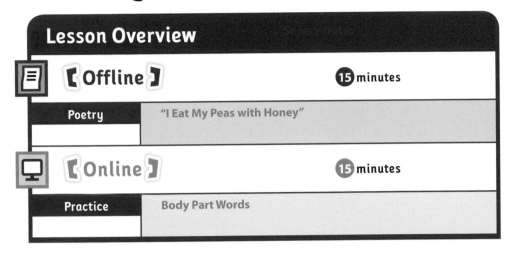

Lesson Overview

Offline		**15** minutes
Poetry	"I Eat My Peas with Honey"	
Online		**15** minutes
Practice	Body Part Words	

[Materials]

Supplied
- *The Rooster Crows*
- *K¹² Language Arts Activity Book*, p. LS 1

Advance Preparation

Before you begin reading the poems in *The Rooster Crows*, you will need to number the pages of the book. Using a pencil, mark the bottom right-hand corner of the title page as page 1. When you have finished numbering all the pages, turn to page 23.

[Offline]  **15** minutes

Work **together** with students to complete an offline Poetry activity.

Poetry

"I Eat My Peas with Honey"

It's time to read the poem "I Eat My Peas with Honey" from *The Rooster Crows*.

1. Tell students that the poem is about peas.

   ▸ Have you ever eaten peas? Answers will vary.
   ▸ Did you eat them with other foods? If so, which foods? Answers will vary.
   ▸ Did you eat them with a spoon, a fork, or a knife? spoon or fork

2. Tell students that honey is a thick, sticky liquid that bees make, but that most people do not eat peas with honey. Then show them the picture next to this poem in *The Rooster Crows*. Point out the jar of honey and the peas. Point out the boy in the picture, too.

3. Tell students to think about why the boy eats his peas with honey as they listen to the poem.

Objectives
- Listen to and discuss poetry.
- Make connections with text: text-to-text, text-to-self, text-to-world.
- Respond to text through art, writing, and/or drama.

4. Have students sit next to you so they can see the picture and words while you read the poem aloud. **Read the entire poem**, and then ask:

▸ Which word in the poem rhymes with *honey*? *funny*
▸ What does the boy in the poem use to eat his peas? a knife
▸ Why does the boy eat his peas with honey when it makes them taste funny? The sticky honey keeps the peas on his knife.

5. Have students complete page LS 1 in *K¹² Language Arts Activity Book*. Before they begin, ask:

▸ What shape is a pea? round or circular
▸ What does a pea look most like: a ball, a box, or a book? a ball
▸ How do peas and balls both move? They roll.
▸ How would *you* keep the peas on the knife? Answers will vary.

 **Online** **15 minutes**

Students will work online **independently** to complete activities on Vocabulary words. Help students locate the online activities, and provide support as needed.

Practice

Body Part Words
Students will practice the body part words *head, neck, shoulders, arm, leg, hips, chest,* and *feet.*

 Objectives
- Increase oral vocabulary.
- Increase concept vocabulary.

Offline Alternative

No computer access? At any time, you can print a list of the unit Vocabulary words and their definitions from the online lesson. Use this list to review the words with students offline. In addition, if students made their own flash cards, these can be used for offline review.

Body Part Words (B)

Lesson Overview

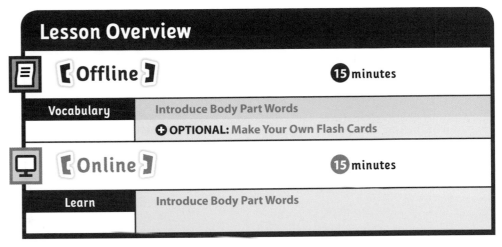

Offline — 15 minutes

Vocabulary	Introduce Body Part Words
	⊕ OPTIONAL: Make Your Own Flash Cards

Online — 15 minutes

Learn	Introduce Body Part Words

Materials

Supplied
- *K¹² Language Arts Activity Book*, p. LS 2

Also Needed
- crayons
- index cards (7) (optional)

Offline — 15 minutes

Work **together** with students to complete an offline Vocabulary activity.

Vocabulary

Introduce Body Part Words

Have students learn these body part words:

ankle	fingers	knee	wrist
elbow	hand	toes	

1. Say each word and point to the corresponding part of your body.

2. Show students how the elbow and wrist are the places where the arm bends and the knee and ankle are the places where the leg bends.

3. Show students how fingers are part of the hand and toes are part of the foot.

4. Have students complete page LS 2 in *K¹² Language Arts Activity Book*.

Objectives
- Increase oral vocabulary.
- Increase concept vocabulary.

⊕ OPTIONAL: Make Your Own Flash Cards

This activity is intended for students who have extra time and would benefit from practicing their vocabulary words with flash cards. Feel free to skip this activity.

Gather seven index cards. Have students create flash cards by writing each vocabulary word on the front of an index card and their own definition for each word on the back. Help students with spelling as necessary.

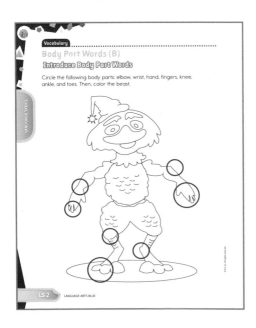

【Online】 15 minutes

Students will work online **independently** to complete activities on Vocabulary words. Help students locate the online activities, and provide support as needed.

Learn ....

Introduce Body Part Words

Students will be introduced to the body part words *elbow, wrist, hand, fingers, knee, ankle,* and *toes.*

Objectives

- Increase oral vocabulary.
- Increase concept vocabulary.
- Use new vocabulary in written and spoken sentences.

My Hand & Foot and Body Part Words

Lesson Overview

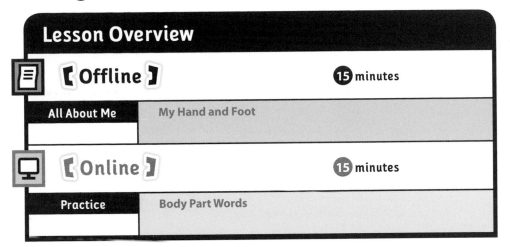

	Offline	15 minutes
All About Me	My Hand and Foot	

	Online	15 minutes
Practice	Body Part Words	

Materials

Supplied
- *K¹² All About Me*, pp. 2–3

Also Needed
- crayons

Offline   15 minutes

Work **together** with students to complete an offline All About Me activity.

All About Me

My Hand and Foot
Students will trace one of their hands and feet.

1. Help students complete pages 2 and 3 in *K¹² All About Me*.

2. Have students trace either foot, but make sure the hand they trace is **not** the hand with which they write. (Right-handed students should trace their left hand, and left-handed students should trace their right hand.) If time permits, have students color their tracings.

3. Write the labels *hand* and *foot* on the top lines under the appropriate picture, spelling aloud the labels as you write them. Point out to students that each letter is lowercase.

4. Have students read aloud the labels and practice writing them on the two lines below your labels. Make sure they use only lowercase letters.

> **Objectives**
> - Draw and label pictures.

 **15** minutes

Students will work online **independently** to complete activities on Vocabulary words. Help students locate the online activities, and provide support as needed.

Practice ....

Body Part Words

Students will practice the body part words *elbow, wrist, hand, fingers, knee, ankle,* and *toes,* and see how these parts combine to make an arm or a leg.

Objectives
- Increase oral vocabulary.
- Increase concept vocabulary.

Offline Alternative

No computer access? At any time, you can print a list of the unit Vocabulary words and their definitions from the online lesson. Use this list to review the words with students offline. In addition, if students made their own flash cards, these can be used for offline review.

"Old Mother Hubbard" and Vocabulary Unit Review

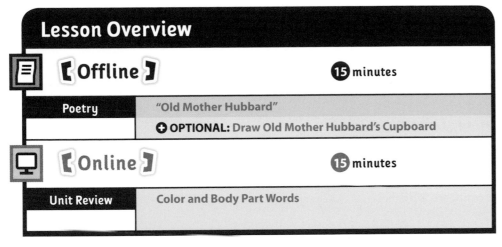

Lesson Overview

☰ **[Offline]** 🕐 **15** minutes

| Poetry | "Old Mother Hubbard" |
| | ➕ OPTIONAL: Draw Old Mother Hubbard's Cupboard |

🖥 **[Online]** 🕐 **15** minutes

| Unit Review | Color and Body Part Words |

[Materials]

Supplied
- *K¹² Read Aloud Treasury*, p. 22–23

Also Needed
- paper, drawing (optional)
- crayons (optional)

[Offline] 🕐 **15** minutes

Work **together** with students to complete an offline Poetry activity.

Poetry ....

"Old Mother Hubbard"

It's time to read the poem "Old Mother Hubbard" from *K¹² Read Aloud Treasury*. When reading this poem, you'll teach about rhyming and the order of events.

1. Tell students that there are some poems that almost all people hear when they are very young. These poems are called *nursery rhymes*. Encourage students to recite a nursery rhyme that they know by heart or recite one for them.

2. Explain that the nursery rhymes we know are sometimes just the beginnings of longer poems, which is the case with "Old Mother Hubbard."

3. Have students sit next to you so they can see the pictures and words while you read the poem aloud. **Read aloud the entire poem**, and then ask:

   ▸ Why does Old Mother Hubbard go to the cupboard? to get her dog a bone
   ▸ Which word rhymes with *there* in this poem: *bare, none,* or *bone*? *bare*
   ▸ Where does Old Mother Hubbard go to buy her dog a coat? the tailor's
   ▸ How would you describe Old Mother Hubbard's dog? Answers will vary.

> **Objectives**
> - Listen to and discuss poetry.
> - Identify rhyme and rhythm in poetry.
> - Sequence events from a text.

4. Reread the lines about Old Mother Hubbard going to the hatter's.

   ▸ Does *hatter's* rhyme with *hat*? No
   ▸ Does *hat* rhyme with *back*? No
   ▸ What word in this part of the poem rhymes with *hat*? cat

5. Reread the lines about Old Mother Hubbard going to the barber's, tailor's, and cobbler's.

   ▸ Where does Old Mother Hubbard go last? the cobbler's

⊕ OPTIONAL: Draw Old Mother Hubbard's Cupboard

This activity is intended for students who have extra time and would benefit from responding to the poem with art. Feel free to skip this activity.

Gather crayons and paper. Have students draw Old Mother Hubbard's cupboard. If necessary, tell them that a cupboard is a cabinet or closet and that *bare* means "empty."

   **[Online] 15 minutes**

Students will work online **independently** to complete an activity on Vocabulary words. Help students locate the online activity, and provide support as needed.

Unit Review

Color and Body Part Words
Students will review all words from the unit to prepare for the Unit Checkpoint.

Objectives
• Increase oral vocabulary.

Offline Alternative

No computer access? At any time, you can print a list of the unit Vocabulary words and their definitions from the online lesson. Use this list to review the words with students offline. In addition, if students made their own flash cards, these can be used for offline review.

Unit Checkpoint

Lesson Overview

 **Online**   **30** minutes

Unit Checkpoint	Color and Body Part Words

 **Materials**

There are no materials to gather for this lesson.

Online **30** minutes

Students will work online to complete the Unit Checkpoint. Help students locate the Unit Checkpoint, and provide support as needed.

Unit Checkpoint ....

Color and Body Part Words
Explain that students are going to show what they have learned about vocabulary words for colors and body parts.

 Objectives

- Increase oral vocabulary.
- Increase reading vocabulary.
- Describe people, places, things, locations, actions, events, and/or feelings.
- Use new vocabulary in written and spoken sentences.
- Increase concept vocabulary.

Body Part Words (C)

Unit Overview

In this unit, students will

- ► Learn words for body parts and jobs.
- ► Complete the *All About Me* pages *How I Use My Arms, Fingers, and Toes* and *When I Grow Up*.
- ► Explore the poems "Teddy Bear, Teddy Bear"; "Monday's Child"; and "Hey, Diddle, Diddle."

[Materials]

Supplied

- ● There are no supplied materials to gather for this lesson.

Also Needed

- ● index cards (8) (optional)

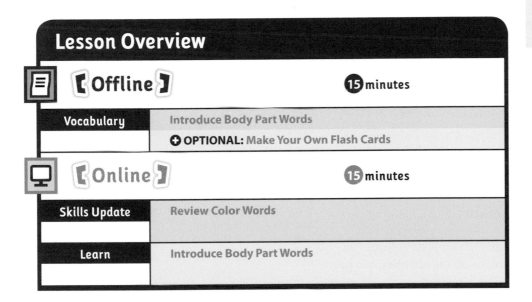

Lesson Overview

	[Offline]	**15** minutes
Vocabulary	Introduce Body Part Words	
	● OPTIONAL: Make Your Own Flash Cards	

	[Online]	**15** minutes
Skills Update	Review Color Words	
Learn	Introduce Body Part Words	

[Offline] **15** minutes

Work **together** with students to complete an offline Vocabulary activity.

Vocabulary ....

Introduce Body Part Words

Play a game with students to introduce the following words:

big	**mouth**	**small**
ears	**nose**	**tall**
eyes	**short**	

For each question, if students answer incorrectly, provide them with the answer. If students get the question correct, have them do one of the following: turn around three times, touch their toes, stand on one leg, hop five times, or make a silly face.

- ► What word means something you see with? *eyes*
- ► What word means something you hear with? *ears*
- ► What word means something you smell with? *nose*

Objectives

- Increase oral vocabulary.
- Increase concept vocabulary.

- ▶ What word means something you talk with? *mouth*
- ▶ What word means a person who is this size [hold hand up high, indicating a tall adult]? *tall*
- ▶ What word means a person who is this size [hold hand down low, indicating a short child]? *short*
- ▶ What word means something this size [hold thumb and index finger slightly apart]? *small*
- ▶ What word means something this size [hold arms wide apart]? *big*

✚ OPTIONAL: Make Your Own Flash Cards

This activity is intended for students who have extra time and would benefit from practicing their vocabulary words with flash cards. Feel free to skip this activity.

Gather eight index cards. Have students create flash cards by writing each vocabulary word on the front of an index card and their own definition for each word on the back. Help students with spelling as necessary.

(TIP) If students are not ready to read and write on their own, skip this optional activity.

 **⑮ minutes**

Students will work online **independently** to complete activities on Vocabulary words. Help students locate the online activities, and provide support as needed.

Skills Update

Review Color Words

Students will answer a few questions to refresh their Vocabulary knowledge.

 Objectives
- Increase oral vocabulary.
- Increase concept vocabulary.

Learn

Introduce Body Part Words

Students will be introduced to the body part words *eyes, ears, nose, mouth, big, tall, short,* and *small.*

 Objectives
- Increase oral vocabulary.
- Increase concept vocabulary.

How I Use My Arms, Fingers, & Legs and Body Part Words

Lesson Overview

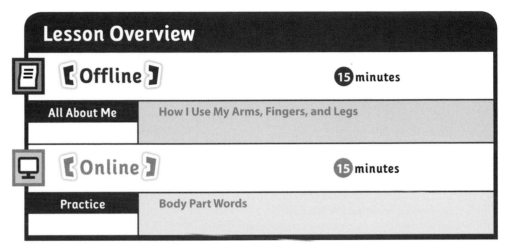

	Offline	15 minutes
All About Me	How I Use My Arms, Fingers, and Legs	

	Online	15 minutes
Practice	Body Part Words	

Materials

Supplied
- *K¹² All About Me*, pp. 4–5

Also Needed
- crayons

Offline 15 minutes

Work **together** with students to complete an offline All About Me activity.

All About Me

How I Use My Arms, Fingers, and Legs

Students will complete sentences about what they can do with their arms, fingers, and legs.

1. Help students complete page 4 in *K¹² All About Me*.

2. For each sentence, read the sentence aloud, pointing to each word as you read.

3. Have students repeat the first part of the sentence and tell you an answer to complete the sentence.

4. Write the words that students say. Read the complete sentences, pointing to each word.

5. Have students repeat the complete sentences.

6. If time permits, have students illustrate one of the sentences in the blank space on page 5.

TIP If students would like to do the writing on their own, spell the word(s) for them.

Objectives
- Dictate or write simple sentences describing experiences, stories, people, objects, or events.
- Write and/or draw narrative text.

[Online] 15 minutes

Students will work online **independently** to complete an activity on Vocabulary words. Help students locate the online activity, and provide support as needed.

Practice ....

Body Part Words

Students will practice using the description words *short, tall, big,* and *small.*

_____

Offline Alternative

No computer access? At any time, you can print a list of the unit Vocabulary words and their definitions from the online lesson. Use this list to review the words with students offline. In addition, if students made their own flash cards, these can be used for offline review.

Objectives
- Increase oral vocabulary.
- Increase concept vocabulary.

"Teddy Bear, Teddy Bear" and Body Part Words

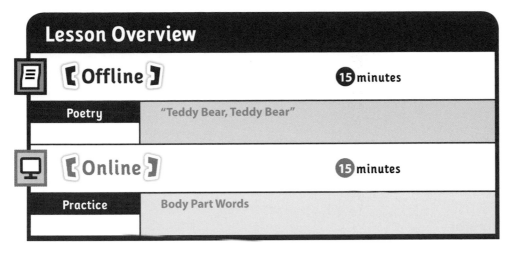

Lesson Overview

Offline — 15 minutes

| Poetry | "Teddy Bear, Teddy Bear" |

Online — 15 minutes

| Practice | Body Part Words |

Materials

Supplied
- *The Rooster Crows*

Advance Preparation

Before reading today's poem, you will need to find the poem in *The Rooster Crows*. If your book has page numbers, turn to page 50. Otherwise, you will need to use a pencil to number the pages in the book. Mark the title page as page 1.

Offline — 15 minutes

Work **together** with students to complete an offline Poetry activity.

Poetry

"Teddy Bear, Teddy Bear"

It's time to read "Teddy Bear, Teddy Bear" from *The Rooster Crows*.

1. Tell students that some poems are meant to be said while people play. Sometimes people say poems while they are skipping rope. Discuss students' experiences with skipping rope or watching others skip rope.

   ▶ Have you ever heard anyone say a poem while skipping rope? Answers will vary.

2. Tell students that "Teddy Bear, Teddy Bear" is a poem that can be said while skipping rope. Encourage them to imagine skipping rope as they listen to the poem.

Objectives
- Listen to and discuss poetry.
- Make connections with text: text-to-text, text-to-self, text-to-world.
- Identify rhyme and rhythm in poetry.
- Identify repetitive text.

3. Have students sit next to you so they can see the picture and words while you read the poem aloud. **Read aloud the entire poem**, and then ask:

   ► Which words from the poem are repeated again and again? *Teddy Bear*
   ► Which word rhymes with *shoe*: *around*, *ground*, or *do*? *do*
   ► Does the poem tell Teddy Bear to stand up straight? No
   ► When would Teddy Bear do the things in the last four lines of the poem? at night, before bed

4. Have students stand up. Tell them to imagine that they are Teddy Bear. Reread the poem and, as much as possible, have students do the things that Teddy Bear is told to do.

 **15 minutes**

Students will work online **independently** to complete an activity on Vocabulary words. Help students locate the online activity, and provide support as needed.

Practice

Body Part Words

Students will practice the body part words *eyes, ears, nose, mouth, big, tall, short,* and *small.*

Objectives
- Increase oral vocabulary.
- Increase concept vocabulary.
- Increase reading vocabulary.

Offline Alternative

No computer access? At any time, you can print a list of the unit Vocabulary words and their definitions from the online lesson. Use this list to review the words with students offline. In addition, if students made their own flash cards, these can be used for offline review.

Job Words (A)

Lesson Overview

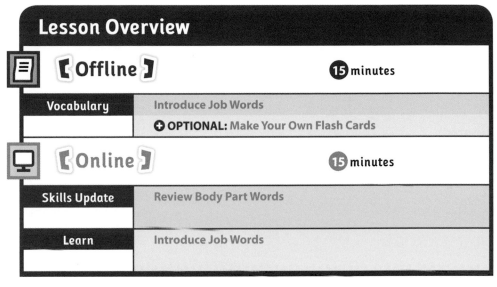

Offline   15 minutes

Vocabulary	Introduce Job Words
	⊕ OPTIONAL: Make Your Own Flash Cards

Online   15 minutes

Skills Update	Review Body Part Words
Learn	Introduce Job Words

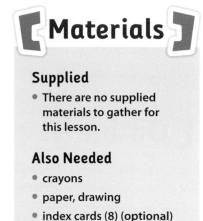

Materials

Supplied
- There are no supplied materials to gather for this lesson.

Also Needed
- crayons
- paper, drawing
- index cards (8) (optional)

Offline   15 minutes

Work **together** with students to complete an offline Vocabulary activity.

Vocabulary

Introduce Job Words

Introduce students to the following vocabulary words for jobs:

dentist	librarian	police officer
doctor	mechanic	teacher
fire fighter	nurse	

Objectives
- Increase oral vocabulary.
- Increase concept vocabulary.

1. Begin by discussing with students what they know about jobs. Answers to questions may vary.

   ▸ Do you know anyone who has a job?
   ▸ Can you name some jobs people might do?

2. Explain to students that people work at jobs to make money. Some jobs are done to help other people.

3. Say each job word, and have students repeat each word after you.

4. For each word, ask students what things someone would use when doing that job. For example, for *fire fighter*, they may respond with *fire truck* or *hose*.

5. Gather crayons and drawing paper. Have students choose one of the jobs discussed and draw pictures of the items or tools needed to do that job. When done, discuss the drawings, and label each picture for students.

6. If time permits, have students choose another job and repeat Step 5.

⊕ OPTIONAL: Make Your Own Flash Cards

This activity is intended for students who have extra time and would benefit from practicing their vocabulary words with flash cards. Feel free to skip this activity.

Gather eight index cards. Have students create flash cards by writing each vocabulary word on the front of an index card and their own definition for each word on the back. Help students with spelling as necessary.

 **15 minutes**

Students will work online **independently** to complete activities on Vocabulary words. Help students locate the online activities, and provide support as needed.

Skills Update

Review Body Part Words
Students will answer a few questions to refresh their Vocabulary knowledge.

 Objectives
- Increase oral vocabulary.

Learn

Introduce Job Words
Students will be introduced to the job words *fire fighter, police officer, doctor, teacher, librarian, nurse, mechanic,* and *dentist.*

 Objectives
- Increase oral vocabulary.
- Increase concept vocabulary.

When I Grow Up and Job Words (A)

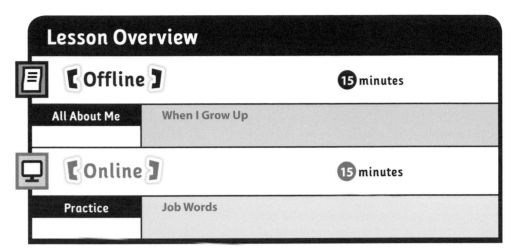

Lesson Overview

[Offline] ⏱ 15 minutes

All About Me	When I Grow Up

[Online] ⏱ 15 minutes

Practice	Job Words

[Materials]

Supplied
- *K¹² All About Me*, p. 6

Also Needed
- crayons

[Offline] ⏱ 15 minutes

Work **together** with students to complete an offline All About Me activity.

When I Grow Up

Students will think about and discuss what they want to be when they grow up. They will complete this page over two lessons.

1. Help students begin page 6 in *K¹² All About Me*. Read aloud the incomplete sentence to students.

2. Discuss with students possible jobs they would like to do when they grow up. Have them repeat the first part of the sentence and tell you what to write in the blank space.

3. Read the complete sentence to students, pointing to each word.

4. Have students explain why they chose that particular job. Answers to questions may vary.

   ▸ What do you think you would do each day at work?
   ▸ Do you know anyone who has that job?

5. Have students begin to draw a picture of themselves as adults working in their chosen profession.

Objectives

- Dictate or write simple sentences describing experiences, stories, people, objects, or events.
- Write and/or draw narrative text.

 **15 minutes**

Students will work online **independently** to complete an activity on Vocabulary words. Help students locate the online activity, and provide support as needed.

Practice

Job Words

Students will practice the job words *fire fighter, police officer, doctor, teacher, librarian, nurse, mechanic,* and *dentist.*

Offline Alternative

No computer access? At any time, you can print a list of the unit Vocabulary words and their definitions from the online lesson. Use this list to review the words with students offline. In addition, if students made their own flash cards, these can be used for offline review.

 Objectives

- Increase oral vocabulary.
- Increase concept vocabulary.
- Identify and use picture clues to define words.

"Monday's Child" and Job Words

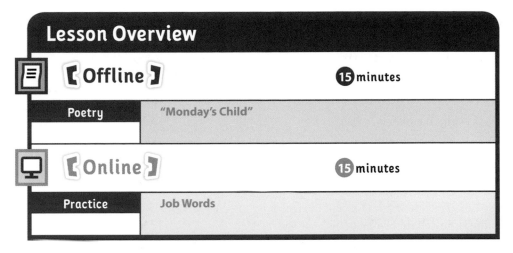

Lesson Overview

	Offline	15 minutes
Poetry	"Monday's Child"	

	Online	15 minutes
Practice	Job Words	

Materials

Supplied
- *The Rooster Crows*

Advance Preparation

Before reading today's poem, you will need to find the poem in *The Rooster Crows*. If your book has page numbers, turn to page 43. Otherwise, you will need to use a pencil to number the pages in the book. Mark the title page as page 1.

Offline 15 minutes

Work **together** with students to complete an offline Poetry activity.

"Monday's Child"

It's time to read "Monday's Child" from *The Rooster Crows*.

1. Tell students they will learn the days of the week in the poem. Recite the days of the week for students.

   ▸ How many days are there in a week? seven
   ▸ What are the days of the week? Monday, Tuesday, Wednesday, Thursday, Friday, Saturday, Sunday

2. Explain to students that sometimes a story or a poem has words that we do not know. If the story or poem has pictures, sometimes we can use the pictures to help us figure out the meaning of those words.

Objectives
- Listen to and discuss poetry.
- Make connections with text: text-to-text, text-to-self, text-to-text world.
- Use visual text features to aid understanding of text.
- Identify rhyme and rhythm in poetry.

3. **Read aloud "Monday's Child."** Have students sit next to you so they can see the pictures and words while you read the poem aloud, and then ask:

  ▸ What word in the poem rhymes with *face: woe, grace,* or *go? grace*
  ▸ Which day's child is full of woe? Wednesday's child
  ▸ How does the poem describe Tuesday's child—"full of woe," "loving and giving," or "full of grace"? "full of grace"
  ▸ What day does the poem call "the Sabbath day?" Sunday

4. Have students look at the picture of Monday's child in *The Rooster Crows.* Remind them that the poem describes Monday's child as "fair of face."

  ▸ What is this girl doing? She is looking in a mirror.
  ▸ What do you think "fair of face" might mean? pretty

5. Have students tell you what day of the week it is today, and what the poem says a child born today would be like.

TIP If students cannot provide a close or correct definition for "fair of face," tell them that the girl in the picture is looking at herself in the mirror because she likes the way she looks. Tell them that *fair* can mean *nice* or *good.* Try once more to get students to state that "fair of face" means *pretty, nice looking,* or *beautiful.*

 **15 minutes**

Students will work online **independently** to complete an activity on Vocabulary words. Help students locate the online activity, and provide support as needed.

Practice

Job Words
Students will practice the job words *fire fighter, police officer, doctor, teacher, librarian, nurse, mechanic,* and *dentist.*

Offline Alternative

No computer access? At any time, you can print a list of the unit Vocabulary words and their definitions from the online lesson. Use this list to review the words with students offline. In addition, if students made their own flash cards, these can be used for offline review.

 Objectives
- Increase oral vocabulary.
- Increase concept vocabulary.
- Identify and use picture clues to define words.

Job Words (B)

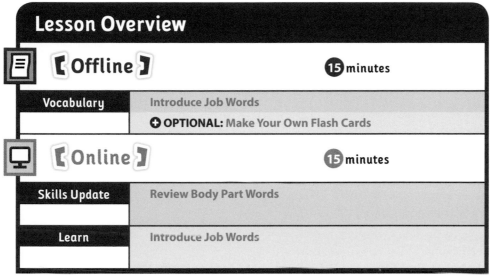

Lesson Overview

Offline — 15 minutes

Vocabulary	Introduce Job Words
	⊕ OPTIONAL: Make Your Own Flash Cards

Online — 15 minutes

Skills Update	Review Body Part Words
Learn	Introduce Job Words

Materials

Supplied
- There are no supplied materials to gather for this lesson.

Also Needed
- crayons
- paper, drawing
- index cards (8) (optional)

Offline — 15 minutes

Work **together** with students to complete an offline Vocabulary activity.

Vocabulary

Introduce Job Words

Introduce students to the following vocabulary words for jobs:

artist	chef	musician
astronaut	farmer	soldier
baker	mail carrier	

Objectives
- Increase oral vocabulary.
- Increase concept vocabulary.

1. Say each job word, and have students repeat the words after you.

2. For each word, ask students what things someone would use when doing that job. For example, for *artist*, they may respond with *paintbrush* or *paint*.

3. Gather crayons and drawing paper. Have students choose one of the jobs discussed and draw pictures of the items or tools needed to do that job. When done, discuss the drawings, and label each picture for students.

4. If time permits, practice these words further by secretly picking a word. Act out the word—for example, pretend to play an instrument or stir a bowl of batter.

5. Give students several tries to guess the word. When they guess correctly, switch roles, and repeat as time allows.

✚ OPTIONAL: Make Your Own Flash Cards

This activity is intended for students who have extra time and would benefit from practicing their vocabulary words with flash cards. Feel free to skip this activity.

Gather eight index cards. Have students create flash cards by writing each vocabulary word on the front of an index card and their own definition for each word on the back. Help students with spelling as necessary.

 **15 minutes**

Students will work online **independently** to complete activities on Vocabulary words. Help students locate the online activities, and provide support as needed.

Skills Update

Review Body Part Words

Students will answer a few questions to refresh their Vocabulary knowledge.

Objectives
- Increase oral vocabulary.

Learn

Introduce Job Words

Students will be introduced to the job words *astronaut, baker, farmer, mail carrier, musician, soldier, artist,* and *chef.*

Objectives
- Increase oral vocabulary.
- Increase concept vocabulary.

When I Grow Up and Job Words (B)

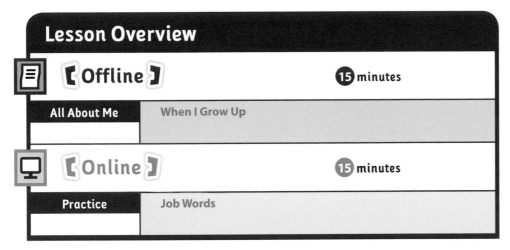

Lesson Overview

Offline		**15** minutes
All About Me	When I Grow Up	
Online		**15** minutes
Practice	Job Words	

Materials

Supplied
- *K¹² All About Me*, p. 6

Also Needed
- crayons

 **Offline** **15** minutes

Work **together** with students to complete an offline All About Me activity.

 All About Me ···

When I Grow Up
Students will complete their illustration of what they want to be when they grow up.

1. Help students complete page 6 in *K¹² All About Me*.

2. Before they begin, ask students to describe their illustration so far.

3. Discuss ways students can add details to their illustration, and encourage them to spend time doing so.

4. When students have completed their illustration, once again ask them to discuss their drawing. Encourage them to share their work with others.

Objectives
- Write and/or draw narrative text.
- Add supporting details to written or drawn work.
- Discuss own drawing.
- Share finished written and drawn works.

 **15 minutes**

Students will work online **independently** to complete an activity on Vocabulary words. Help students locate the online activity, and provide support as needed.

Practice

Job Words

Students will practice the job words *astronaut, baker, farmer, mail carrier, musician, soldier, artist,* and *chef.*

 Objectives

- Increase oral vocabulary.
- Increase concept vocabulary.
- Classify and sort common words into categories.

Offline Alternative

No computer access? At any time, you can print a list of the unit Vocabulary words and their definitions from the online lesson. Use this list to review the words with students offline. In addition, if students made their own flash cards, these can be used for offline review.

"Hey, Diddle, Diddle" and Vocabulary Unit Review

Lesson Overview

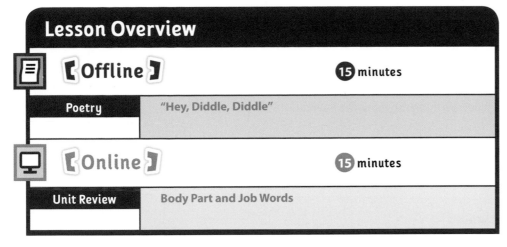

 **Offline**		15 minutes
Poetry	"Hey, Diddle, Diddle"	

Online		15 minutes
Unit Review	Body Part and Job Words	

Materials

Supplied
- *K¹² Read Aloud Treasury*, p. 29
- *K¹² Language Arts Activity Book*, p. LS 3

Also Needed
- crayons

Offline 15 minutes

Work **together** with students to complete an offline Poetry activity.

Poetry

"Hey Diddle, Diddle"

It's time to read "Hey, Diddle, Diddle," a nursery rhyme, from *K¹² Read Aloud Treasury*.

1. Explain to students that there are poems that almost all people hear when they are very young, and those poems are called *nursery rhymes*. Tell students that they will hear a very famous nursery rhyme, "Hey, Diddle, Diddle."

2. Explain to students that one way to learn a nursery rhyme or any other kind of poem is to say it aloud.

3. Have students sit next to you so they can see the picture and words while you read the poem aloud. Read aloud the entire poem and then ask:

   ▸ How many animals are in the poem? three: the cat, the dog, and the cow
   ▸ What word in the poem rhymes with *moon*: *fiddle*, *sport*, or *spoon*? *spoon*
   ▸ What does the little dog do in the poem? laughs
   ▸ Who runs away with the spoon? dish
   ▸ Could the things in this poem really happen? No
   ▸ If you could be one of the things in this poem, which would it be? Why? Answers will vary.

4. Have students choose one of the things in the poem and show you how that thing acts. For example, the cat *played the fiddle*, the cow *jumped*, and so on.

Objectives
- Listen to and discuss poetry.
- Recite short poems or rhymes.
- Make connections with text: text-to-text, text-to-self, text-to-world.
- Respond to text through art, writing, and/or drama.
- Identify rhyme and rhythm in poetry.

5. Help students recite the poem and, possibly, memorize it. Begin by reading the poem's first line and having students repeat it. Then read the first two lines and have students repeat them. Continue this pattern until students are repeating the entire poem.

6. Have students color page LS 3 in *K¹² Language Arts Activity Book*. They should recite the poem while coloring the pictures in the same order as the poem (the cat and the fiddle first, the cow and the moon second, the little dog third, and the dish and the spoon last).

TIP Point out that rhymes can help us remember the lines of a poem. Additionally, reciting a poem often will help with memorizing the poem.

 **15 minutes**

Students will work online **independently** to complete an activity on Vocabulary words. Help students locate the online activity, and provide support as needed.

Unit Review •

Body Part and Job Words
Students will review all words from the unit to prepare for the Unit Checkpoint.

 Objectives
- Increase oral vocabulary.

Offline Alternative

No computer access? At any time, you can print a list of the unit Vocabulary words and their definitions from the online lesson. Use this list to review the words with students offline. In addition, if students made their own flash cards, these can be used for offline review.

Unit Checkpoint

Lesson Overview

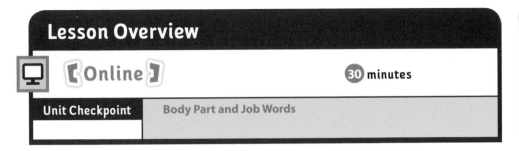

🖥 **[Online]**		**30** minutes
Unit Checkpoint	Body Part and Job Words	

[Materials]

There are no materials to gather for this lesson.

[Online] **30** minutes

Students will work online to complete the Unit Checkpoint. Help students locate the Unit Checkpoint, and provide support as needed.

Unit Checkpoint ....

Body Part and Job Words
Explain that students are going to show what they have learned about vocabulary words for body parts and jobs.

Objectives
- Increase oral vocabulary.
- Increase reading vocabulary.
- Increase concept vocabulary.
- Identify and use picture clues to define words.
- Classify and sort common words into categories.

Family Words (A)

Unit Overview

In this unit, students will
- ► Learn family and friend vocabulary words.
- ► Complete the *All About Me* pages *Family Portrait* and *Fun With My Friends.*
- ► Explore the poems "Open Hydrant," "The Wheels on the Bus," and "The Secret Place."

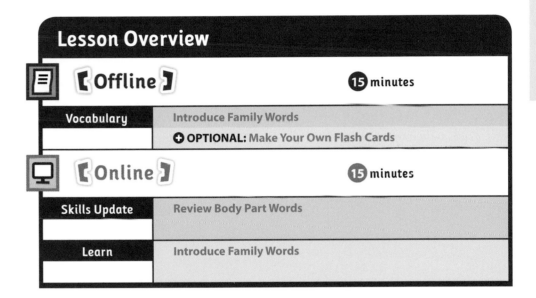

Lesson Overview

【Offline】	15 minutes
Vocabulary	**Introduce Family Words**
	➕ **OPTIONAL: Make Your Own Flash Cards**

【Online】	15 minutes
Skills Update	**Review Body Part Words**
Learn	**Introduce Family Words**

【Materials】

Supplied
- There are no supplied materials to gather for this lesson.

Also Needed
- household objects – magazine or family photos
- index cards (10) (optional)

【Offline】 15 minutes

Work **together** with students to complete an offline Vocabulary activity.

Vocabulary

Introduce Family Words
Tell students they are going to learn words for family members:

brother	mama	mother
dad	mom	pop
daddy	mommy	sister
father		

★ Objectives
- Increase oral vocabulary.
- Increase concept vocabulary.
- Use synonyms.

1. Say each word, and have students repeat the word after you.

2. Gather a magazine or family photos. With students, browse the magazine or photos and point out people who represent, or could represent, each vocabulary word. Prompt students to use the vocabulary words as they find examples of them.

   ▸ Point out that *mother, mom, mommy,* and *mama* all are different words for the same person.
   ▸ Point out that *father, pop, dad,* and *daddy* all are different words for the same person.

✪ OPTIONAL: Make Your Own Flash Cards

This activity is intended for students who have extra time and would benefit from practicing their vocabulary words with flash cards. Feel free to skip this activity.

Gather 10 index cards. Have students create flash cards by writing each vocabulary word on the front of an index card and their own definition for each word on the back. Help students with spelling as necessary.

TIP If students are not ready to read and write on their own, skip this optional activity.

 **(Online)** **15 minutes**

Students will work online **independently** to complete activities on Vocabulary words. Help students locate the online activities, and provide support as needed.

Skills Update ....

Review Body Part Words
Students will answer a few questions to refresh their Vocabulary knowledge.

> **Objectives**
> • Increase oral vocabulary.

Learn ....

Introduce Family Words
Students will be introduced to the family words *mother, mom, mommy, mama, father, pop, dad, daddy, brother,* and *sister.*

> **Objectives**
> • Increase oral vocabulary.
> • Increase reading vocabulary.
> • Increase concept vocabulary.

My Family and Family Words (A)

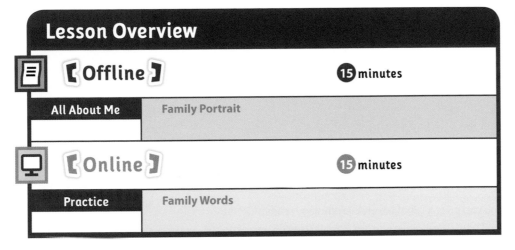

Lesson Overview

Offline		**15** minutes
All About Me	Family Portrait	
Online		**15** minutes
Practice	Family Words	

Materials

Supplied
- *K¹² All About Me*, p. 7

Also Needed
- crayons

Offline · **15** minutes

Work **together** with students to complete an offline All About Me activity.

All About Me

Family Portrait

Students will begin page 7 in *K¹² All About Me*. They will complete this page over two lessons.

1. Discuss with students the family members that live in their home. Have students tell you who each person is, using the vocabulary words *mother*, *father*, *brother*, and *sister* as applicable.

2. Discuss with students the family members they would like to include in a family portrait. If necessary, make note of students' responses, as you will need this information to finish the *K¹² All About Me* page.

3. Have students begin drawing their family portrait.

Objectives
- Draw and label pictures.
- Discuss own drawing.

 **Online** **15 minutes**

Students will work online **independently** to complete an activity on Vocabulary words. Help students locate the online activity, and provide support as needed.

Practice

Family Words

Students will practice the family words *mother, mom, mommy, mama, father, pop, dad, daddy, brother,* and *sister*.

Offline Alternative

No computer access? At any time, you can print a list of the unit Vocabulary words and their definitions from the online lesson. Use this list to review the words with students offline. In addition, if students made their own flash cards, these can be used for offline review.

 Objectives

- Increase oral vocabulary.
- Increase concept vocabulary.
- Use synonyms.

"Open Hydrant" and Family Words

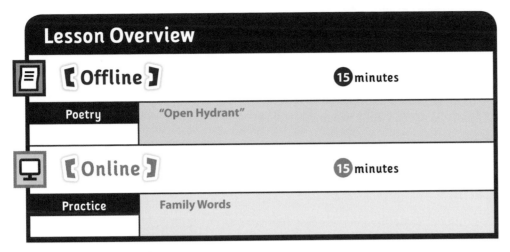

Lesson Overview

Offline		**15** minutes
Poetry	"Open Hydrant"	

Online		**15** minutes
Practice	Family Words	

Materials

Supplied

- *Tomie dePaola's Rhyme Time*

Advance Preparation

Before you begin reading the poems in *Tomie dePaolo's Rhyme Time*, you will need to number the pages of the book. Using a pencil, mark the bottom right-hand corner of the first title page as page 1. When you have finished numbering all the pages, turn to page 25.

Offline **15** minutes

Work **together** with students to complete an offline Poetry activity.

Poetry

"Open Hydrant"
It's time to read "Open Hydrant" from *Tomie dePaolo's Rhyme Time*.

1. Talk with students about summer weather. Ask them how they like to cool off when it's hot outside. Then tell students that the poem is about how some children in the city like to cool off.

2. Have students sit next to you so they can see the picture and words while you read the poem aloud. Tell students to listen for words in the poem that help us imagine how a summer day and cool water feel and sound.

Objectives

- Listen to and discuss poetry.
- Make connections with text: text-to-text, text-to self, text-to-world.
- Identify author's use of sensory language.

3. **Read aloud the entire poem**, and then ask:
   ▶ Is the water in the poem hot or cool? cool
   ▶ Does the water from the hydrant move fast or slow? fast
   ▶ Who are the "city fishes" in the poem? The children who play in the hydrant's water.
   ▶ Why do you think the author uses "city fishes" instead of "children"? Answers will vary.

4. **Say:** Many words in this poem help us imagine how a summer day and cool water feel and sound. When I hear the word *sizzle*, I think of something hot, like eggs in a frying pan or hamburgers on the grill.
   ▶ Does the word *sizzle* describe the summer weather or the water from the hydrant? the summer weather
   ▶ Name something else that could sizzle. Answers will vary.

5. **Say:** When I hear the word *whoosh*, I think of something moving fast, like a car speeding by.
   ▶ What does the word *whoosh* describe? the water rushing out of the fire hydrant
   ▶ Name something else that could *whoosh*. Answers will vary.

6. Ask students to listen as you reread the poem. As you read, emphasize the following words: *rushes, gushes, sizzle, whoosh, drizzle, hush, crashes, swishes, luscious,* and *city fishes.*
   ▶ Do you think the poem would be as much fun to listen to if the words were plain? Answers will vary.
   ▶ What helps you imagine the poem better: "water rushes up and gushes" or "water came out"? "water rushes up and gushes"

7. Reread the third stanza of the poem.
   ▶ Which three words help us imagine how the water sounds as it comes out of the hydrant? *hush, crashes, swishes*

 **15 minutes**

Students will work online **independently** to complete an activity on Vocabulary words. Help students locate the online activity, and provide support as needed.

Practice

Family Words

Students will practice the family words *mother, mom, mommy, mama, father, pop, dad, daddy, brother,* and *sister,* and learn synonyms for *mother* and *father*.

Objectives

- Increase oral vocabulary.
- Increase concept vocabulary.
- Use synonyms.

Offline Alternative

No computer access? At any time, you can print a list of the unit Vocabulary words and their definitions from the online lesson. Use this list to review the words with students offline. In addition, If students made their own flash cards, these can be used for offline review.

Family Words (B)

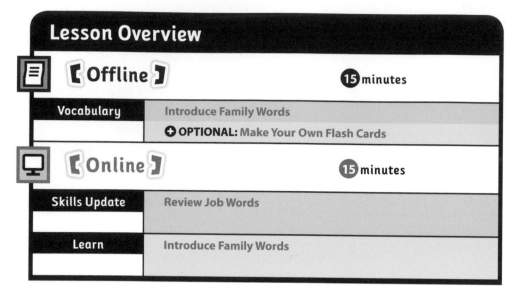

Lesson Overview

Offline		15 minutes
Vocabulary	Introduce Family Words	
	⊕ OPTIONAL: Make Your Own Flash Cards	

Online		15 minutes
Skills Update	Review Job Words	
Learn	Introduce Family Words	

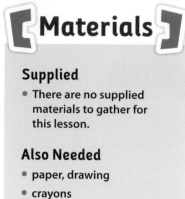

Materials

Supplied
- There are no supplied materials to gather for this lesson.

Also Needed
- paper, drawing
- crayons
- index cards (7) (optional)

Offline 15 minutes

Work **together** with students to complete an offline Vocabulary activity.

Vocabulary

Introduce Family Words

Introduce students to the following vocabulary words:

aunt	grandfather	nephew	uncle
cousin	grandmother	niece	

Objectives
- Increase oral vocabulary.
- Increase reading vocabulary.
- Increase concept vocabulary.

1. Gather paper and crayons. Ask students to draw a picture of their extended family (grandparents, aunts, uncles, and cousins).

2. Ask students to point out family members. Prompt them to use the vocabulary words. Label the people in the picture with the correct vocabulary words.

TIP Vary the questions you ask based on each student's family. For example, if a student doesn't have any cousins, omit that question.

⊕ **OPTIONAL: Make Your Own Flash Cards**

This activity is intended for students who have extra time and would benefit from practicing their vocabulary words with flash cards. Feel free to skip this activity.

Gather seven index cards. Have students create flash cards by writing each vocabulary word on the front of an index card and their own definition for each word on the back. Help students with spelling as necessary.

 **[Online]** minutes

Students will work online **independently** to complete activities on Vocabulary words. Help students locate the online activities, and provide support as needed.

Skills Update

Review Job Words

Students will answer a few questions to refresh their Vocabulary knowledge.

Objectives
- Increase oral vocabulary.
- Identify and use picture clues to define words.
- Classify and sort words into categories.

Learn

Introduce Family Words

Students will be introduced to the family words *aunt, uncle, cousin, niece, nephew, grandmother,* and *grandfather.*

Objectives
- Increase oral vocabulary.
- Increase reading vocabulary.
- Increase concept vocabulary.

My Family and Family Words (B)

Lesson Overview

Offline   15 minutes

All About Me	Family Portrait

Online   15 minutes

Practice	Family Words

Materials

Supplied
- *K¹² All About Me*, p. 7

Also Needed
- crayons

Offline   15 minutes

Work **together** with students to complete an offline All About Me activity.

All About Me

Family Portrait

Students will complete page 7 in *K¹² All About Me*.

1. Have students explain their drawing of family members. Encourage them to add details to their drawing to make each person as accurate and identifiable as possible.

2. Help students label each person in their drawing. If necessary, label the pictures for students.

3. If you labeled the pictures for students, have students practice writing the words below your writing. Make sure they use lowercase letters and proper letter formation.

4. If time permits, have students add family members who do not live with them to their drawing. Have them tell you the name of each person.

5. Encourage students to share their drawing with others.

Objectives
- Draw and label pictures.
- Add supporting details to written or drawn work.
- Discuss own drawing.

 **15 minutes**

Students will work online **independently** to complete an activity on Vocabulary words. Help students locate the online activity, and provide support as needed.

Practice

Family Words

Students will practice the family words *aunt, uncle, cousin, niece, nephew, grandmother,* and *grandfather,* and learn about the concept of a family tree.

Objectives
- Increase oral vocabulary.
- Increase concept vocabulary.

Offline Alternative

No computer access? At any time, you can print a list of the unit Vocabulary words and their definitions from the online lesson. Use this list to review the words with students offline. In addition, if students made their own flash cards, these can be used for offline review.

"The Wheels on the Bus" and Family Words

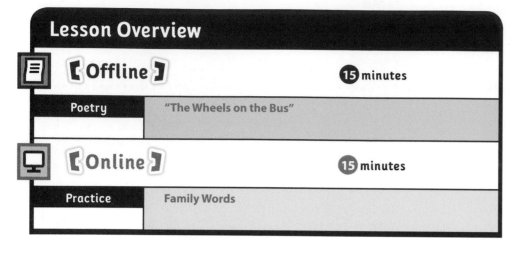

Lesson Overview

Offline		**15** minutes
Poetry	"The Wheels on the Bus"	

Online		**15** minutes
Practice	Family Words	

Materials

Supplied
- *K¹² Read Aloud Treasury*, pp. 30–33
- *K¹² Language Arts Activity Book*, p. LS 5

Also Needed
- crayons

[Offline] ⏱ **15** minutes

Work **together** with students to complete an offline Poetry activity.

Poetry

"The Wheels on the Bus"

It's time to read "The Wheels on the Bus" from *K¹² Read Aloud Treasury*.

1. Tell students that the poem is about a bus.

   ▸ Have you ever ridden on a bus? Answers will vary.
   ▸ What do buses do? They drive around and take people to places.

2. Have students sit next to you so they can see the picture and the words while you read the poem aloud. Tell students to listen for words in the poem that help us imagine how things and people sound.

3. **Read aloud the entire poem**, and then ask:

   ▸ What do the wheels on the bus do? They go round and round.
   ▸ Which phrase is repeated in the part of the poem that describes the wipers—*shh, shh, shh*; *waa, waa, waa*; or *swish, swish, swish*? *swish, swish, swish*
   ▸ What does the driver of the bus say? "move on back"
   ▸ What do the babies on the bus do? They cry.
   ▸ Where does the bus go in this poem? all through the town

4. Remind students that this poem, like others, has words that help us imagine how things and people sound.

Objectives

- Listen to and discuss poetry.
- Make connections with text: text-to-text, text-to-self, text-to-world.
- Identify author's use of sensory language.
- Respond to text through art, writing, and/or drama.
- Identify repetitive text.

5. **Say:** "The wipers on the bus say *swish, swish, swish*." The words *swish, swish, swish* make me think of water—it must be raining outside during this poem.

   ► What sound do the babies make? *waa, waa, waa*
   ► What does that make you think about the babies? Answers will vary.
   ► What sound do the mommies make? *shh, shh, shh*
   ► Have you heard these sounds in your life? Answers will vary.

6. Turn to page LS 5 in *K¹² Language Arts Activity Book*. Reread the poem. As students listen, they should point to each corresponding part of the picture. Then, have students color the page and tell you what each part of the bus does and what each person on the bus says.

Poetry

"The Wheels on the Bus" and Family Words
"The Wheels on the Bus"

Color the picture.

LANGUAGE ARTS BLUE   LS 5

[Online] 🕒 minutes

Students will work online **independently** to complete an activity on Vocabulary words. Help students locate the online activity, and provide support as needed.

Practice

Family Words
Students will practice the family words *aunt, uncle, cousin, niece, nephew, grandmother,* and *grandfather*.

Offline Alternative

No computer access? At any time, you can print a list of the unit Vocabulary words and their definitions from the online lesson. Use this list to review the words with students offline. In addition, if students made their own flash cards, these can be used for offline review.

 Objectives
- Increase oral vocabulary.
- Increase concept vocabulary.

Friend Words

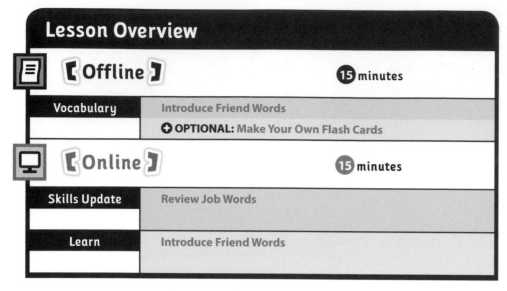

Lesson Overview

Offline		15 minutes
Vocabulary	Introduce Friend Words	
	⊕ OPTIONAL: Make Your Own Flash Cards	

Online		15 minutes
Skills Update	Review Job Words	
Learn	Introduce Friend Words	

Materials

Supplied
- There are no supplied materials to gather for this lesson.

Also Needed
- index cards (16) (8 optional)

Advance Preparation

Gather eight index cards. Write each of these words on an index card, one word per card: *friend, buddy, pal, toy, playmate, play, game,* and *share.* If students cannot read easily, also draw a simple picture of the object or action.

Offline 15 minutes

Work **together** with students to complete an offline Vocabulary activity.

Vocabulary ....

Introduce Friend Words

Play a game to introduce students to the following vocabulary words:

buddy	**game**	**play**	**share**
friend	**pal**	**playmate**	**toy**

1. Say each word, and have students repeat the word after you.

2. Gather the index cards you prepared. Show each one to students, and discuss the definitions of the words, providing examples from students' lives. For example, when explaining the definitions of *friend, buddy,* and *pal,* you might name one of the student's friends.

Objectives
- Increase oral vocabulary.
- Increase reading vocabulary.
- Use synonyms.

3. Put the cards on a flat surface, with the words/pictures face up. Ask students to

   ▸ Find the card that has another word for *friend*. buddy, pal
   ▸ Find the card that has another word for *buddy*. friend, pal
   ▸ Find the card that has another word for *pal*. friend, pal
   ▸ Find the card that has a word for something to play with. toy
   ▸ Find the card that has a word for a child who joins a person in playing and having fun. playmate
   ▸ Find the card that has a word for having fun or taking part in a game or sport. play
   ▸ Find the card that has a word for a way of playing with rules that the players agree on. game
   ▸ Find the card that has a word for letting someone else enjoy something, too. share

---

⊕ OPTIONAL: Make Your Own Flash Cards

This activity is intended for students who have extra time and would benefit from practicing their vocabulary words with flash cards. Feel free to skip this activity.

Gather eight index cards. Have students create flash cards by writing each vocabulary word on the front of an index card and their own definition for each word on the back. Help students with spelling as necessary.

 **15 minutes**

Students will work online **independently** to complete activities on Vocabulary words. Help students locate the online activities, and provide support as needed.

Skills Update ··

Review Job Words
Students will answer a few questions to refresh their Vocabulary knowledge.

 Objectives
- Increase oral vocabulary.
- Identify and use picture clues to define words.
- Classify and sort words into categories.

Learn ··

Introduce Friend Words
Students will be introduced to the friend words *friend, buddy, pal, toy, playmate, play, game,* and *share*.

 Objectives
- Increase oral vocabulary.
- Increase reading vocabulary.
- Increase concept vocabulary.

My Friends and Friend Words

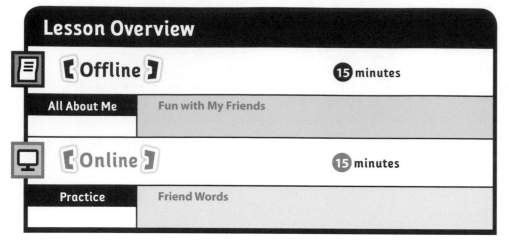

Lesson Overview

【Offline】		**15** minutes
All About Me	Fun with My Friends	
【Online】		**15** minutes
Practice	Friend Words	

【Materials】

Supplied
- *K¹² All About Me*, p. 8

Also Needed
- crayons

【Offline】 **15** minutes

Work **together** with students to complete an offline All About Me activity.

All About Me

Fun with My Friends

Students will complete sentences and illustrate them to practice vocabulary. They will complete this page over two lessons.

1. Help students begin page 8 in *K¹² All About Me*. Read aloud the first incomplete sentence to students, pointing to each word as you read.

2. Have students repeat the first part of the sentence and tell you an answer to write in the blank. Read the complete sentence to students.

3. Ask students to point to the words *friends* and *play*.

4. Repeat these steps for the remaining sentences. Have students point to the words *share*, *friends*, and *toys*.

5. Discuss answers with students. Ask them what they'd like to draw to go with the sentences. If time permits, have students begin their drawing.

Objectives
- Dictate or write simple sentences describing experiences, stories, people, objects, or events.
- Write and/or draw narrative text.

 **15 minutes**

Students will work online **independently** to complete an activity on Vocabulary words. Help students locate the online activity, and provide support as needed.

Practice

Friend Words

Students will review the friend words *friend, buddy, pal, toy, playmate, play, game,* and *share,* and learn synonyms for the word *friend.*

Objectives
- Increase oral vocabulary.
- Increase concept vocabulary.
- Use synonyms.

Offline Alternative

No computer access? At any time, you can print a list of the unit Vocabulary words and their definitions from the online lesson. Use this list to review the words with students offline. In addition, if students made their own flash cards, these can be used for offline review.

"The Secret Place" and Vocabulary Unit Review

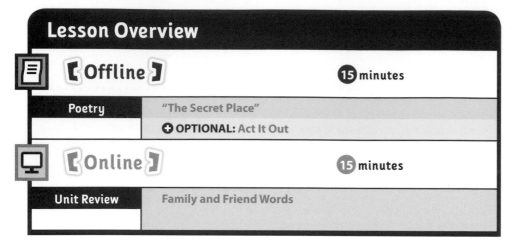

Lesson Overview

	Offline	15 minutes
Poetry	"The Secret Place"	
	⊕ OPTIONAL: Act It Out	

	Online	15 minutes
Unit Review	Family and Friend Words	

Materials

Supplied

● *Tomie dePaola's Rhyme Time*

Advance Preparation

Before reading today's poem, you will need to find the poem in *Tomie dePaola's Rhyme Time*. If your book has page numbers, turn to page 13. Otherwise, you will need to use a pencil to number the pages in the book. Mark the title page as page 1.

Offline 15 minutes

Work **together** with students to complete an offline Poetry activity.

Poetry

"The Secret Place"

It's time to read "The Secret Place" from *Tomie dePaola's Rhyme Time*.

1. Have students tell you their meaning of the word *secret*. As necessary, tell them that a secret is something you keep to yourself. Tell them that a secret can be special, something that is yours and no one else's.

2. Have students sit next to you so they can see the picture and words while you read the poem aloud.

3. **Read aloud the entire poem**, and then ask:
   ▶ Where is the child's secret place? under the covers, at the bottom of the bed
   ▶ What does the child do in his secret place? read and draw pictures
   ▶ What does the child draw pictures on? the sheets
   ▶ How long is the child's secret place a secret? about a week

Objectives
● Listen to and discuss poetry.
● Make connections with text: text-to-text, text-to-self, text-to-world.
● Use visual text features to aid understanding of text.

4. Point to the illustration in *Tomie dePaola's Rhyme Time*.

   ▸ How does the mother look in the picture? Possible answer: unhappy
   ▸ Why does the mother look this way? Possible answer: because the little boy shouldn't have drawn on his sheets

5. Discuss whether students have a secret place of their own, a place where they like to go to draw, color, listen to music, or spend time alone.

   Say: You don't have to tell where your special place is—it's a secret! But tell me why your secret place is special.

⊕ OPTIONAL: Act It Out

This activity is intended for students who have extra time and would benefit from role-playing as the people in the picture. Feel free to skip this activity.

   Have students imagine that they are the mother in the poem and you are the child. Act out the conversation you two might have after the secret place has been discovered and the sheets have been drawn on.

 **minutes**

Students will work online **independently** to complete an activity on Vocabulary words. Help students locate the online activity, and provide support as needed.

Unit Review •

Family and Friend Words
Students will review all words from the unit to prepare for the Unit Checkpoint.

Objectives
• Increase oral vocabulary.

Offline Alternative

No computer access? At any time, you can print a list of the unit Vocabulary words and their definitions from the online lesson. Use this list to review the words with students offline. In addition, if students made their own flash cards, these can be used for offline review.

Unit Checkpoint

Lesson Overview

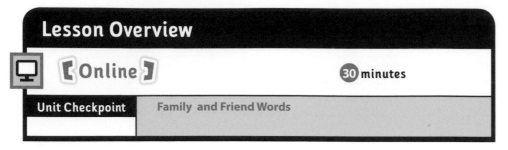

[Online]	30 minutes
Unit Checkpoint	Family and Friend Words

[Materials]

There are no materials to gather for this lesson.

[Online] 30 minutes

Students will work online to complete the Unit Checkpoint. Help students locate the Unit Checkpoint, and provide support as needed.

Unit Checkpoint

Family and Friend Words

Explain that students are going to show what they have learned about vocabulary words for family members and friends.

Objectives
- Increase oral vocabulary.
- Increase reading vocabulary.
- Increase concept vocabulary.
- Use synonyms.

Community Words (A)

Unit Overview

In this unit, students will
- Learn community vocabulary words.
- Complete the *All About Me* pages *Fun with My Friends* and *My Street*.
- Explore the poems "Mary Had a Little Lamb," "Time to Rise," and "Old King Cole."

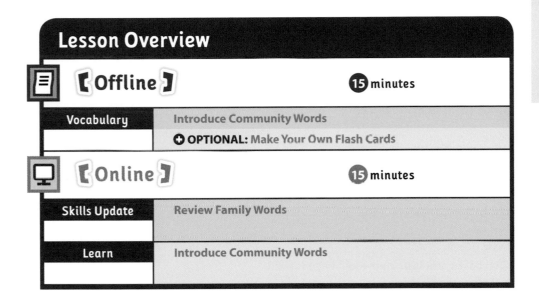

Lesson Overview

[Offline] — 15 minutes

| Vocabulary | Introduce Community Words |
| | ⊕ OPTIONAL: Make Your Own Flash Cards |

[Online] — 15 minutes

| Skills Update | Review Family Words |
| Learn | Introduce Community Words |

[Offline] 15 minutes

Work **together** with students to complete an offline Vocabulary activity.

Vocabulary

Introduce Community Words
Have students learn the following community words:

city	house	room	town
door	map	stairs	wall

Materials

Supplied
- There are no supplied materials to gather for this lesson.

Also Needed
- household objects – state map
- index cards (8) (optional)

Objectives
- Increase oral vocabulary.
- Increase concept vocabulary.

1. Gather a state map that shows cities and towns, or go to a website with a state map. (A map of your own state would be ideal.) Tell students that a map is a drawing of a place that shows where things are. Explain that some maps show cities and towns.

2. Point to a city on the map. Tell students that a city is a place where many people live and work. If students live in, have visited, or are familiar with a city, use that city as an example. Have them try to give more examples of cities they know.

3. Point to a town on the map. Explain that towns are also places where people live and work, but that towns are smaller than cities.

4. Explain to students that within cities and towns are communities. Communities are like neighborhoods, where a small group of people live and work. Within a community are houses, stores, schools, post offices, libraries, and other places.

5. Discuss with students what they know about their own community.

   ▸ What kinds of places and things do you see in your community?
     Answers will vary.

6. Tell students that many houses and other buildings in a community have things in common: They have rooms, doors, walls, and sometimes stairs. Have students point to any rooms, doors, walls, and stairs around them.

⊕ OPTIONAL: Make Your Own Flash Cards

This activity is intended for students who have extra time and would benefit from practicing their vocabulary words with flash cards. Feel free to skip this activity.

Gather eight index cards. Have students create flash cards by writing each vocabulary word on the front of an index card and their own definition for each word on the back. Help students with spelling as necessary.

(TIP) If students are not ready to read and write on their own, skip this optional activity.

[Online] minutes

Students will work online **independently** to complete activities on Vocabulary words. Help students locate the online activities, and provide support as needed.

Skills Update

Review Family Words
Students will answer a few questions to refresh their Vocabulary knowledge.

Objectives
- Increase oral vocabulary.
- Increase reading vocabulary.
- Increase concept vocabulary.

Learn

Introduce Community Words
Students will be introduced to the community words *map, city, town, house, wall, room, door,* and *stairs.*

Objectives
- Increase oral vocabulary.
- Increase reading vocabulary.
- Increase concept vocabulary.

My Friends and Community Words

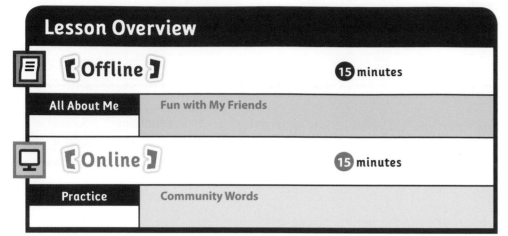

Lesson Overview

[Offline]   **15** minutes

All About Me	Fun with My Friends

[Online]   **15** minutes

Practice	Community Words

[Materials]

Supplied
● *K¹² All About Me*, p. 8

Also Needed
● crayons

[Offline] **15** minutes

Work **together** with students to complete an offline All About Me activity.

All About Me ···

Fun with My Friends
Students will complete page 8 in *K¹² All About Me*.

1. Read aloud each sentence, pointing to each word as you read.

2. Have students finalize their drawing of a scene with their friends and explain their illustration when done. Encourage them to use vocabulary words they've learned (*friend, play, game, toy, share,* and others) in their description.

Objectives
● Write and/or draw narrative text.
● Add supporting details to written or drawn work.
● Discuss own drawing.
● Share finished written and drawn works.

 **15 minutes**

Students will work online **independently** to complete an activity on Vocabulary words. Help students locate the online activity, and provide support as needed.

Practice ....

Community Words

Students will practice the community words *map, city, town, house, wall, room, door,* and *stairs.*

Objectives
- Increase oral vocabulary.
- Increase reading vocabulary.
- Increase concept vocabulary.

Offline Alternative

No computer access? At any time, you can print a list of the unit Vocabulary words and their definitions from the online lesson. Use this list to review the words with students offline. In addition, if students made their own flash cards, these can be used for offline review.

"Mary Had a Little Lamb" and Community Words

Lesson Overview

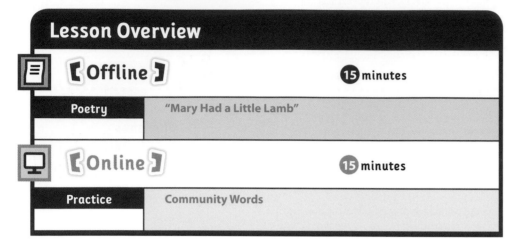

Offline — 15 minutes

| Poetry | "Mary Had a Little Lamb" |

Online — 15 minutes

| Practice | Community Words |

Materials

Supplied
- *The Rooster Crows*
- *K¹² Language Arts Activity Book*, p. LS 7

Also Needed
- crayons

Advance Preparation

Before reading today's poem, you will need to find the poem in *The Rooster Crows*. If your book has page numbers, turn to page 8. Otherwise, you will need to use a pencil to number the pages in the book. Mark the title page as page 1.

Offline 15 minutes

Work **together** with students to complete an offline Poetry activity.

 **Poetry**

"Mary Had a Little Lamb"

It's time to read "Mary Had a Little Lamb" from *The Rooster Crows*. Before you begin this activity, read the poem to yourself. Note that *b-a-a-r* is pronounced like the word *bar*.

1. Ask students if they've ever heard "Mary Had a Little Lamb." If so, ask them to recite the poem.

2. If students don't know the more-familiar "fleece as white as snow" version, recite the following for them: "Mary had a little lamb, its fleece was white as snow; and everywhere that Mary went, the lamb was sure to go."
   Say: This is not the only poem that begins with "Mary had a little lamb." Today you'll hear another poem that begins with those same words.

3. Have students sit next to you so they can see the picture and words while you read the poem aloud.

Objectives
- Listen to and discuss poetry.
- Use prior knowledge to aid understanding of text.
- Identify and use picture clues to define words.
- Respond to text through art, writing, and/or drama.

4. Point to the illustration of the black sheep.

   ▸ What color is the lamb's fleece in this version of the poem? black
   Say: *B-a-a-r* is an old-fashioned spelling of *bear*.
   ▸ Do you think the author is telling us that everywhere Mary went, people thought she had a little bear with her? Yes
   ▸ What word in the poem rhymes with *b-a-a-r*? *tar*
   ▸ What do you think the word *fleece* means? Possible answers: wool; fur

5. Have students complete page LS 7 in *K¹² Language Arts Activity Book*. Before students color the picture, ask:

   ▸ Why is the little girl hiding from the lamb? She's afraid.
   ▸ Why is the little girl afraid of the little lamb? She thinks the lamb is a bear.
   ▸ What color should you use for the lamb's fleece? black

6. Encourage students to practice reciting the poem as they color the picture. Remind them that rhyming words can be clues to help remember the words in a poem.

[Online] ⏱ 15 minutes

Students will work online **independently** to complete an activity on Vocabulary words. Help students locate the online activity, and provide support as needed.

Practice ●

Community Words
Students will practice the community words *map*, *city*, *town*, *house*, *wall*, *room*, *door*, and *stairs*.

Offline Alternative

No computer access? At any time, you can print a list of the unit Vocabulary words and their definitions from the online lesson. Use this list to review the words with students offline. In addition, if students made their own flash cards, these can be used for offline review.

Objectives
• Increase oral vocabulary.
• Increase reading vocabulary.
• Increase concept vocabulary.

Community Words (B)

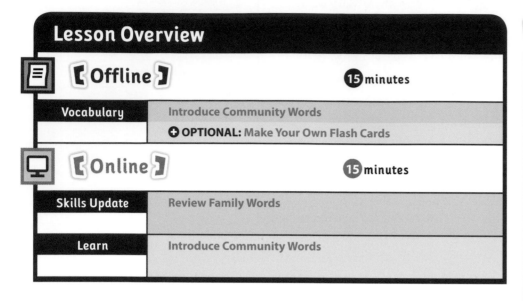

Lesson Overview

Offline 15 minutes

Vocabulary	Introduce Community Words
	✚ OPTIONAL: Make Your Own Flash Cards

Online 15 minutes

Skills Update	Review Family Words
Learn	Introduce Community Words

Materials

Supplied

- There are no supplied materials to gather for this lesson.

Also Needed

- household objects – magazines
- scissors, round-end safety
- glue stick
- paper, construction
- crayons
- index cards (8) (optional)

Offline 15 minutes

Work **together** with students to complete an offline Vocabulary activity.

Vocabulary

Introduce Community Words

Help students learn the following community words by making a community poster:

car	mailbox	road	sign
fence	neighborhood	sidewalk	street

1. Gather some magazines, scissors, construction paper, glue, and crayons. Tell students they are going to make a community poster.

2. Have students flip through the magazines, cutting out pictures that represent each community word. Have them glue the pictures to their paper to make a community scene. As students find each picture, make sure they use the vocabulary words. For example, if students see a picture of a mailbox, have them say, "I found a mailbox." (If students cannot find a picture for a word, have them draw a picture instead.)

3. When students look for a street and a road, explain that the two words can mean the same thing.

4. Once the poster is complete, have students explain their poster by naming each item, saying, "In this community, there is a [vocabulary word]."

Objectives
- Increase oral vocabulary.
- Increase concept vocabulary.

⊕ OPTIONAL: Make Your Own Flash Cards

This activity is intended for students who have extra time and would benefit from practicing their vocabulary words with flash cards. Feel free to skip this activity.

Gather eight index cards. Have students create flash cards by writing each vocabulary word on the front of an index card and their own definition for each word on the back. Help students with spelling as necessary.

 **15 minutes**

Students will work online **independently** to complete activities on Vocabulary words. Help students locate the online activities, and provide support as needed.

Skills Update ••

Review Family Words
Students will answer a few questions to refresh their Vocabulary knowledge.

Objectives
- Increase reading vocabulary.
- Increase oral vocabulary.
- Increase concept vocabulary.

Learn ••

Introduce Community Words
Students will be introduced to the community words *mailbox, neighborhood, street, car, fence, road, sidewalk,* and *sign.*

Objectives
- Increase oral vocabulary.
- Increase reading vocabulary.
- Increase concept vocabulary.

My Neighborhood and Community Words (A)

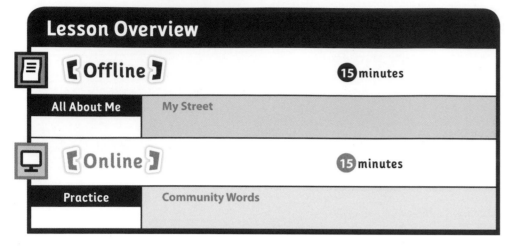

Lesson Overview

[Offline]	15 minutes
All About Me	My Street

[Online]	15 minutes
Practice	Community Words

Supplied
- *K¹² All About Me*, p. 9

Also Needed
- crayons

[Offline] 15 minutes

Work **together** with students to complete an offline All About Me activity.

 All About Me ....

My Street

Students will complete a sentence and describe their street. They will complete this page over two lessons.

1. Help students begin page 9 in *K¹² All About Me*. Ask them to describe the street they live on. Encourage students to use details to describe the houses, buildings, restaurants, signs, or common activities they see in their neighborhood.

2. Read aloud the incomplete sentence to students, pointing to each word as you read.

3. Have students repeat the first part of the sentence and tell you the answer to write in the blank space.

4. Read the complete sentence to students, and have students repeat it.

5. If time permits, have students begin their drawing of their street.

Objectives
- Describe familiar and common objects and events.
- Write and /or draw narrative text.
- Describe people, places, things, locations, actions, events, and/or feelings.

 Online ⑮ minutes

Students will work online **independently** to complete an activity on
Vocabulary words. Help students locate the online activity, and provide
support as needed.

Practice ···

Community Words
Students will practice the community words *mailbox, neighborhood, street, car, fence,*
road, sidewalk, and *sign.*

Objectives
- Increase oral vocabulary.
- Increase reading vocabulary.
- Increase concept vocabulary.

Offline Alternative

No computer access? At any time, you can print a list of the unit Vocabulary words
and their definitions from the online lesson. Use this list to review the words with
students offline. In addition, if students made their own flash cards, these can be used
for offline review.

"Time to Rise" and Community Words

Lesson Overview

[Offline] **15** minutes

Poetry	"Time to Rise"
	⊕ OPTIONAL: More Rhymes

[Online] **15** minutes

Practice	Community Words

[Materials]

Supplied

- *Tomie dePaola's Rhyme Time*

Keywords

prediction – a guess about what might happen that is based on information in a story and what you already know

Advance Preparation

Before reading today's poem, you will need to find the poem in *Tomie dePaola's Rhyme Time*. If your book has page numbers, turn to page 26. Otherwise, you will need to use a pencil to number the pages in the book. Mark the title page as page 1.

[Offline] **15** minutes

Work **together** with students to complete an offline Poetry activity.

Poetry

"Time to Rise"

It's time to read "Time to Rise" in *Tomie dePaola's Rhyme Time*.

1. Ask students if they know the word **prediction.** Explain that a prediction is a type of guess.

2. Tell students that today's poem is called "Time to Rise."

   ▸ What do you think this poem might be about? Answers will vary.

3. Have students sit next to you so they can see the picture, and read aloud the poem.
   Say: Think about your prediction. Now tell me, what was the poem about? Does that match your prediction? Answers will vary.

4. Reread the poem. Then ask:

Objectives

- Listen to and discuss poetry.
- Make predictions based on title, illustrations, and/or context clues.
- Make connections with text: text-to-text, text-to-self, text-to-world.
- Identify rhyme and rhythm in poetry.

- ▶ What color is the birdie's bill? yellow
- ▶ Which word in the poem rhymes with *bill*: *said*, *sill*, or *sleepyhead*? *sill*
- ▶ Which two words rhyme in the poem's last two lines? *said* and *sleepyhead*
- ▶ Is it probably morning, afternoon, or night in this poem? morning

5. Discuss with students how they feel when it's time for them to rise in the morning. Encourage them to talk about any morning routines they have and how those routines make them feel.

➕ OPTIONAL: More Rhymes

This activity is intended for students who have extra time and would benefit from practicing rhyming words. Feel free to skip this activity.

Have students say words that rhyme with *bill* or *sill*. Repeat, using *said* or *sleepyhead*.

 **15 minutes**

Students will work online **independently** to complete an activity on Vocabulary words. Help students locate the online activity, and provide support as needed.

Practice ....

Community Words

Students will practice the community words *mailbox*, *neighborhood*, *street*, *car*, *fence*, *road*, *sidewalk*, and *sign*.

Offline Alternative

No computer access? At any time, you can print a list of the unit Vocabulary words and their definitions from the online lesson. Use this list to review the words with students offline. In addition, if students made their own flash cards, these can be used for offline review.

> **Objectives**
> - Increase oral vocabulary.
> - Increase reading vocabulary.
> - Increase concept vocabulary.

Community Words (C)

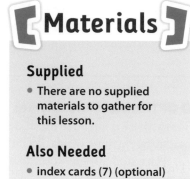

Lesson Overview

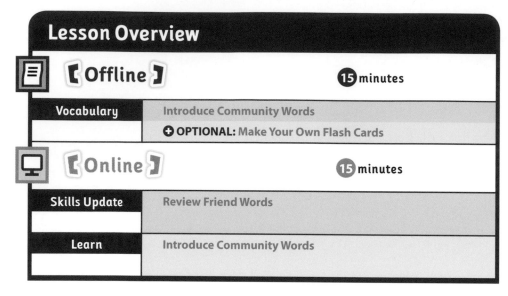

[Offline]   **15** minutes

Vocabulary	Introduce Community Words
	⊕ OPTIONAL: Make Your Own Flash Cards

[Online]   **15** minutes

Skills Update	Review Friend Words
Learn	Introduce Community Words

[Materials]

Supplied
- There are no supplied materials to gather for this lesson.

Also Needed
- index cards (7) (optional)

[Offline]   **15** minutes

Work **together** with students to complete an offline Vocabulary activity.

Introduce Community Words

Introduce the following community words to students:

grocery store	**park**	**restaurant**
library	**playground**	**toy store**
office		

Objectives
- Increase oral vocabulary.
- Increase concept vocabulary.

1. Ask students to name some places they go or see in their community. List these places on a sheet of paper. If students do not name all the vocabulary words, prompt them to say the words. For example, "How about a library? Do you ever go to a library?" Then add the words to the list. If students do not know what a place is, provide an explanation.

2. Ask students the following questions. If students give the correct answer, have them circle the word(s) on your list and then do one of the following: turn around three times, touch their toes, or stand on one leg. If students do not give the correct answer, provide a definition and have them try again.

   ▸ Where do people check out books? library
   ▸ Where might people have a picnic? park
   ▸ Where do people buy food? grocery store
   ▸ Where do some people go to work? office

- ▶ Where do people go to eat? restaurant
- ▶ Where do children play on a slide or swings? playground
- ▶ Where do people buy toys? toy store

3. If time permits, discuss with students the library, park, grocery store, office buildings, restaurants, playgrounds, and toy stores in their community. You might ask questions such as the following:

- ▶ What do you play on at your playground?
- ▶ What is your favorite restaurant?
- ▶ Do you know anyone who works in an office?

⊕ OPTIONAL: Make Your Own Flash Cards

This activity is intended for students who have extra time and would benefit from practicing their vocabulary words with flash cards. Feel free to skip this activity.

Gather seven index cards. Have students create flash cards by writing each vocabulary word on the front of an index card and their own definition for each word on the back. Help students with spelling as necessary.

 **15 minutes**

Students will work online **independently** to complete activities on Vocabulary words. Help students locate the online activities, and provide support as needed.

Skills Update

Review Friend Words
Students will answer a few questions to refresh their Vocabulary knowledge.

Objectives
- Increase oral vocabulary.
- Increase reading vocabulary.
- Increase concept vocabulary.

Learn

Introduce Community Words
Students will be introduced to the community words *library, park, grocery store, office, restaurant, playground,* and *toy store.*

Objectives
- Increase oral vocabulary.
- Increase reading vocabulary.
- Increase concept vocabulary.

My Neighborhood and Community Words (B)

Lesson Overview

[Offline]		**15** minutes
All About Me	My Street	
[Online]		**15** minutes
Practice	Community Words	

[Materials]

Supplied
- *K¹² All About Me*, p. 9

Also Needed
- crayons

[Offline] **15** minutes

Work **together** with students to complete an offline All About Me activity.

All About Me

My Street

Students will complete a drawing and describe their street.

1. Have students finish their drawing on page 9 in *K¹² All About Me*.

2. When students have completed the picture, have them explain their illustration. Encourage them to use vocabulary words they've learned (*house, apartment, mailbox, car, fence, sidewalk, sign, park, grocery store*, and others) in their description.

3. If possible, encourage students to share their completed drawing with others.

Objectives

- Describe familiar and common objects and events.
- Write and/or draw narrative text.
- Describe people, places, things, locations, actions, events, and/or feelings.
- Add supporting details to written or drawn work.
- Discuss own drawing.
- Share finished written and drawn works.

 **[Online]** **15** minutes

Students will work online **independently** to complete an activity on Vocabulary words. Help students locate the online activity, and provide support as needed.

Practice ....

Community Words

Students will practice the community words *library, park, grocery store, office, restaurant, playground,* and *toy store.*

Offline Alternative

No computer access? At any time, you can print a list of the unit Vocabulary words and their definitions from the online lesson. Use this list to review the words with students offline. In addition, if students made their own flash cards, these can be used for offline review.

Objectives
- Increase oral vocabulary.
- Increase reading vocabulary.
- Increase concept vocabulary.

"Old King Cole" and Vocabulary Unit Review

Lesson Overview

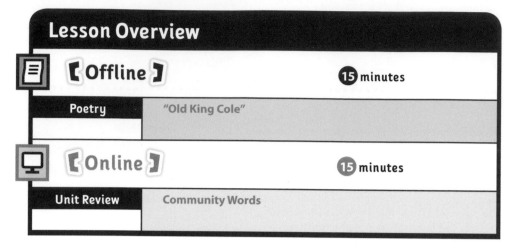

[Offline]		**15** minutes
Poetry	"Old King Cole"	

[Online]		**15** minutes
Unit Review	Community Words	

[Materials]

Supplied
- *K¹² Read Aloud Treasury,* p. 61

Keywords

character – a person or animal in a story or poem

[Offline] **15** minutes

Work **together** with students to complete an offline Poetry activity.

Poetry

"Old King Cole"

It's time to read "Old King Cole" from *K¹² Read Aloud Treasury.*

1. Tell students that nursery rhymes are poems that almost everyone hears when they are very young. They will hear a nursery rhyme about a man named Old King Cole.

   Say: The people and animals in poems are called **characters**. We learn about characters from what they do, what they say, and what the poem or story says about them.

2. Have students sit next to you so they can see the picture and words while you **read aloud** "Old King Cole," and then ask:
   - ▸ What word rhymes with *Cole: soul, three,* or *pipe*? *soul*
   - ▸ What does Old King Cole call for first? his pipe
   - ▸ How many fiddlers does Old King Cole call for? three

3. Remind students what a character is.
   - ▸ Who is the character in this poem? Old King Cole

Objectives
- Listen to and discuss poetry.
- Identify rhyme and rhythm.
- Identify character(s).
- Describe character(s).

4. Remind students that we learn about characters from what they do, what they say, and what the poem or story says about them.

   ▶ What does Old King Cole say and do in the poem? He calls for his pipe, his bowl, and his fiddlers three.
   ▶ Does the poem say that Old King Cole is happy or sad? happy (merry)

5. Reread the poem a final time. If possible, encourage students to recite the poem with you.

 **15** minutes

Students will work online **independently** to complete an activity on Vocabulary words. Help students locate the online activity, and provide support as needed.

Unit Review

Community Words

Students will review all words from the unit to prepare for the Unit Checkpoint.

Offline Alternative

No computer access? At any time, you can print a list of the unit Vocabulary words and their definitions from the online lesson. Use this list to review the words with students offline. In addition, if students made their own flash cards, these can be used for offline review.

Objectives
- Increase oral vocabulary.
- Increase reading vocabulary.
- Increase concept vocabulary.

Unit Checkpoint

Lesson Overview

 [Online]   **30** minutes

Unit Checkpoint	Community Words

[Materials]

There are no materials to gather for this lesson.

[Online] **30** minutes

Students will work online to complete the Unit Checkpoint. Help students locate the Unit Checkpoint, and provide support as needed.

Unit Checkpoint ....

Community Words

Explain that students are going to show what they have learned about vocabulary words for community.

Objectives
- Increase oral vocabulary.
- Increase reading vocabulary.
- Increase concept vocabulary.

Color Words (B)

Unit Overview

In this unit, students will
- ▸ Learn vocabulary words for colors.
- ▸ Complete the *All About Me* pages *My Favorite Color* and *My Favorite Shape*.
- ▸ Explore the poems "Engine, Engine, Number Nine"; "How Much Wood Would a Woodchuck Chuck?"; and "Baa Baa, Black Sheep."

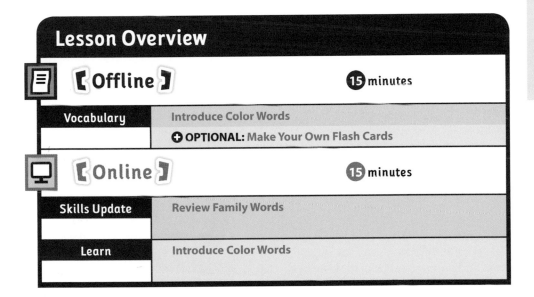

Lesson Overview

▤	**【 Offline 】**	**15** minutes
Vocabulary	Introduce Color Words	
	⊕ OPTIONAL: Make Your Own Flash Cards	

🖥	**【 Online 】**	**15** minutes
Skills Update	Review Family Words	
Learn	Introduce Color Words	

【 Materials 】

Supplied
- *K¹² Language Arts Activity Book*, p. LS 9

Also Needed
- household objects – buttons or other small, round objects
- index cards (7) (optional)
- crayons (optional)

[Offline] ⓵⓹ minutes

Work **together** with students to complete an offline Vocabulary activity.

Vocabulary •

Introduce Color Words

Play a game on page LS 9 in *K¹² Language Arts Activity Book* to help students learn the following color words:

apricot	**hot pink**	**maroon**
burnt orange	**lavender**	**pink**
gray		

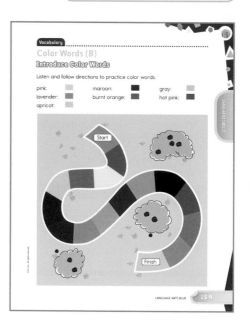

> **Objectives**
> • Increase oral vocabulary.
> • Increase concept vocabulary.

1. Gather buttons or other small, round objects that students can use as markers. You will need one object per player.

2. Tell students the name of each color at the top of the Activity Book page.

3. Ask students to move their markers to each of these squares:

   ▶ burnt orange
   ▶ pink
   ▶ maroon
   ▶ gray
   ▶ hot pink
   ▶ lavender
   ▶ apricot

4. Have students look around the room and point out objects they see in each of these colors.

⊕ OPTIONAL: Make Your Own Flash Cards

This activity is intended for students who have extra time and would benefit from practicing their vocabulary words with flash cards. Feel free to skip this activity.

Gather seven index cards and crayons. Have students create flash cards by writing each vocabulary word on the front of an index card and drawing a shape on the back in the corresponding color. (For example, on the back of the card for *pink*, students might draw a pink circle.)

TIP If students are not ready to read and write on their own, skip this optional activity.

 **15 minutes**

Students will work online **independently** to complete activities on Vocabulary words. Help students locate the online activities, and provide support as needed.

Skills Update ·

Review Family Words
Students will answer a few questions to refresh their Vocabulary knowledge.

 Objectives
• Increase oral vocabulary.

Learn ·

Introduce Color Words
Students will be introduced to the color words *pink, maroon, gray, lavender, burnt orange, hot pink,* and *apricot.*

 Objectives
• Increase oral vocabulary.
• Increase concept vocabulary.

[Online] 15 minutes

Students will work online **independently** to complete activities on Vocabulary words. Help students locate the online activities, and provide support as needed.

Practice ....

Color Words
Students will practice the color words *pink, maroon, gray, lavender, burnt orange, hot pink,* and *apricot*.

Offline Alternative

No computer access? At any time, you can print a list of the unit Vocabulary words and their definitions from the online lesson. Use this list to review the words with students offline. In addition, if students made their own flash cards, these can be used for offline review.

Objectives
- Increase oral vocabulary.
- Increase concept vocabulary.
- Identify words that create mental imagery.

"Engine, Engine, Number Nine" and Color Words

Lesson Overview

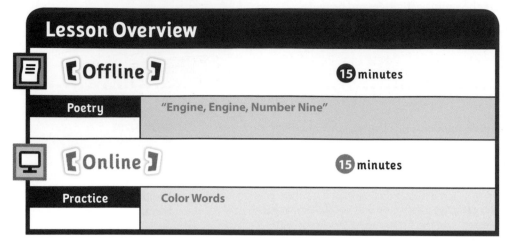

	Offline	15 minutes
Poetry	"Engine, Engine, Number Nine"	

	Online	15 minutes
Practice	Color Words	

[Materials]

Supplied
- *The Rooster Crows*
- *K¹² Language Arts Activity Book*, p. LS 11

Also Needed
- scissors, round-end safety
- crayons

Advance Preparation

Before reading today's poem, you will need to find the poem in *The Rooster Crows*. If your book has page numbers, turn to page 9. Otherwise, you will need to use a pencil to number the pages in the book. Mark the title page as page 1.

[Offline] 15 minutes

Work **together** with students to complete an offline Poetry activity.

Poetry ....

"Engine, Engine, Number Nine"

It's time to read "Engine, Engine, Number Nine" from *The Rooster Crows*.

1. Tell students that the poem they will hear is about the first car of a train, which is called an *engine*. Explain that the engine pulls all the other cars of the train.

   ▸ Have you ever been on a train? Answers will vary.
   ▸ What noise do trains make? "choo-choo"

> **Objectives**
> - Listen to and discuss poetry.
> - Identify rhyme and rhythm in poetry.
> - Identify repetitive text.
> - Respond to text through art, writing, and/or drama.

2. Have students sit next to you so they can see the picture and words while you **read the poem aloud**, and then ask:

 ▸ How many lines of this poem rhyme? four
 ▸ Name another word that rhymes with *nine*, *line*, and *shine*. Answers will vary.
 ▸ What number is in this poem twice? nine

3. Show students the picture above the poem in *The Rooster Crows*. Have them point to the engine, and then to all three 9s in the picture.

4. Gather scissors and crayons. Have students complete page LS 11 in *K¹² Language Arts Activity Book*. Have them color the picture of the engine while reciting the poem. Reread the poem as students color, if necessary.

5. Have students cut out the picture of the engine. Have them draw the number 9 anywhere on the engine.

6. Have students recite the poem one final time.

 **Online** **15** minutes

Students will work online **independently** to complete activities on Vocabulary words. Help students locate the online activity, and provide support as needed.

Practice

Color Words
Students will practice the color words *pink*, *maroon*, *gray*, *lavender*, *burnt orange*, *hot pink*, and *apricot*.

 Objectives
• Increase oral vocabulary.
• Increase concept vocabulary.

Offline Alternative

No computer access? At any time, you can print a list of the unit Vocabulary words and their definitions from the online lesson. Use this list to review the words with students offline. In addition, if students made their own flash cards, these can be used for offline review.

Color Words (C)

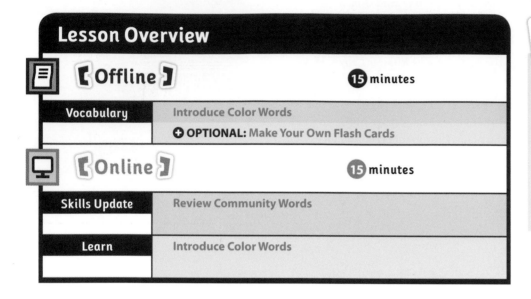

Lesson Overview

[Offline]		**15** minutes
Vocabulary	Introduce Color Words	
	⊕ OPTIONAL: Make Your Own Flash Cards	
[Online]		**15** minutes
Skills Update	Review Community Words	
Learn	Introduce Color Words	

[Materials]

Supplied
- *K¹² Language Arts Activity Book,* p. LS 13

Also Needed
- scissors, adult
- index cards (6) (optional)
- crayons (optional)

Advance Preparation

Cut out the color cards on the Activity Book page.

[Offline] **15** minutes

Work **together** with students to complete an offline Vocabulary activity.

Vocabulary

Introduce Color Words

Play a game to help students learn the following color words:

baby blue	**kelly green**	**navy blue**
forest green	**lime green**	**sky blue**

Objectives
- Increase oral vocabulary.
- Increase concept vocabulary.

1. Gather the cut-out cards from page LS 13 in *K¹² Language Arts Activity Book*.

2. Point out the colors on the cards, and read the color names to students.

3. Have students put the cards in two piles—blue cards and green cards. Have them arrange the cards in each pile from lightest to darkest.

   ▸ Is it better to describe an object as "baby blue" rather than just "blue"? Why or why not? Answers will vary.

4. Have students look around the room and point out objects they see in each of these colors.

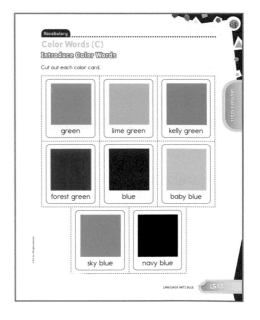

✛ OPTIONAL: Make Your Own Flash Cards

This activity is intended for students who have extra time and would benefit from practicing their vocabulary words with flash cards. Feel free to skip this activity.

Gather six index cards and crayons. Have students create flash cards by writing each vocabulary word on the front of an index card and drawing a shape on the back in the corresponding color. (For example, on the back of the card for *kelly green*, students might draw a kelly green circle.)

 **⟨ Online ⟩** **15** minutes

Students will work online **independently** to complete activities on Vocabulary words. Help students locate the online activities, and provide support as needed.

Skills Update ●

Review Community Words
Students will answer a few questions to refresh their Vocabulary knowledge.

Objectives
• Increase oral vocabulary.

Learn ●

Introduce Color Words
Students will be introduced to the color words *kelly green, forest green, lime green, baby blue, navy blue,* and *sky blue*.

Objectives
• Increase oral vocabulary.
• Increase concept vocabulary.
• Describe people, places, things, locations, actions, events, and/or feelings.

My Favorite Color and Color Words (B)

Lesson Overview

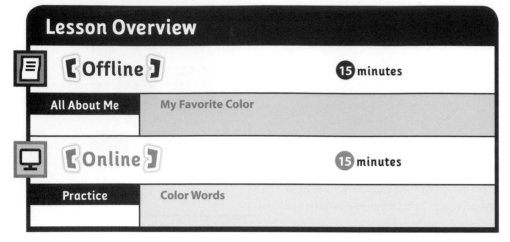

	Offline	15 minutes
All About Me	My Favorite Color	

	Online	15 minutes
Practice	Color Words	

Materials

Supplied
- *K¹² All About Me*, p. 10

Also Needed
- crayons

Offline 15 minutes

Work **together** with students to complete an offline All About Me activity.

All About Me

My Favorite Color

Students will complete page 10 in *K¹² All About Me*.

1. Have students finalize their drawing of items that are usually their favorite color.

2. Have students explain their illustration. Encourage students to use all relevant color words in their descriptions, rather than focusing only on their favorite color. For example, a student who likes red could say: "My favorite color is red. Strawberries are mostly red, but they have green leaves on top. Sometimes you can see tiny black dots on them, too. When you cut them open, strawberries are light pink or white on the inside."

Objectives

- Describe familiar and common objects and events.
- Describe people, places, things, locations, actions, events, and/or feelings.
- Add supporting details to written or drawn work.
- Discuss own drawing.
- Share finished written and drawn works.

[Online] ⏱ minutes

Students will work online **independently** to complete an activity on Vocabulary words. Help students locate the online activity, and provide support as needed.

Practice ●●●

Color Words

Students will practice the color words *kelly green, forest green, lime green, baby blue, navy blue,* and *sky blue*.

Objectives
- Increase oral vocabulary.
- Increase concept vocabulary.
- Describe people, places, things, locations, actions, events, and/or feelings.

Offline Alternative

No computer access? At any time, you can print a list of the unit Vocabulary words and their definitions from the online lesson. Use this list to review the words with students offline. In addition, if students made their own flash cards, these can be used for offline review.

"How Much Wood Would a Woodchuck Chuck?" and Color Words

Lesson Overview

[Offline]		**15** minutes
Poetry	"How Much Wood Would a Woodchuck Chuck?"	
	⊕ **OPTIONAL:** Another Tongue Twister	
[Online]		**15** minutes
Practice	Color Words	

[Materials]

Supplied
- *The Rooster Crows*

Advance Preparation

Before reading today's poem, you will need to find the poem in *The Rooster Crows*. If your book has page numbers, turn to page 7. Otherwise, you will need to use a pencil to number the pages in the book. Mark the title page as page 1.

[Offline] **15** minutes

Work **together** with students to complete an offline Poetry activity.

Poetry •••

"How Much Wood Would a Woodchuck Chuck?"
It's time to read a tongue twister from *The Rooster Crows*. Tongue twisters can be hard, but they are a fun way to help students further develop their speech skills.

1. Tell students that tongue twisters are poems that are very hard to say because they are filled with sounds and words that are almost the same.

2. **Say:** This is a tongue twister: *She sells seashells by the seashore.*

3. Have students try to say the tongue twister a few times. Point out that the words of the tongue twister have many /s/ and /sh/ sounds.

Objectives
- Listen to and discuss poetry.
- Recite short poems or rhymes.
- Use visual text features to aid understanding of text.

4. Have students sit next to you so they can see the picture and words while you **read aloud** "How Much Wood Would a Woodchuck Chuck?" and then ask:

   ▸ What word rhymes with *would* in this poem? *could*
   ▸ What two words sound the same in the poem? *would* and *wood*
   ▸ Which sound do the words *much, woodchuck,* and *chuck* all have: /m/, /w/, or /ch/? /ch/
   ▸ Look at the picture. What is a woodchuck? Answers will vary, but students should understand that a woodchuck is an animal.

5. Tell students that now they will practice saying the tongue twister. Read the first line and have students repeat it. Then read the first two lines and have them repeat both. Continue to add lines 3 and 4.

6. As students grow familiar with the language, encourage them to say the lines faster. Point out that it's easy to stumble on the words, but that's part of the fun.

⊕ OPTIONAL: Another Tongue Twister

This activity is intended for students who have extra time and would benefit from more practice with tongue twisters. Feel free to skip this activity.

Have students repeat after you the following tongue twister:

> *Peter Piper picked a peck of pickled peppers,*
> *A peck of pickled peppers Peter Piper picked.*
> *If Peter Piper picked a peck of pickled peppers,*
> *Where's the peck of pickled peppers Peter Piper picked?*

 **15 minutes**

Students will work online **independently** to complete an activity on Vocabulary words. Help students locate the online activities, and provide support as needed.

Practice •

Color Words

Students will practice the color words *kelly green, forest green, lime green, baby blue, navy blue,* and *sky blue.*

Offline Alternative

No computer access? At any time, you can print a list of the unit Vocabulary words and their definitions from the online lesson. Use this list to review the words with students offline. In addition, if students made their own flash cards, these can be used for offline review.

Objectives
• Increase oral vocabulary.
• Increase concept vocabulary.
• Describe people, places, things, locations, actions, events, and/or feelings.

Shape Words

Lesson Overview

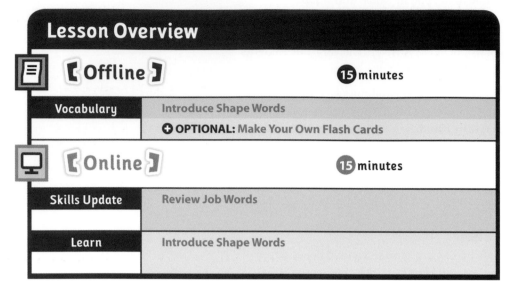

	Offline	15 minutes
Vocabulary	Introduce Shape Words	
	➕ OPTIONAL: Make Your Own Flash Cards	

	Online	15 minutes
Skills Update	Review Job Words	
Learn	Introduce Shape Words	

Materials

Supplied
- There are no supplied materials to gather for this lesson.

Also Needed
- index cards (7)
- crayons

Advance Preparation

Gather seven index cards and crayons. On the front of each card, draw a simple picture of one of these shapes: triangle, circle, oval, square, rectangle, star, and octagon.

Offline  15 minutes

Work **together** with students to complete an offline Vocabulary activity.

Vocabulary

Introduce Shape Words

Play a game to introduce students to the following words for shapes:

circle	rectangle	star
octagon	square	triangle
oval		

Objectives
- Increase oral vocabulary.
- Increase concept vocabulary.

1. Gather the seven prepared index cards. Show each card to students, and say the name of the shape. Have students repeat the word after you.

2. Spread out the index cards picture-side up. Ask students to find the triangle. Then turn that card face down.

3. Continue with the rest of the shape words until all the cards are face down.

4. Have students look around the room and point out objects they see in each of these shapes.

⊕ OPTIONAL: Make Your Own Flash Cards

This activity is intended for students who have extra time and would benefit from practicing their vocabulary words with flash cards. Feel free to skip this activity.

Gather the seven prepared index cards. Have students create flash cards by writing the name of each shape on the blank side of the card. Help students with spelling as necessary.

 **Online** 🕖 **minutes**

Students will work online **independently** to complete activities on Vocabulary words. Help students locate the online activities, and provide support as needed.

Skills Update ....

Review Job Words
Students will answer a few questions to refresh their Vocabulary knowledge.

Objectives
*   Increase oral vocabulary.

Learn ....

Introduce Shape Words
Students will be introduced to the shape words *triangle, circle, oval, square, rectangle, star,* and *octagon*.

Objectives
*   Increase oral vocabulary.
*   Increase concept vocabulary.

My Favorite Shape and Shape Words

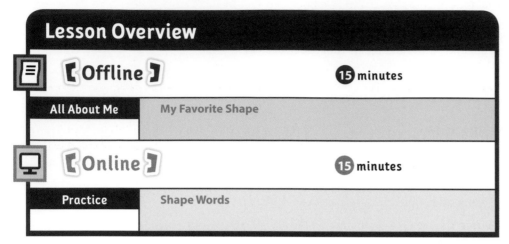

Lesson Overview

[Offline]		**15** minutes
All About Me	My Favorite Shape	
[Online]		**15** minutes
Practice	Shape Words	

[Materials]

Supplied
- *K¹² All About Me*, p. 11

Also Needed
- crayons

[Offline] **15** minutes

Work **together** with students to complete an offline All About Me activity.

All About Me

My Favorite Shape

Students will complete a sentence to practice vocabulary. They will begin page 11 in *K¹² All About Me*; they will complete this page over two lessons.

1. Read aloud the incomplete sentence to students, pointing to each word as you read.

2. Have students repeat the first part of the sentence and tell you the answer to write in the blank space. Read the complete sentence to them, pointing to each word.

3. Have students repeat the complete sentence and draw their favorite shape next to the sentence.

4. Ask students to think of everyday objects that are their favorite shape. Provide examples if necessary.

5. If time permits, have students begin to draw a picture that includes some of the objects discussed. For example, if a student's favorite shape is a circle, the picture could show a person riding a bicycle with round wheels, with a round sun in the sky, and a tree with round apples in the background.

Objectives
- Describe familiar and common objects and events.
- Dictate or write simple sentences describing experiences, stories, people, objects, or events.
- Generate ideas for writing and drawing through discussion.
- Draw a picture or write about an idea generated through discussion.

 **15** minutes

Students will work online **independently** to complete activities on Vocabulary words. Help students locate the online activities, and provide support as needed.

Practice ....

Shape Words

Students will practice the shape words *triangle, circle, oval, square, rectangle, star,* and *octagon*.

Objectives
- Increase oral vocabulary.
- Increase concept vocabulary.

Offline Alternative

No computer access? At any time, you can print a list of the unit Vocabulary words and their definitions from the online lesson. Use this list to review the words with students offline. In addition, if students made their own flash cards, these can be used for offline review.

"Baa Baa, Black Sheep" and Vocabulary Unit Review

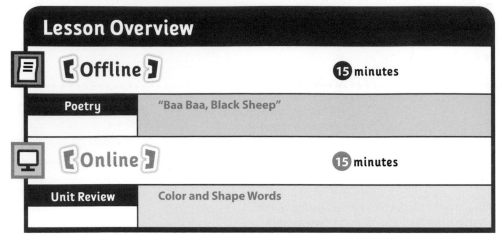

Lesson Overview

[Offline]		**15** minutes
Poetry	"Baa Baa, Black Sheep"	
[Online]		**15** minutes
Unit Review	Color and Shape Words	

[Materials]

Supplied
- *K¹² Read Aloud Treasury*, p. 62

Also Needed
- household objects – wool items

Advance Preparation

Gather wool items.

[Offline] **15** minutes

Work **together** with students to complete an offline Poetry activity.

"Baa Baa, Black Sheep"

It's time to read "Baa Baa, Black Sheep" from *K¹² Read Aloud Treasury*.

1. Remind students that the people and animals in poems are called **characters**. Tell them that we learn about characters from what they do, what they say, and what the poem says about them.

   ▶ Who might be a character in "Baa Baa, Black Sheep? a sheep

2. Have students sit next to you so they can see the picture and words while you read the poem aloud. **Read aloud the entire poem**, and then ask:

   ▶ How many bags of wool does the black sheep have? three
   ▶ Who are the bags of wool for? the master, the dame, and the little boy who lives down the lane
   ▶ Which word rhymes with *wool: dame, full,* or *lane*? *full*

Objectives
- Listen to and discuss poetry.
- Identify rhyme and rhythm in poetry.
- Identify character(s).
- Make connections with text: text-to-text, text-to-self, text-to-world.

3. Tell students that the black sheep is one of four characters in the poem. Have them name the other three. As necessary, tell them that the other characters are the master, the dame, and the little boy.

4. Show students the wool item(s) you gathered. Tell them that the wool of sheep—which is like their fur—is used to make many types of clothing.

5. Encourage students to imagine what clothes the master, the dame, and the little boy in the poem might have made with the wool.

   ▸ If you had one of the black sheep's bags of wool, what would you make with it? Answers will vary.

 **minutes**

Students will work online **independently** to complete an activity on Vocabulary words. Help students locate the online activity, and provide support as needed.

Unit Review

Color and Shape Words
Students will review all words from the unit to prepare for the Unit Checkpoint.

Objectives
- Increase oral vocabulary.
- Increase concept vocabulary.

Offline Alternative

No computer access? At any time, you can print a list of the unit Vocabulary words and their definitions from the online lesson. Use this list to review the words with students offline. In addition, if students made their own flash cards, these can be used for offline review.

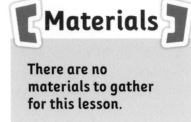

Unit Checkpoint

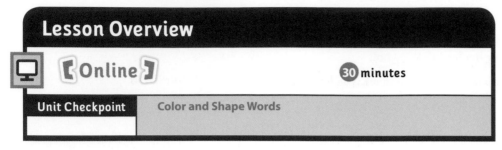

Lesson Overview

[Online]		30 minutes
Unit Checkpoint	Color and Shape Words	

[Online] 30 minutes

Students will work online to complete the Unit Checkpoint. Help students locate the Unit Checkpoint, and provide support as needed.

Unit Checkpoint

Color and Shape Words
Explain that students are going to show what they have learned about vocabulary words for colors and shapes.

Objectives
- Increase oral vocabulary.
- Increase reading vocabulary.
- Increase concept vocabulary.
- Identify words that create mental imagery.
- Describe people, places, things, locations, actions, events, and/or feelings.

Kitchen Words (A)

Unit Overview

In this unit, students will
- ▶ Learn vocabulary words for kitchen items and food.
- ▶ Complete the *All About Me* pages *My Favorite Shape* and *My Favorite Foods*.
- ▶ Explore the poems "Jack and Jill," "Jack Be Nimble," and "Little Jack Horner."

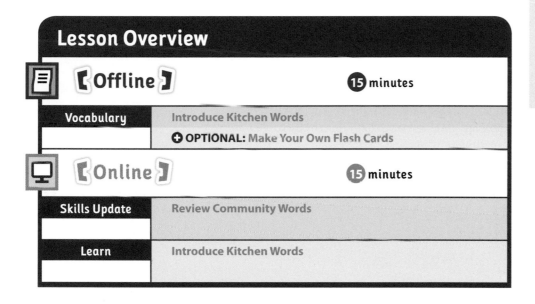

Lesson Overview

📄	**[Offline]**		⓯ minutes
Vocabulary	Introduce Kitchen Words		
	⊕ OPTIONAL: Make Your Own Flash Cards		

🖥	**[Online]**		⓯ minutes
Skills Update	Review Community Words		
Learn	Introduce Kitchen Words		

[Materials]

Supplied
- *K¹² Language Arts Activity Book*, p. LS 15

Also Needed
- scissors, round-end safety
- glue stick
- index cards (7) (optional)

[Offline] ⓯ minutes

Work **together** with students to complete an offline Vocabulary activity.

Vocabulary ....

Introduce Kitchen Words
Introduce students to the following kitchen words:

bowl	jar	stool
chair	plate	table
cup		

⭐ Objectives
- Increase oral vocabulary.
- Increase concept vocabulary.

1. Tell students that they are going to learn some words for things in the kitchen.

2. Turn to page LS 15 in *K¹² Language Arts Activity Book*. Point to each kitchen item at the bottom of the page. Tell students the name of each item. Ask them to repeat the names and describe what each item is used for. If they do not know what an item is used for, give a definition or example.

3. Have students cut out each kitchen item and glue it where it might go in the kitchen scene. Have them say sentences describing each item. For example, "The cup is on the shelf" or "The chair is next to the table."

⊕ OPTIONAL: Make Your Own Flash Cards

This activity is intended for students who have extra time and would benefit from practicing vocabulary words with flash cards. Feel free to skip this activity.

Gather seven index cards. Have students create flash cards by writing each vocabulary word on the front of an index card and their own definition for each word on the back. Help students with spelling as necessary.

TIP If students are not ready to read and write on their own, skip this optional activity.

〖 Online 〗 ⑮ minutes

Students will work online **independently** to complete Vocabulary activities. Help students locate the online activities, and provide support as needed.

Skills Update

Review Community Words
Students will answer a few questions to refresh their Vocabulary knowledge.

Objectives
- Increase oral vocabulary.
- Increase reading vocabulary.
- Increase concept vocabulary.

Learn

Introduce Kitchen Words
Students will be introduced to the kitchen words *cup, jar, plate, table, bowl, chair,* and *stool*.

Objectives
- Increase oral vocabulary.
- Increase reading vocabulary.
- Increase concept vocabulary.

My Favorite Shape and Kitchen Words

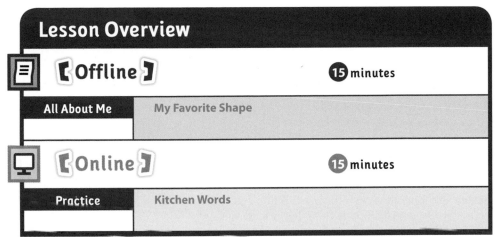

Lesson Overview

[Offline]   **15** minutes

| All About Me | My Favorite Shape |

[Online]   **15** minutes

| Practice | Kitchen Words |

[Materials]

Supplied
- *K¹² All About Me*, p. 11

Also Needed
- crayons

[Offline] **15** minutes

Work **together** with students to complete an offline All About Me activity.

All About Me

My Favorite Shape

Students will complete page 11 in *K¹² All About Me*.

1. Have students finalize their drawing of a scene that includes everyday items that are their favorite shape.

2. Ask students to explain their picture, pointing out the objects that are their favorite shape. Encourage them to use a variety of shape words in their descriptions, rather than focusing only on their favorite shape. Sample student description: My favorite shape is a square. In my picture, the house is square. It has two square windows and a roof that looks like a triangle. The door is a rectangle and has a doorknob that is a circle. I drew a square table in the backyard. I am sitting at the table reading a square book.

Objectives
- Describe familiar and common objects and events.
- Describe people, places, things, locations, actions, events, and/or feelings.
- Add supporting details to written or drawn work.
- Discuss own drawing.
- Share finished written and drawn works.

 **15 minutes**

Students will work online **independently** to complete activities on Vocabulary words. Help students locate the online activities, and provide support as needed.

Practice

Kitchen Words

Students will practice the kitchen words *cup, jar, plate, table, bowl, chair,* and *stool.*

___

Offline Alternative

No computer access? At any time, you can print a list of the unit Vocabulary words and their definitions from the online lesson. Use this list to review the words with students offline. In addition, if students made their own flash cards, these can be used for offline review.

Objectives
- Increase oral vocabulary.
- Increase reading vocabulary.
- Increase concept vocabulary.

"Jack and Jill" and Kitchen Words

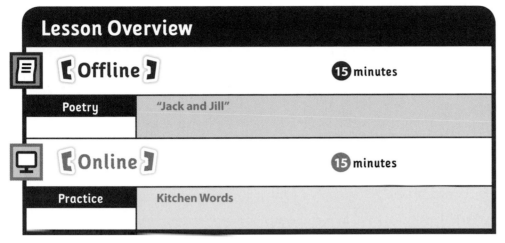

Lesson Overview

Offline   15 minutes

Poetry	"Jack and Jill"

Online   15 minutes

Practice	Kitchen Words

Materials

Supplied
- *The Rooster Crows*
- *K¹² Language Arts Activity Book*, p. LS 17

Also Needed
- crayons

Advance Preparation

Before reading today's poem, you will need to find the poem in *The Rooster Crows*. If your book has page numbers, turn to page 24. Otherwise, you will need to use a pencil to number the pages in the book. Mark the title page as page 1.

Offline   15 minutes

Work **together** with students to complete an offline Poetry activity.

Poetry

"Jack and Jill"

It's time to read "Jack and Jill" from *The Rooster Crows*.

1. Tell students that rhyming words do not just come at the ends of lines in poetry. Sometimes one line of poetry has two or more rhyming words.

   ► Which two words rhyme in this line? *I was glad to see my dad. glad* and *dad*

2. Tell students that today's poem has two lines with rhyming words in them. **Say:** The poem also has a word used in a way you may not have heard before. Later, we will talk about the word to figure out what it means.

Objectives
- Listen to and discuss poetry.
- Build vocabulary through listening, reading, and discussion.
- Identify rhyme and rhythm in poetry.
- Describe character(s).

3. Have students sit next to you so they can see the picture and words while you **read aloud the entire poem**, and then ask:

   ▸ Which two words rhyme in the first line of the poem, *Jack and Jill went up the hill*? *Jill* and *hill*
   ▸ Why do Jack and Jill go up the hill? to fetch a pail of water
   ▸ What happens to Jack and Jill? They both fall.

4. Reread the third line of the poem. Tell students that the word *crown* is used in a way they may not have heard before.
   Say: Jack is not wearing a crown. The word *crown* describes the part of Jack's body that he hurts when he falls.

5. Tell students to think about what a crown is and where people wear crowns.

   ▸ Where would you wear a crown? on my head
   ▸ So what body part does Jack hurt when he falls? his head

6. Turn to page LS 17 of *K¹² Language Arts Activity Book* and have students color the picture. As they work, have them describe where Jack and Jill are, what they went there to do, and what Jack hurts when he falls.

 **15 minutes**

Students will work online **independently** to complete activities on Vocabulary words. Help students locate the online activities, and provide support as needed.

 Practice ●

Kitchen Words
Students will practice the kitchen words *cup, jar, plate, table, bowl, chair,* and *stool*.

Objectives
• Increase oral vocabulary.
• Increase reading vocabulary.
• Increase concept vocabulary.

Offline Alternative

No computer access? At any time, you can print a list of the unit Vocabulary words and their definitions from the online lesson. Use this list to review the words with students offline. In addition, if students made their own flash cards, these can be used for offline review.

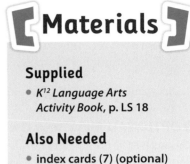

Food Words

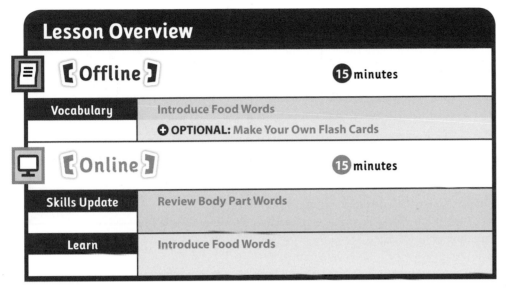

Lesson Overview

Offline — 15 minutes

Vocabulary	Introduce Food Words
	⊕ OPTIONAL: Make Your Own Flash Cards

Online — 15 minutes

Skills Update	Review Body Part Words
Learn	Introduce Food Words

Materials

Supplied
- *K¹² Language Arts Activity Book*, p. LS 18

Also Needed
- index cards (7) (optional)

Offline — 15 minutes

Work **together** with students to complete an offline Vocabulary activity.

Vocabulary

Introduce Food Words

Help students learn the following food words and how they are related:

apple	bread	flour
applesauce	cream	ice cream

1. Tell students that some foods are made from other foods. For example, peanut butter is made from peanuts, and grape jelly is made from grapes.

   ▸ What is applesauce made from? apples
   ▸ Do you know what bread is made from? flour

2. If students do not know what bread is made from, explain that it is made from flour mixed with other ingredients, and that flour is a powder made by grinding wheat.

   ▸ What is ice cream made from? cream

Objectives
- Increase oral vocabulary.
- Increase reading vocabulary.
- Increase concept vocabulary.

3. If students do not know what ice cream is made from, explain that it is made from cream mixed with other ingredients, and that cream is the part of milk that is thick and yellowish.

4. Turn to page LS 18 in *K¹² Language Arts Activity Book*. Have students write the name of each food item and draw lines to match the related foods. Help them with writing and spelling as necessary. Once students have finished matching the related foods, have them state the relationships. For example, "Applesauce is made from apples."

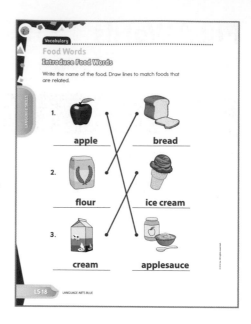

⊕ **OPTIONAL: Make Your Own Flash Cards**

This activity is intended for students who have extra time and would benefit from practicing their vocabulary words with flash cards. Feel free to skip this activity.

Gather seven index cards. Have students create flash cards by writing each vocabulary word on the front of an index card and their own definition for each word on the back. Help students with spelling as necessary.

〖 Online 〗 ⓕ minutes

Students will work online **independently** to complete activities on Vocabulary words. Help students locate the online activities, and provide support as needed.

Skills Update

Review Body Part Words
Students will answer a few questions to refresh their Vocabulary knowledge.

Objectives
- Increase oral vocabulary.
- Increase reading vocabulary.
- Increase concept vocabulary.

Learn

Introduce Food Words
Students will be introduced to the food words *flour, bread, apple, applesauce, cream,* and *ice cream.*

Objectives
- Increase oral vocabulary.
- Increase reading vocabulary.
- Increase concept vocabulary.

My Favorite Foods and Food Words

Lesson Overview

【 Offline 】		⏱ 15 minutes
All About Me	My Favorite Foods	
【 Online 】		⏱ 15 minutes
Practice	Food Words	

【 Materials 】

Supplied
- *K¹² All About Me*, pp. 12–14

Also Needed
- crayons

【 Offline 】 ⏱ 15 minutes

Work **together** with students to complete an offline All About Me activity.

All About Me

My Favorite Foods

Students will discuss their favorite foods. They will begin page 12 in *K¹² All About Me*; they will complete this page over two lessons.

1. Read aloud the first incomplete sentence to students, pointing to each word as you read.

2. Have students repeat the first part of the sentence and tell you the answer to write in the blank space. Read the complete sentence to them, pointing to each word.

3. Have students repeat the complete sentence and point to the word *breakfast*.

4. Repeat this procedure with the remaining three sentences and the words *lunch*, *dinner*, and *dessert*.

5. If time permits, have students begin to illustrate each sentence.

Objectives
- Dictate or write simple sentences describing experiences, stories, people, objects, or events.
- Generate ideas for writing and drawing through discussion.
- Draw a picture or write about an idea generated through discussion.

[Online] ⏱ 15 minutes

Students will work online **independently** to complete activities on Vocabulary words. Help students locate the online activities, and provide support as needed.

Practice ●●●

Food Words

Students will practice the food words *flour, bread, apple, applesauce, cream,* and *ice cream*.

Objectives
- Increase oral vocabulary.
- Increase reading vocabulary.
- Increase concept vocabulary.

Offline Alternative

No computer access? At any time, you can print a list of the unit Vocabulary words and their definitions from the online lesson. Use this list to review the words with students offline. In addition, if students made their own flash cards, these can be used for offline review.

"Jack Be Nimble" and Food Words

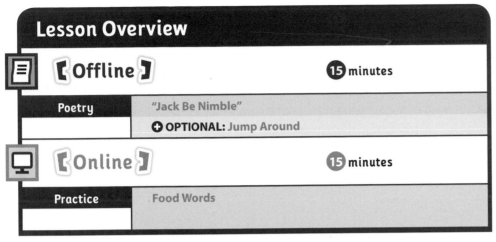

Lesson Overview

[Offline] **15** minutes

Poetry	"Jack Be Nimble"
	✚ OPTIONAL: **Jump Around**

[Online] **15** minutes

Practice	Food Words

〔 Materials 〕

Supplied
- *K¹² Read Aloud Treasury*, p. 63

Also Needed
- household objects – pencil, book, candlestick (optional)

[Offline] **15** minutes

Work **together** with students to complete an offline Poetry activity.

Poetry ....

"Jack Be Nimble"

It's time to read "Jack Be Nimble" from *K¹² Read Aloud Treasury*.

1. Remind students that reading poetry is a great way to learn new words. Tell students that when we see a word we don't know in a poem, sometimes we can figure out the word's meaning by looking at other words in the poem.

2. **Say:** After we read the poem, we will use the other words in the poem to figure out what the word *nimble* means.

3. Have students sit next to you so they can see the words and the picture while you **read the entire poem aloud**, and then ask:

   ▸ Which word rhymes with *quick* in the poem: *nimble, over,* or *candlestick*? *candlestick*

   ▸ What does the poem say Jack does in line 3? He jumps.

   ▸ What does Jack jump over in the poem? the candlestick

4. Tell students that they can learn what *nimble* means by looking at other words in the poem.

   ▸ Who is nimble in the poem? Jack

   ▸ What other word describes Jack? *quick*

   ▸ What can Jack do **because** he is nimble and quick? He can jump over the candlestick.

Objectives

- Listen to and discuss poetry.
- Identify and use context clues to define words.
- Identify rhyme and rhythm in poetry.
- Describe character(s).

5. **Say:** We know that being nimble helps Jack to jump. We also know that jumping is a quick movement. So the word *nimble* must have something to do with movement.

6. Point out that the poem does not say that it is hard for Jack to jump over the candlestick. Rather, it is easy. Tell students that being *nimble* means being able to move easily.

⊕ OPTIONAL: Jump Around

This activity is intended for students who have extra time and would benefit from an activity that reinforces what it is to be *nimble*. Feel free to skip this activity.

Have students jump over a pencil, a book, and a candlestick (if one is available). As students jump over each item, tell them how quick and nimble they are—just like Jack.

 **minutes**

Students will work online **independently** to complete activities on Vocabulary words. Help students locate the online activities, and provide support as needed.

Practice

Food Words
Students will practice the food words *flour, bread, apple, applesauce, cream,* and *ice cream*.

Offline Alternative

No computer access? At any time, you can print a list of the unit Vocabulary words and their definitions from the online lesson. Use this list to review the words with students offline. In addition, if students made their own flash cards, these can be used for offline review.

 Objectives
- Increase oral vocabulary.
- Increase reading vocabulary.
- Increase concept vocabulary.

Kitchen Words (B)

Lesson Overview

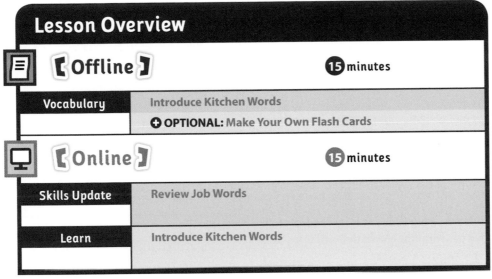

[Offline] **15** minutes

Vocabulary	Introduce Kitchen Words
	✚ OPTIONAL: Make Your Own Flash Cards

[Online] **15** minutes

Skills Update	Review Job Words
Learn	Introduce Kitchen Words

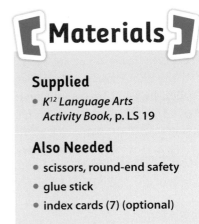

[Materials]

Supplied
- *K¹² Language Arts Activity Book*, p. LS 19

Also Needed
- scissors, round-end safety
- glue stick
- index cards (7) (optional)

[Offline] **15** minutes

Work **together** with students to complete an offline Vocabulary activity.

Vocabulary ....

Introduce Kitchen Words
Introduce students to the following kitchen words:

fork	mixer	spoon
knife	skillet	whisk
ladle		

Objectives
- Increase oral vocabulary.
- Increase reading vocabulary.
- Increase concept vocabulary.

1. Tell students that they are going to learn some more words for things in the kitchen.

2. Turn to page LS 19 in *K¹² Language Arts Activity Book*. Point to each kitchen item and tell students the name of each item. Have students repeat the names and describe what each item is used for. If they do not know what an item is used for, give a definition or example.

3. Have students cut out each kitchen item and glue it where it might go in the kitchen scene. Have them say sentences describing each item. For example, "The skillet is on the stove" or "The ladle is in the bowl."

⊕ OPTIONAL: Make Your Own Flash Cards
This activity is intended for students who have extra time and would benefit from practicing their vocabulary words with flash cards. Feel free to skip this activity.

Gather seven index cards. Have students create flash cards by writing each vocabulary word on the front of an index card and their own definition for each word on the back. Help students with spelling as necessary.

 **Online** ⏱ **minutes**

Students will work online **independently** to complete activities on Vocabulary words. Help students locate the online activities, and provide support as needed.

Skills Update

Review Job Words
Students will answer a few questions to refresh their Vocabulary knowledge.

> **Objectives**
> - Increase oral vocabulary.
> - Increase reading vocabulary.
> - Increase concept vocabulary.

Learn

Introduce Kitchen Words
Students will be introduced to the kitchen words *skillet, whisk, mixer, spoon, fork, knife,* and *ladle.*

> **Objectives**
> - Increase oral vocabulary.
> - Increase reading vocabulary.
> - Increase concept vocabulary.

My Favorite Foods and Kitchen Words

Lesson Overview

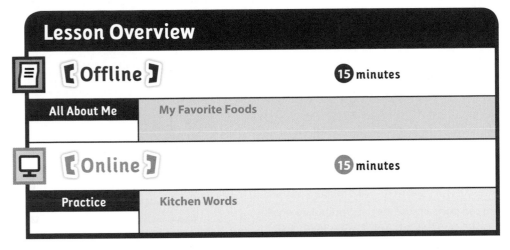

Offline		**15** minutes
All About Me	My Favorite Foods	

Online		**15** minutes
Practice	Kitchen Words	

Materials

Supplied
- *K¹² All About Me*, pp. 12–14

Also Needed
- crayons

Offline   **15** minutes

Work **together** with students to complete an offline All About Me activity.

All About Me

My Favorite Foods

Students will complete sentences on pages 12–14 in *K¹² All About Me* to practice vocabulary.

1. Have students finalize their drawings of their favorite breakfast, lunch, dinner, and dessert foods.

2. Have students explain their drawings and why those particular foods are their favorites. Encourage them to describe smells, tastes, textures, and colors they associate with the foods.

Objectives
- Add supporting details to written or drawn work.
- Discuss own drawing.
- Share finished written and drawn works.

 ⟦Online⟧ ⑮ minutes

Students will work online **independently** to complete activities on Vocabulary words. Help students locate the online activities, and provide support as needed.

Practice

Kitchen Words

Students will practice the kitchen words *skillet, whisk, mixer, spoon, fork, knife,* and *ladle.*

Offline Alternative

No computer access? At any time, you can print a list of the unit Vocabulary words and their definitions from the online lesson. Use this list to review the words with students offline. In addition, if students made their own flash cards, these can be used for offline review.

Objectives
- Increase oral vocabulary.
- Increase reading vocabulary.
- Increase concept vocabulary.

"Little Jack Horner" and Vocabulary Unit Review

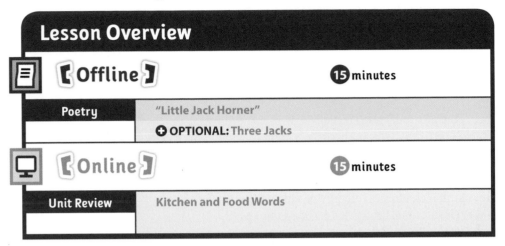

Lesson Overview

📄 [Offline] 🕐15 minutes

Poetry	"Little Jack Horner"
	➕ OPTIONAL: Three Jacks

🖥 [Online] 🕐15 minutes

Unit Review	Kitchen and Food Words

[Materials]

Supplied
- *The Rooster Crows*

Advance Preparation

Before reading today's poem, you will need to find the poem in *The Rooster Crows*. If your book has page numbers, turn to page 29. Otherwise, you will need to use a pencil to number the pages in the book. Mark the title page as page 1.

[Offline] 🕐15 minutes

Work **together** with students to complete an offline Poetry activity.

Poetry ....

"Little Jack Horner"

It's time to read "Little Jack Horner" from *The Rooster Crows*.

1. Tell students that poems can have rhyming words at the ends of lines or within the same line. Tell them that some poems have both types of rhymes.

2. Tell students that the people and animals in poems are called **characters**. We learn about characters from what they do, what they say, and what the poem says about them.

Objectives
- Listen to and discuss poetry.
- Identify rhyme and rhythm in poetry.
- Describe character(s).

3. Have students sit next to you so they can see the picture and words while you **read the poem aloud**, and then ask:

   ▸ Where does Little Jack Horner sit? in a corner
   ▸ What word rhymes with *pie* in this poem: *corner*, *plum*, or *I*? *I*
   ▸ What word rhymes with *thumb* in line 3: *stuck*, *pulled*, or *plum*? *plum*
   ▸ Where does Jack Horner put his thumb in the poem? in the pie

4. Tell students that it is time to see what we learn about Jack Horner from the poem. We learn about characters from what they do, what they say, and what the poem says about them.

   ▸ Does the poem say Jack Horner is big or small? small (little)
   ▸ What four things does Jack Horner do in this poem? He sits in a corner, eats pie, sticks his thumb in the pie, and pulls out a plum.
   ▸ What does Jack Horner say in this poem? He says he is "a good boy."

5. Discuss with students whether they think Jack Horner is happy or sad and why. Help them use evidence from the text (he eats pie, he says he is a good boy) to support their answers.

✚ OPTIONAL: Three Jacks

This activity is intended for students who have extra time and would benefit from reviewing the poems from this unit. Feel free to skip this activity.

Remind students that all three poems in this unit have boys named Jack in them. Ask them to describe each Jack, stating what he does and what happens to him.

 15 minutes

Students will work online **independently** to complete an activity on Vocabulary words. Help students locate the online activity and provide support as needed.

Unit Review ●●

Kitchen and Food Words
Students will review all words from the unit to prepare for the Unit Checkpoint.

Offline Alternative

No computer access? At any time, you can print a list of the unit Vocabulary words and their definitions from the online lesson. Use this list to review the words with students offline. In addition, if students made their own flash cards, these can be used for offline review.

 Objectives
• Increase oral vocabulary.
• Increase reading vocabulary.
• Increase concept vocabulary.

Unit Checkpoint

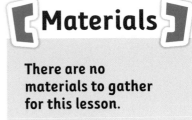

Lesson Overview

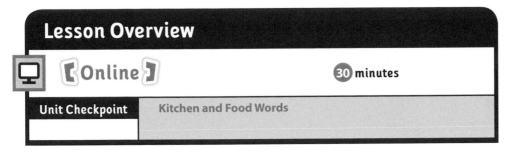

Online	30 minutes
Unit Checkpoint	Kitchen and Food Words

Materials

There are no materials to gather for this lesson.

Online 30 minutes

Students will work online to complete the Unit Checkpoint. Help students locate the Unit Checkpoint, and provide support as needed.

Unit Checkpoint

Kitchen and Food Words
Explain that students are going to show what they have learned about vocabulary words for kitchen and food items.

Objectives
- Increase oral vocabulary.
- Increase reading vocabulary.
- Increase concept vocabulary.

Animal Words (A)

Unit Overview

In this unit, students will
- ▶ Learn animal and subject vocabulary words.
- ▶ Complete the *All About Me* pages *My Favorite Animal* and *My Favorite Subject.*
- ▶ Explore the poems "Star Bright, Star Light"; "Jack Sprat"; and "Evening Red and Morning Gray."

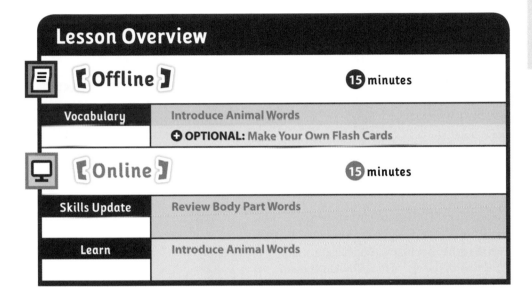

Lesson Overview

【Offline 】   **15** minutes

| Vocabulary | **Introduce Animal Words** |
| | **⊕ OPTIONAL:** Make Your Own Flash Cards |

【Online 】   **15** minutes

| Skills Update | **Review Body Part Words** |
| Learn | **Introduce Animal Words** |

Materials

Supplied
- *K¹² Language Arts Activity Book,* p. LS 21

Also Needed
- scissors, round-end safety
- index cards (7) (optional)

 **Offline** ⏱ **15 minutes**

Work **together** with students to complete an offline Vocabulary activity.

Vocabulary ·

Introduce Animal Words

Introduce students to the following animal words:

cat	**dog**	**horse**
chicken	**goat**	**sheep**
cow		

1. Point to each animal on page LS 21 from *K¹² Language Arts Activity Book*. Ask students to name each animal and the sound it makes. Tell them the name and sound of any animal they don't know. Help them cut out the animal cards.

2. Spread the animal cards on the floor or table. Ask students to sort the cards into two groups: animals that are bigger than an adult, and animals that are smaller than an adult. Have them say the name of each animal as they sort the cards. bigger: cow, horse; smaller: cat, chicken, goat, dog, sheep

3. Shuffle the cards, and then ask students to sort the cards into two new groups: animals that have fur, and animals that do not have fur. Have students say the name of each animal as they sort the cards. have fur: cat, dog; have no fur: chicken, goat, cow, horse, sheep   Discuss what type of coverings chickens and sheep have. feathers and wool

4. Shuffle the cards again, and then ask students to sort them into two new groups: animals that might live on a farm, and animals that might live in a house. Have them say the name of each animal as they sort the cards. live on a farm: sheep, goat, chicken, cow, horse; live in a house: cat, dog

> ★ **Objectives**
> * Increase oral vocabulary.
> * Increase concept vocabulary.
> * Classify and sort common words into categories.

Vocabulary
Animal Words (A)
Introduce Animal Words
Cut out each animal card.

LANGUAGE ARTS BLUE   LS 21

➕ OPTIONAL: Make Your Own Flash Cards

This activity is intended for students who have extra time and would benefit from practicing their vocabulary words with flash cards. Feel free to skip this activity.

Gather seven index cards. Have students create flash cards by writing each vocabulary word on the front of an index card and their own definition for each word on the back. Help students with spelling as necessary.

TIP If students are not ready to read and write on their own, skip this optional activity.

 **[Online]** **15 minutes**

Students will work online **independently** to complete activities on Vocabulary words. Help students locate the online activities, and provide support as needed.

Skills Update ....

Review Body Part Words
Students will answer a few questions to refresh their Vocabulary knowledge.

Objectives
- Increase oral vocabulary.

Learn ....

Introduce Animal Words
Students will be introduced to the animal words *cat, cow, chicken, dog, goat, horse,* and *sheep*.

Objectives
- Increase oral vocabulary.
- Increase concept vocabulary.

My Favorite Animal and Animal Words (A)

Lesson Overview

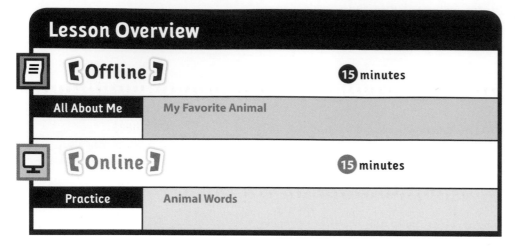

	Offline	15 minutes
All About Me	My Favorite Animal	

	Online	15 minutes
Practice	Animal Words	

Materials

Supplied
- *K¹² All About Me*, p. 15

Also Needed
- crayons

Offline 15 minutes

Work **together** with students to complete an offline All About Me activity.

 All About Me •

My Favorite Animal

Students will begin page 15 in *All About Me*. They will complete this page over two lessons.

1. Discuss with students their favorite animal. Guide students to describe the animal in as much detail as possible by asking questions about the animal's size and color, how it moves, where it lives, and so on.

2. Have students begin their illustration.

 Objectives
- Describe people, places, things, locations, events, and/or feelings.

 **15 minutes**

Students will work online **independently** to complete an activity on Vocabulary words. Help students locate the online activity, and provide support as needed.

Practice

....

Animal Words
Students will practice the animal words *cat, chicken, cow, dog, goat, horse,* and *sheep.*

Offline Alternative

No computer access? At any time, you can print a list of the unit Vocabulary words and their definitions from the online lesson. Use this list to review the words with students offline. In addition, if students made their own flash cards, these can be used for offline review.

Objectives
- Increase oral vocabulary.
- Increase concept vocabulary.
- Classify and sort common words into categories.

"Star Bright, Star Light" and Animal Words

Lesson Overview

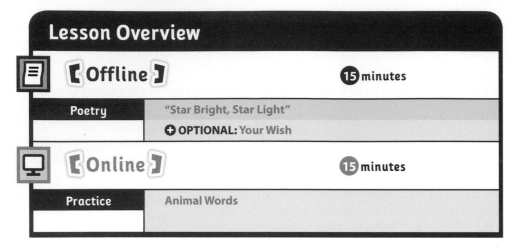

[Offline] 15 minutes

Poetry	"Star Bright, Star Light"
	⊕ OPTIONAL: Your Wish

[Online] 15 minutes

Practice	Animal Words

Materials

Supplied
- *The Rooster Crows*

Advance Preparation

Before reading today's poem, you will need to find the poem in *The Rooster Crows*. If your book has page numbers, turn to page 15. Otherwise, you will need to use a pencil to number the pages in the book. Mark the title page as page 1.

[Offline] 15 minutes

Work **together** with students to complete an offline Poetry activity.

"Star Bright, Star Light"

It's time to read "Star Bright, Star Light" from *The Rooster Crows*.

1. Tell students that poems contain specific words to help them picture what they are reading or hearing. Some words make the pictures in our minds more clear than others.

2. **Say:** Listen to these two sentences and the words in them: *The car drove by us going fast. The car roared by us in a flash.*

   ▸ Which sentence makes the picture in your mind clearer?
   The second one.   Why? Answers will vary; guide students to understand that the words in the second sentence create a clearer picture. The words help us use more of our senses—what it sounded like, what it looked like.

Objectives
- Listen to and discuss poetry.
- Identify words that create mental imagery.
- Identify rhyme and rhythm in poetry.

3. Have students sit next to you so they can see the picture and words while you **read the poem aloud**, and then ask:

   ▶ Which two words rhyme in the first line of the poem? *bright* and *light*
   ▶ What is the person in the poem doing? Answers will vary; students should understand that the speaker is looking at the sky and is about to make a wish.
   ▶ At what time of day does this poem happen? at night

4. Reread the first line of the poem. Tell students to picture in their minds what is being described.

   ▶ How would the picture in your mind change if the words *bright* and *light* were changed to *fright* and *fight*? Answers will vary.

5. Talk with students about how they feel when they picture a dark night sky with one shining star in it. Explain that the words *bright* and *light* help create this feeling.

➕ **OPTIONAL: Your Wish**
This activity is intended for students who have extra time and would benefit from making a more personal connection to the text. Feel free to skip this activity.

Have students imagine looking upon the first star that they see in the night sky. Talk with them about what they would wish for, and why.

 **15 minutes**

Students will work online **independently** to complete an activity on Vocabulary words. Help students locate the online activity, and provide support as needed.

Practice

Animal Words
Students will practice the animal words *cat, chicken, cow, dog, goat, horse,* and *sheep*.

Offline Alternative

No computer access? At any time, you can print a list of the unit Vocabulary words and their definitions from the online lesson. Use this list to review the words with students offline. In addition, if students made their own flash cards, these can be used for offline review.

Objectives
- Increase oral vocabulary.
- Increase concept vocabulary.
- Classify and sort common words into categories.

Animal Words (B)

Lesson Overview

[Offline]   ⓯ minutes

Vocabulary	Introduce Animal Words
	➕ **OPTIONAL:** Make Your Own Flash Cards

[Online]   ⓯ minutes

Skills Update	Review Family Words
Learn	Introduce Animal Words

[Materials]

Supplied
- *K¹² Language Arts Activity Book*, p. LS 23

Also Needed
- scissors, round-end safety
- index cards (7) (optional)

[Offline]   ⓯ minutes

Work **together** with students to complete an offline Vocabulary activity.

Vocabulary ·

Introduce Animal Words

Introduce students to the following animal words:

camel	**moth**	**trout**
eagle	**tiger**	**zebra**
lizard		

1. Point to each animal on page LS 23 from *K¹² Language Arts Activity Book*. Ask students to name each animal. Tell them the name of any animal they don't know. Help them cut out the animal cards.

2. Spread the animal cards on the floor or table. Ask students to sort the cards into two groups: animals with stripes, and animals without stripes. Have students say the name of each animal as they sort the cards. with stripes: tiger, zebra; without stripes: camel, moth, trout, eagle, lizard

> ⭐ **Objectives**
> - Increase oral vocabulary.
> - Increase concept vocabulary.
> - Classify and sort common words into categories.

3. Shuffle the cards, and then ask students to sort them into four groups: animals that fly, animals that walk, animals that crawl, and animals that swim. Have them say the name of each animal as they sort the cards. those that fly: eagle, moth; those that walk: camel, tiger, zebra; those that crawl: lizard; those that swim: trout

4. Shuffle the cards again, and then ask students to sort them into groups according to how many legs each animal has: zero, two, four, or six. (Note: Fish have no legs; mammals typically have four legs; and insects have six legs.) Have them say the name of each animal as they sort the cards. zero: trout; two: eagle; four: camel, tiger, zebra, lizard; six: moth

5. If time permits, discuss where each animal might live.

⊕ OPTIONAL: Make Your Own Flash Cards

This activity is intended for students who have extra time and would benefit from practicing their vocabulary words with flash cards. Feel free to skip this activity.

Gather seven index cards. Have students create flash cards by writing each vocabulary word on the front of an index card and their own definition for each word on the back. Help students with spelling as necessary.

[Online] 🕓 minutes

Students will work online **independently** to complete activities on Vocabulary words. Help students locate the online activities, and provide support as needed.

Skills Update ●

Review Family Words
Students will answer a few questions to refresh their Vocabulary knowledge.

Objectives
- Increase oral vocabulary.

Learn ●

Introduce Animal Words
Students will be introduced to the animal words *camel, eagle, lizard, moth, tiger, trout,* and *zebra.*

Objectives
- Increase oral vocabulary.
- Increase concept vocabulary.

My Favorite Animal and Animal Words (B)

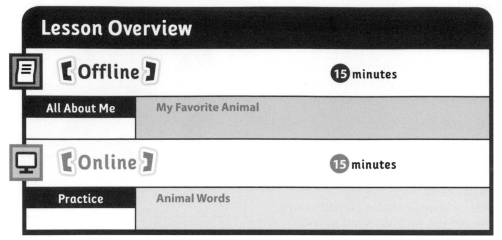

Lesson Overview

Offline · 15 minutes

All About Me	My Favorite Animal

Online · 15 minutes

Practice	Animal Words

Materials

Supplied
- *K¹² All About Me*, p. 15

Also Needed
- crayons

Offline · 15 minutes

Work **together** with students to complete an offline All About Me activity.

All About Me

My Favorite Animal

Students will complete page 15 in *K¹² All About Me*.

1. Give students time to add any other important details to the picture of their favorite animal.

2. Label the animal for students, spelling aloud as you write the word.

3. Read aloud the label, and have students point to the label and say the word.

4. Have students explain their drawing of their favorite animal using the details of the picture. For example, a student may say: "My favorite animal is a horse. This is a very big, chocolate brown horse. He likes to eat hay and apples. He has a very black mane and tail. He lives in the country, where he can run in the green grass and eat all the hay he wants."

5. Encourage students to share their finished work with others.

 Objectives
- Describe people, places, things, locations, actions, events, and/or feelings.
- Add supporting details to written or drawn work.
- Discuss own drawing.
- Share finished written and drawn works.

 **15 minutes**

Students will work online **independently** to complete an activity on Vocabulary words. Help students locate the online activity, and provide support as needed.

Practice ···

Animal Words

Students will practice the animal words *camel, eagle, lizard, moth, tiger, trout,* and *zebra.*

Objectives
- Increase oral vocabulary.
- Increase concept vocabulary.
- Classify and sort common words into categories.

Offline Alternative

No computer access? At any time, you can print a list of the unit Vocabulary words and their definitions from the online lesson. Use this list to review the words with students offline. In addition, if students made their own flash cards, these can be used for offline review.

"Jack Sprat" and Animal Words

Lesson Overview

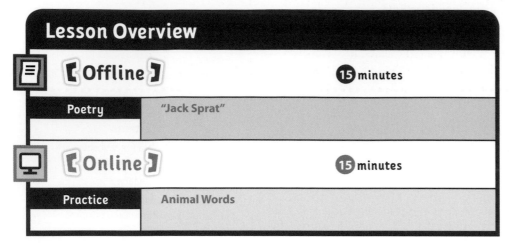

[Offline] **15** minutes

| Poetry | "Jack Sprat" |

[Online] **15** minutes

| Practice | Animal Words |

[Materials]

Supplied
- *K¹² Read Aloud Treasury*, p. 81
- *K¹² Language Arts Activity Book*, p. LS 25

Also Needed
- crayons

[Offline] **15** minutes

Work **together** with students to complete an offline Poetry activity.

Poetry ....

"Jack Sprat"

It's time to read "Jack Sprat" from *K¹² Read Aloud Treasury*.

1. Remind students that the people and animals in poems are called **characters**. We learn about characters from what they do, what they say, and what the poem says about them.

2. **Say:** There are two characters in our poem today, and they are *very* different. Listen carefully so you can tell me *how* they are different.

3. Have students sit next to you so they can see the picture and the words while you read the poem aloud. Tell students that *lean* in this poem means "food without fat" or "healthy food."

Objectives
- Listen to and discuss poetry.
- Identify rhyme and rhythm in poetry.
- Describe character(s).

4. **Reread the poem**, and then ask:

   ▶ What can Jack Sprat not eat? fat
   ▶ What can Jack Sprat's wife not eat? lean
   ▶ What word in the poem rhymes with *lean—fat, them,* or *clean? clean*
   ▶ How are Jack Sprat and his wife different? One cannot eat any fat and one cannot eat any lean.
   ▶ Do their differences cause problems when they eat? No   Why not? Answers will vary; guide students to understand that Jack Sprat and his wife eat different things, so together they clean the platter.

5. Turn to page LS 25 in *K¹² Language Arts Activity Book,* and have students color the platter of food. As students work, discuss the foods, explaining which foods are full of fats and which foods are lean. Have students tell you which foods Jack Sprat would eat and which foods his wife would eat.

Online ⑮ minutes

Students will work online **independently** to complete an activity on Vocabulary words. Help students locate the online activity, and provide support as needed.

Practice

Animal Words
Students will practice the animal words *camel, eagle, lizard, moth, tiger, trout,* and *zebra.*

Offline Alternative

No computer access? At any time, you can print a list of the unit Vocabulary words and their definitions from the online lesson. Use this list to review the words with students offline. In addition, if students made their own flash cards, these can be used for offline review.

Objectives
- Increase oral vocabulary.
- Increase concept vocabulary.
- Classify and sort common words into categories.

Subject Words

Lesson Overview

[Offline] 🕐 **15** minutes

Vocabulary	Introduce Subject Words
	➕ OPTIONAL: Make Your Own Flash Cards

[Online] 🕐 **15** minutes

Skills Update	Review Community Words
Learn	Introduce Subject Words

[Materials]

Supplied
- *K¹² Language Arts Activity Book*, p. LS 26

Also Needed
- index cards (5) (optional)

[Offline] 🕐 **15** minutes

Work **together** with students to complete an offline Vocabulary activity.

Vocabulary

Introduce Subject Words
Introduce students to the following subject words:

history	music	science
math	reading	

Objectives
- Increase oral vocabulary.
- Increase concept vocabulary.

1. Read each word to students, and talk about each subject. For example, tell students that history is the study of important past events. Ask students what important past events they might study.

2. Have students complete page LS 26 in *K¹² Language Arts Activity Book*. They should draw lines to match the subject words with the pictures that represent those subjects. Provide support as necessary.

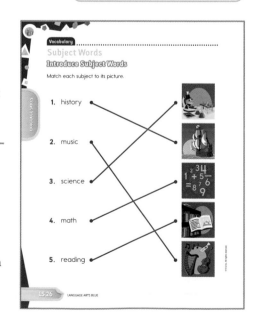

➕ **OPTIONAL: Make Your Own Flash Cards**
This activity is intended for students who have extra time and would benefit from practicing their vocabulary words with flash cards. Feel free to skip this activity.

Gather five index cards. Have students create flash cards by writing each vocabulary word on the front of an index card and their own definition for each word on the back. Help students with spelling as necessary.

 **15 minutes**

Students will work online **independently** to complete activities on Vocabulary words. Help students locate the online activities, and provide support as needed.

Skills Update ....

Review Community Words
Students will answer a few questions to refresh their Vocabulary knowledge.

Objectives
- Increase oral vocabulary.

Learn ....

Introduce Subject Words
Students will be introduced to the subject words *history, math, music, reading,* and *science.*

Objectives
- Increase oral vocabulary.
- Increase concept vocabulary.

My Favorite Subject and Subject Words (A)

Lesson Overview

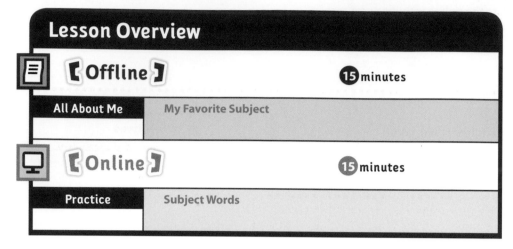

[Offline]		**15** minutes
All About Me	My Favorite Subject	
[Online]		**15** minutes
Practice	Subject Words	

[Materials]

Supplied
- *K¹² All About Me*, p. 16

Also Needed
- crayons

[Offline] **15** minutes

Work **together** with students to complete an offline All About Me activity.

All About Me

My Favorite Subject

Students will begin page 16 in *All About Me*. They will complete this page over two lessons.

1. Point to and read aloud the first sentence on the page.

2. Ask students what things come to mind when they think about their favorite subject. If necessary, prompt students with questions such as "What people or places make you think of your favorite subject? Why?" or "What books or games make you think of your favorite subject? Why?"

3. Have students tell you the answers to write in the blank spaces. Read the complete sentences to students, pointing to each word.

4. If time permits, have students begin to illustrate their sentences.

Objectives

- Dictate or write simple sentences describing experiences, stories, people, objects, or events.
- Generate ideas for writing and drawing through discussion.
- Draw a picture or write about an idea generated through discussion.
- Describe people, places, things, locations, actions, events, and/or feelings.

 **Online** 🕐 **minutes**

Students will work online **independently** to complete an activity on Vocabulary words. Help students locate the online activity, and provide support as needed.

Practice ....

Subject Words

Students will practice the subject words *history*, *math*, *music*, *reading*, and *science*.

Objectives

- Increase oral vocabulary.
- Increase concept vocabulary.

Offline Alternative

No computer access? At any time, you can print a list of the unit Vocabulary words and their definitions from the online lesson. Use this list to review the words with students offline. In addition, if students made their own flash cards, these can be used for offline review.

"Evening Red and Morning Gray" and Vocabulary Unit Review

Lesson Overview

📄 **[Offline]**		🕐 **15** minutes
Poetry	"Evening Red and Morning Gray"	
🖥️ **[Online]**		🕐 **15** minutes
Unit Review	Animal and Subject Words	

[Materials]

Supplied
- *The Rooster Crows*
- *K¹² Language Arts Activity Book*, p. LS 27

Also Needed
- crayons

Advance Preparation

Before reading today's poem, you will need to find the poem in *The Rooster Crows*. If your book has page numbers, turn to page 28. Otherwise, you will need to use a pencil to number the pages in the book. Mark the title page as page 1.

[Offline] 🕐 15 minutes

Work **together** with students to complete an offline Poetry activity.

Poetry ....

"Evening Red and Morning Gray"

It's time to read "Evening Red and Morning Gray" from *The Rooster Crows*.

1. Tell students that some poems were written to help people remember things. Ask them if they have ever heard the short rhyme "An apple a day keeps the doctor away." Tell students that this particular rhyme was written to help people remember to eat healthy foods.

2. Have students sit next to you so they can see the picture and words while you **read the poem aloud**, and then ask:

   ▸ Which word in the poem rhymes with *gray: way, red,* or *head*? *way*
   ▸ What color morning sends the traveler on his way? gray
   ▸ What color morning brings rain upon the traveler's head? red

⭐ **Objectives**
- Listen to and discuss poetry.
- Respond to text through art, writing, and/or drama.
- Identify rhyme and rhythm in poetry.
- Identify the purpose of a text.

3. Tell students to think about what this poem is supposed to help people remember. Reread the poem, and then read the first two lines again.

   ▸ Is a gray morning a good morning for travelers? Yes   How do you know? The poem says it "sends a traveler on his way."

4. Reread the last two lines of the poem.

   ▸ If you were traveling, would you rather travel when the morning is gray or when the morning is red? when the morning is gray
   ▸ What happens when the morning is red? it rains
   ▸ What is this poem supposed to help people remember? when the weather will be best for traveling

5. Turn to page LS 27 in *K¹² Language Arts Activity Book*. Point to the picture of a traveler walking down a path. Have students draw weather and color the picture as they practice reciting the rhyme. When they have finished, ask them what kind of sky their traveler would have seen that morning. If students colored the picture to show the traveler walking in the rain, the sky would be red. If students colored the picture to show the traveler walking on a nice day, the sky would be gray.

Poetry
"Evening Red and Morning Gray" and Vocabulary Unit Review
"Evening Red and Morning Gray"
Draw the weather. Color the picture.

LANGUAGE ARTS BLUE   LS 27

[Online] 15 minutes

Students will work online **independently** to complete an activity on Vocabulary words. Help students locate the online activity, and provide support as needed.

Unit Review

Animal and Subject Words
Students will review all words from the unit to prepare for the Unit Checkpoint.

Objectives
• Increase oral vocabulary.
• Increase concept vocabulary.

Offline Alternative

No computer access? At any time, you can print a list of the unit Vocabulary words and their definitions from the online lesson. Use this list to review the words with students offline. In addition, if students made their own flash cards, these can be used for offline review.

Unit Checkpoint

Lesson Overview

🖥 **[Online]**   **30** minutes

Unit Checkpoint	Animal and Subject Words

[Materials]

There are no materials to gather for this lesson.

[Online] **30** minutes

Students will work online to complete the Unit Checkpoint. Help students locate the Unit Checkpoint, and provide support as needed.

Unit Checkpoint ....

Animal and Subject Words

Explain that students are going to show what they have learned about vocabulary words for animals and subjects.

Objectives
- Increase oral vocabulary.
- Increase concept vocabulary.
- Classify and sort common words into categories.

Music Words

Unit Overview

In this unit, students will

▸ Learn vocabulary words for music and reading.

▸ Complete the *All About Me* pages *My Favorite Subject* and *My Favorite Book.*

▸ Explore the poems "Three Blind Mice," "There Was a Little Girl," "Mackerel Sky," and "Rain Before Seven."

Materials

Supplied

● *K¹² Language Arts Activity Book,* p. LS 29

Also Needed

● scissors, round-end safety

● glue stick

● index cards (7) (optional)

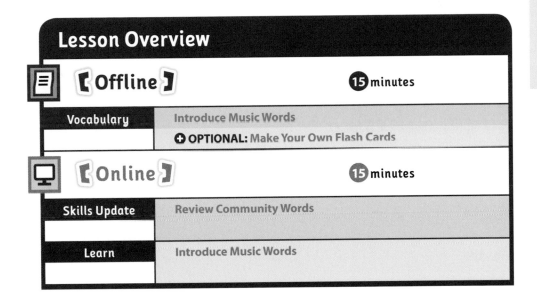

Lesson Overview

▤	**Offline**		15 minutes
Vocabulary	Introduce Music Words		
	⊕ OPTIONAL: Make Your Own Flash Cards		

🖥	**Online**		15 minutes
Skills Update	Review Community Words		
Learn	Introduce Music Words		

Offline — 15 minutes

Work **together** with students to complete an offline Vocabulary activity.

Vocabulary ....

Introduce Music Words

Help students learn the following music words:

drum	**song**	**tuba**
flute	**trumpet**	**violin**
orchestra		

Objectives

● Increase oral vocabulary.

● Increase concept vocabulary.

1. Gather page LS 29 from *K¹² Language Arts Activity Book*. Explain to students that they will learn some music words.

2. Show students the page and explain that an *orchestra* is a large band, or group of people, playing different instruments. Point to each instrument as you say its name. For the word *song*, point to the person singing.

3. Have students point to each picture and help them name each item.

4. Have students cut out each item and glue it on the stage scene. Have them point to and name each item one more time.

___

⊕ OPTIONAL: Make Your Own Flash Cards

This activity is intended for students who have extra time and would benefit from practicing vocabulary words with flash cards. Feel free to skip this activity.

Gather seven index cards. Have students create flash cards by writing each vocabulary word on the front of an index card and drawing a picture of each word on the back. Help students with spelling and drawings as necessary.

TIP If students are not ready to read and write on their own, skip this optional activity.

 **Online** ⑮ **minutes**

Students will work online **independently** to complete Vocabulary activities. Help students locate the online activities, and provide support as needed.

Skills Update •

Review Community Words
Students will answer a few questions to refresh their Vocabulary knowledge.

Objectives
- Increase oral vocabulary.
- Increase reading vocabulary.
- Increase concept vocabulary.

Learn •

Introduce Music Words
Students will be introduced to the music words *drum, flute, orchestra, song, trumpet, tuba,* and *violin.*

Objectives
- Increase oral vocabulary.
- Increase reading vocabulary.
- Increase concept vocabulary.

My Favorite Subject and Music Words

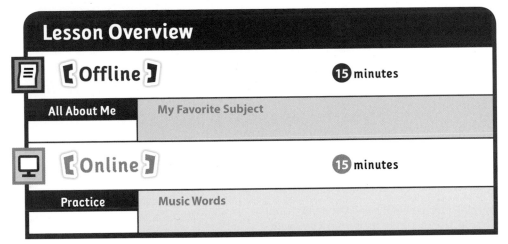

Lesson Overview

Offline — 15 minutes

All About Me	My Favorite Subject

Online — 15 minutes

Practice	Music Words

Materials

Supplied
- *K¹² All About Me*, p. 16

Also Needed
- crayons

Offline — 15 minutes

Work **together** with students to complete an offline All About Me activity.

All About Me

My Favorite Subject

Students will complete page 16 in *K¹² All About Me*.

1. Give students time to complete their illustration. Encourage them to add supporting details to their picture.

2. Reread the first sentence, pointing to each word as you read. Have students repeat the sentence. Repeat this process for the second sentence, and then ask:

   ▸ Would it make sense to draw a picture of your favorite pet on this page? No   Why? Answers will vary; students should understand that the topic is their favorite subject, so the illustration should support the sentences that talk about their favorite subject.

3. Have students finalize and then explain their drawing. Encourage them to share their drawing with others.

Objectives
- Add supporting details to written or drawn work.
- Discuss own drawing.

[Online] minutes

Students will work online **independently** to complete an activity on Vocabulary words. Help students locate the online activity, and provide support as needed.

Practice

Music Words

Students will practice the music words *drum, flute, orchestra, song, trumpet, tuba,* and *violin.*

Objectives
- Increase oral vocabulary.
- Increase reading vocabulary.
- Increase concept vocabulary.

Offline Alternative

No computer access? At any time, you can print a list of the unit Vocabulary words and their definitions from the online lesson. Use this list to review the words with students offline. In addition, if students made their own flash cards, these can be used for offline review.

"Three Blind Mice" and Music Words

Lesson Overview

[Offline] ⏱ **15** minutes

Poetry	"Three Blind Mice"

[Online] ⏱ **15** minutes

Practice	Music Words

[Materials]

Supplied
- *K¹² Read Aloud Treasury*, p. 87

[Offline] ⏱ **15** minutes

Work **together** with students to complete an offline Poetry activity.

Poetry

"Three Blind Mice"

It's time to read "Three Blind Mice" from *K¹² Read Aloud Treasury*.

1. Remind students that **nursery rhymes** are poems that many people hear when they are very young. Tell them that today they will hear a nursery rhyme called "Three Blind Mice." Like many nursery rhymes, "Three Blind Mice" can be sung as well as read.

2. Before you begin reading, ask:
   - ▶ What does it mean to be blind? You're not able to see.
   - ▶ What do you think will happen to the blind mice in this poem? Answers will vary.

3. Have students sit next to you so they can see the picture and the words while you **read aloud the entire poem**, and then ask:
   - ▶ Who do the blind mice run after? the farmer's wife
   - ▶ What happens to the mice in the poem? Their tails are cut off.
   - ▶ Do you think the farmer's wife liked mice? No   Why? Answers will vary. The farmer's wife may be afraid of mice or worried that they will eat some of the family's food.
   - ▶ What two words in the poem rhyme with *wife*? *knife* and *life*
   - ▶ Were you surprised by what happened to the three blind mice? Answers will vary.

> ⭐ **Objectives**
> - Listen to and discuss poetry.
> - Listen and respond to texts representing a variety of cultures, time periods, and traditions.
> - Identify rhyme and rhythm in poetry.
> - Make predictions based on title, illustrations, and/or context clues.

4. Remind students of the predictions they made about the mice before hearing the poem.

   ▸ What did you predict would happen to the blind mice? Answers will vary.
   ▸ What really happened to the mice? They tried to chase the farmer's wife, but she caught them and cut off their tails.

5. **Say:** Good readers always make predictions about what will happen before they read. What makes reading so much fun is checking to see if your prediction was correct or if the author was able to surprise you. We'll want to remember that the next time we read together.

TIP Predictions are never *right* or *wrong*. Predictions help focus a reader's attention and assist in comprehension. The foundational work done with predicting in this course will help students as they grow into independent readers.

 **[Online]** **15** minutes

Students will work online **independently** to complete an activity on Vocabulary words. Help students locate the online activity, and provide support as needed.

Practice ••

Music Words
Students will practice the music words *drum, flute, orchestra, song, trumpet, tuba,* and *violin.*

Objectives
- Increase oral vocabulary.
- Increase reading vocabulary.
- Increase concept vocabulary.

Offline Alternative

No computer access? At any time, you can print a list of the unit Vocabulary words and their definitions from the online lesson. Use this list to review the words with students offline. In addition, if students made their own flash cards, these can be used for offline review.

Reading Words (A)

Lesson Overview

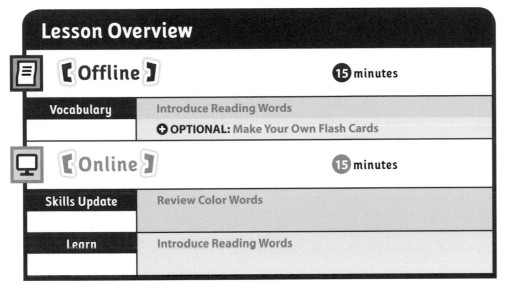

Offline		15 minutes
Vocabulary	Introduce Reading Words	
	⊕ OPTIONAL: Make Your Own Flash Cards	

Online		15 minutes
Skills Update	Review Color Words	
Learn	Introduce Reading Words	

Materials

Supplied
- There are no supplied materials to gather for this lesson.

Also Needed
- household objects – book
- index cards (7) (optional)

Advance Preparation

Select a fiction book from your own library. Make sure the book includes chapters and an author's name.

 **Offline** 15 minutes

Work **together** with students to complete an offline Vocabulary activity.

 Vocabulary ....

Introduce Reading Words
Help students learn the following reading words and how they are related:

author	cover	spine
book	page	story
chapter		

Objectives
- Increase oral vocabulary.
- Increase reading vocabulary.
- Increase concept vocabulary.

1. Gather the book you selected from your home library. Tell students that you are taking them on a Book Walk, where you will talk about the parts of a book.

2. Scan the book together. Point out the different parts of the book and where they are located.

    ▸ Point to the **book**.
      Say: This is a book. A book is sheets of paper that are put together between two covers. The paper can have writing or be blank.
    ▸ Point to the **cover** of the book.
      Say: This is a cover. A cover is something put over the pages of a book to protect it.
    ▸ Point to the name of the **author**.
      Say: This is the author. An author is a writer. Authors write all kinds of books.
    ▸ Point to the **spine**.
      Say: This is a spine. The spine is the part of a book that the pages are attached to.
    ▸ Point to the title of the book and flip through the pages. Point to a **story**.
      Say: This is a story. A story is a tale of something that happened that is either true or made up.
    ▸ Point to a **chapter** title in the book.
      Say: This is a chapter. A chapter is one of the main parts of a book. It usually has a number or a title.
    ▸ Point to a **page** in the book.
      Say: This is a page. A page is one sheet of paper in a book, magazine, or newspaper.

3. If time permits, have students explain each part of the book as they do their own Book Walk.

⊕ OPTIONAL: Make Your Own Flash Cards

This activity is intended for students who have extra time and would benefit from practicing their vocabulary words with flash cards. Feel free to skip this activity.

Gather seven index cards. Have students create flash cards by writing each vocabulary word on the front of an index card and their own definition for each word on the back. Help students with spelling as necessary.

 **minutes**

Students will work online **independently** to complete activities on Vocabulary words. Help students locate the online activities, and provide support as needed.

Skills Update ....

Review Color Words
Students will answer a few questions to refresh their Vocabulary knowledge.

Objectives
- Increase reading vocabulary.
- Increase concept vocabulary.

Learn ....

Introduce Reading Words
Students will be introduced to the reading words *author, book, chapter, cover, page, spine,* and *story.*

Objectives
- Increase oral vocabulary.
- Increase reading vocabulary.
- Increase concept vocabulary.

My Favorite Book and Reading Words (A)

Lesson Overview

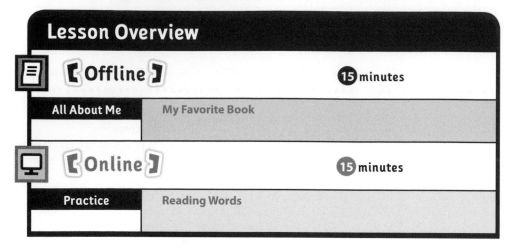 **Offline**		**15** minutes
All About Me	My Favorite Book	
Online		**15** minutes
Practice	Reading Words	

Materials

Supplied
- *K12 All About Me*, p. 17

Also Needed
- crayons

Offline   **15** minutes

Work **together** with students to complete an offline All About Me activity.

All About Me

My Favorite Book

Students will begin page 17 in *K12 All About Me*. They will complete this page over two lessons.

1. Point to and read aloud the sentence on the page.

2. Have students tell you the answer to write in the blank space. Read the complete sentence to them, pointing to each word.

3. Ask students to tell you about their favorite book and explain why it is their favorite. Prompt them by asking about details of the story. Answers to questions may vary.

   ▸ Who are the characters?
   ▸ Where does the story take place?
   ▸ What happens in the story?
   ▸ What do you like best about the book?

4. If time permits, have students begin to illustrate a scene from their favorite book.

Objectives
- Dictate or write simple sentences describing experiences, stories, people, objects, or events.
- Write and/or draw narrative text.

 **15 minutes**

Students will work online **independently** to complete activities on Vocabulary words. Help students locate the online activities, and provide support as needed.

Practice

Reading Words

Students will practice the reading words *author, book, chapter, cover, page, spine,* and *story.*

Objectives
- Increase oral vocabulary.
- Increase concept vocabulary.

Offline Alternative

No computer access? At any time, you can print a list of the unit Vocabulary words and their definitions from the online lesson. Use this list to review the words with students offline. In addition, if students made their own flash cards, these can be used for offline review.

"There Was a Little Girl" and Reading Words

Lesson Overview

📄 [Offline]   🕐 15 minutes

Poetry	"There Was a Little Girl"

🖥 [Online]   🕐 15 minutes

Practice	Reading Words

[Materials]

Supplied
- *The Rooster Crows*

Also Needed
- paper, drawing
- crayons

Advance Preparation

Before reading today's poem, you will need to find the poem in *The Rooster Crows*. If your book has page numbers, turn to page 34. Otherwise, you will need to use a pencil to number the pages in the book. Mark the title page as page 1.

[Offline] 🕐 15 minutes

Work **together** with students to complete an offline Poetry activity.

Poetry ....

"There Was a Little Girl"

It's time to read "There Was a Little Girl" from *The Rooster Crows*.

1. Remind students that the people and animals in poems are called **characters**. We learn about characters from what they do, what they say, and what the poem says about them.

    ▶ Who or what do you think is the main character in the poem? a little girl

2. Remind students that poems sometimes contain words we do not know, but we can figure out the meanings of these words by looking at other words in the poem.

Objectives
- Listen to and discuss poetry.
- Identify and use context clues to define words.
- Respond to text through art, writing, and/or drama.
- Identify rhyme and rhythm in poetry.
- Describe character(s).

3. Have students sit next to you so they can see the picture and words while you **read aloud the entire poem**, and then ask:

    ▶ Who is the character in the poem? the little girl
    ▶ What hangs down on the little girl's forehead? a curl of hair
    ▶ Is the little girl always good? No
    ▶ How would you describe the little girl? Answers will vary.
    ▶ What word in the poem rhymes with *forehead*? *horrid*

4. Point to the word *horrid* in the poem.

    Say: This is a word that many people do not know. Yet we can figure out what it means.

5. Reread lines 4 and 5.

    ▶ How does the little girl act when she is good? She acts "very good indeed."

6. Tell students that *good* and *bad* are opposites—they are as different as can be.

    Say: We can guess that *very good* and *horrid* must be opposites, too. *Horrid* must mean *very bad*.

7. Have students gather paper and crayons and draw the little girl. If possible, have them practice reciting the poem as they draw. Remind them that she should have a curl of hair on her forehead. When students have finished their drawing, help them recite the poem. Then have them say whether the girl is being good or bad in their drawing.

 **15 minutes**

Students will work online **independently** to complete activities on Vocabulary words. Help students locate the online activities, and provide support as needed.

Practice •

Reading Words
Students will practice the reading words *author*, *book*, *chapter*, *cover*, *page*, *spine*, and *story*.

 Objectives
- Increase oral vocabulary.
- Increase concept vocabulary.

Offline Alternative

No computer access? At any time, you can print a list of the unit Vocabulary words and their definitions from the online lesson. Use this list to review the words with students offline. In addition, if students made their own flash cards, these can be used for offline review.

Reading Words (B)

Lesson Overview

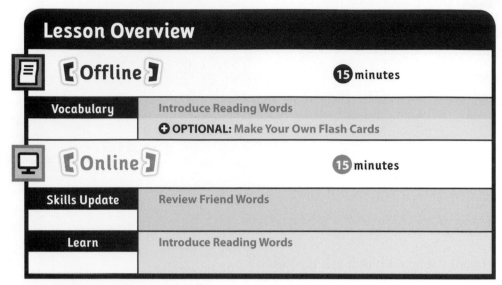

Offline		**15** minutes
Vocabulary	Introduce Reading Words	
	O OPTIONAL: Make Your Own Flash Cards	
Online		**15** minutes
Skills Update	Review Friend Words	
Learn	Introduce Reading Words	

[Materials]

Supplied
- *K¹² Language Arts Activity Book*, p. LS 31

Also Needed
- household objects – dictionary, newspaper, magazine, letter
- index cards (6) (optional)

Advance Preparation

Gather a dictionary, a newspaper, a magazine, and a letter.

[Offline] **15** minutes

Work **together** with students to complete an offline Vocabulary activity.

Introduce Reading Words

Have students learn the following reading words:

dictionary	**magazine**	**sentence**
letter	**newspaper**	**word**

1. Tell students that they are going to learn some words related to reading. Show examples of each of the following: dictionary, newspaper, magazine, and letter.

2. Explain what a dictionary, newspaper, magazine, and letter are used for. For example, "A dictionary is used to look up the meaning of a word" or "A letter is written to someone. It tells something and is usually sent through the mail."

Objectives
- Increase oral vocabulary.
- Increase concept vocabulary.
- Identify and use new meanings for known words.

3. Tell students that one of the words is a tricky word because it has two meanings. Show them the example of the letter.
Say: The word *letter* can mean something we write to someone to tell them news or say hello. But the word *letter* has another meaning. Can you guess what it is?

4. If necessary, tell students that a letter can also be from the alphabet, such as *a, b, c, d,* and so on. Explain that these kinds of letters are put together to make words.

5. Explain that words are put together to make sentences. A sentence begins with a capital letter and ends with a period, a question mark, or an exclamation point. Point to a sentence in the magazine or letter.

6. Gather page LS 31 from *K¹² Language Arts Activity Book*. Read the sentences on the page to the students. Encourage students to read the sentences on their own.

7. Have students underline each sentence. Have them put a circle around each word.

⊕ OPTIONAL: Make Your Own Flash Cards
This activity is intended for students who have extra time and would benefit from practicing their vocabulary words with flash cards. Feel free to skip this activity.

Gather six index cards. Have students create flash cards by writing each vocabulary word on the front of an index card and their own definition for each word on the back. Help students with spelling as necessary.

 **15 minutes**

Students will work online **independently** to complete activities on Vocabulary words. Help students locate the online activities, and provide support as needed.

Skills Update

Review Friend Words

Students will answer a few questions to refresh their Vocabulary knowledge.

 Objectives

- Increase oral vocabulary.
- Increase concept vocabulary.

Learn

Introduce Reading Words

Students will be introduced to the reading words *dictionary, letter, magazine, newspaper, sentence,* and *word.*

 Objectives

- Increase oral vocabulary.
- Increase concept vocabulary.

My Favorite Book and Reading Words (B)

Lesson Overview

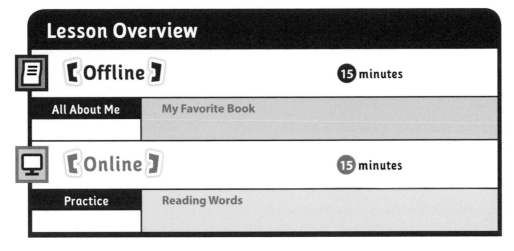

Offline		**15** minutes
All About Me	My Favorite Book	

Online		**15** minutes
Practice	Reading Words	

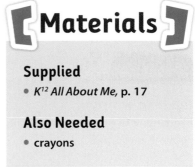

Offline **15** minutes

Work **together** with students to complete an offline All About Me activity.

All About Me

My Favorite Book

Students will complete page 17 in *K¹² All About Me*.

1. Give students time to complete the illustration of a scene from their favorite book.

2. As necessary, help students label items in the picture (for example, the name of the main character).

3. Have students explain their drawing, using details of the picture to help them.

4. Encourage students to share their finished work with others.

Objectives
- Add supporting details to written or drawn work.
- Discuss own drawing.
- Share finished written and drawn works.

 **[Online]** ⏱ **minutes**

Students will work online **independently** to complete an activity on Vocabulary words. Help students locate the online activity, and provide support as needed.

Practice

Reading Words

Students will practice the reading words *dictionary, letter, magazine, newspaper, sentence,* and *word.*

Objectives
- Increase oral vocabulary.
- Increase concept vocabulary.

Offline Alternative

No computer access? At any time, you can print a list of the unit Vocabulary words and their definitions from the online lesson. Use this list to review the words with students offline. In addition, if students made their own flash cards, these can be used for offline review.

"Mackerel Sky" & "Rain Before Seven" and Vocabulary Unit Review

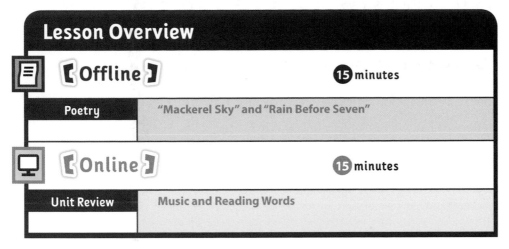

Lesson Overview

	Offline	15 minutes
Poetry	"Mackerel Sky" and "Rain Before Seven"	

	Online	15 minutes
Unit Review	Music and Reading Words	

Advance Preparation

Before reading today's poems, you will need to find the poems in *The Rooster Crows*. If your book has page numbers, turn to page 28. Otherwise, you will need to use a pencil to number the pages in the book. Mark the title page as page 1.

Offline   15 minutes

Work **together** with students to complete an offline Poetry activity.

Poetry ....

"Mackerel Sky" and "Rain Before Seven"
It's time to read two weather-related poems from *The Rooster Crows*.

1. Discuss with students the weather you are having. Explain that some poems were written a long time ago to help people predict the weather. Ask students if they can recall other poems they may have heard that help people predict the weather, such as "Evening Red and Morning Gray."

2. Tell students they will hear two poems that help people predict the weather. The first is called "Mackerel Sky." Explain that a *mackerel* is a type of fish. A mackerel sky looks like the skin of a mackerel, with many small spots—clouds—everywhere.

Objectives
- Listen to and discuss poetry.
- Identify the purpose of a text.
- Respond to text through art, writing, and/or drama.
- Identify rhyme and rhythm in poetry.

3. Have students sit next to you so they can see the pictures and the words while you **read the poems aloud**.

4. **Say:** In "Mackerel Sky," the line "never long wet, never long dry" means that it won't be long until there is a short storm.

   ▸ In "Mackerel Sky," what word rhymes with *sky*? *dry*
   ▸ In "Rain Before Seven," what two words rhyme? *seven* and *eleven*
   ▸ What does "Rain Before Seven" say the weather will be like if it rains early in the morning? *clear*

5. Talk with students about predicting the weather. Answers to questions may vary.

   ▸ Would you like to know what the weather will be like later today? Why?
   ▸ What if you were going on a picnic tomorrow? Would it be helpful to know what the weather would be like ahead of time?

TIP It may be helpful to do an Internet search on the phrase "mackerel sky" to better see the similarities between a mackerel and a mackerel sky.

 **15 minutes**

Students will work online **independently** to complete an activity on Vocabulary words. Help students locate the online activity, and provide support as needed.

Unit Review

Music and Reading Words
Students will review all words from the unit to prepare for the Unit Checkpoint.

Objectives
• Increase oral vocabulary.
• Increase reading vocabulary.
• Increase concept vocabulary.

Offline Alternative

No computer access? At any time, you can print a list of the unit Vocabulary words and their definitions from the online lesson. Use this list to review the words with students offline. In addition, if students made their own flash cards, these can be used for offline review.

Unit Checkpoint

Lesson Overview

 Online **30** minutes

Unit Checkpoint	Music and Reading Words

Materials

There are no materials to gather for this lesson.

Online **30** minutes

Students will work online to complete the Unit Checkpoint. Help students locate the Unit Checkpoint, and provide support as needed.

Unit Checkpoint

Music and Reading Words

Explain that students are going to show what they have learned about vocabulary words for music and reading.

Objectives
- Increase oral vocabulary.
- Increase reading vocabulary.
- Increase concept vocabulary.
- Identify and use new meanings for known words.

Travel Words (A)

Unit Overview

In this unit, students will
- ▶ Learn travel and comparison vocabulary words.
- ▶ Complete the *All About Me* pages *My Best Day* and *My Best Friend*.
- ▶ Explore the poems "Red at Night, Sailors Delight," "The Little Elf," and "This Little Pig Goes to Market."

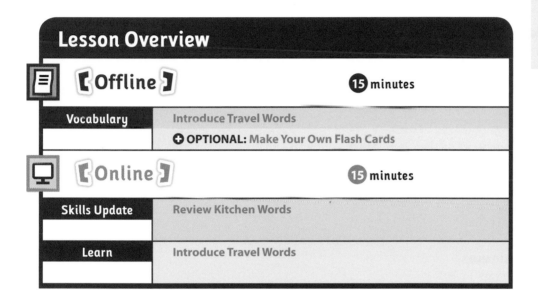

Lesson Overview

▤	**[Offline]**		**15** minutes
Vocabulary	Introduce Travel Words		
	✚ OPTIONAL: Make Your Own Flash Cards		

🖥	**[Online]**		**15** minutes
Skills Update	Review Kitchen Words		
Learn	Introduce Travel Words		

 **[Offline]** **15** minutes

Work **together** with students to complete an offline Vocabulary activity.

Vocabulary ....

Introduce Travel Words

Introduce students to the following travel words:

atlas	avenue	signal
automobile	driver	trip

1. Say the words *atlas*, *automobile*, *avenue*, and *driver* to students. Have them repeat the words. Discuss the words by talking about where you might find each of these things. For example, you might see an atlas in the library or in a car. *Automobile* is another word for *car*, so you might see an automobile on the street. You might see an avenue in the city, or a driver in a bus or taxicab.

Objectives
- Increase oral vocabulary.
- Increase reading vocabulary.
- Increase concept vocabulary.
- Identify and use new meanings for known words.

2. Say the word *signal* to students and have them repeat it. Explain that there many kinds of signals. For example, there are traffic signals and railroad-crossing signals. And in sports, a referee may make a signal. Although there are different kinds of signals, they are all things that direct, warn, or remind.

3. Say the word *trip* and have students repeat it. Explain that unlike the word *signal*, which always means "to direct, warn, or remind," the word *trip* has two completely different meanings. Ask students if they can think of any definitions for the word *trip*. If necessary, explain that sometimes *trip* means "to stumble or fall over something on the ground" and sometimes it means "travel from one place to another."

⊕ OPTIONAL: Make Your Own Flash Cards

This activity is intended for students who have extra time and would benefit from practicing their vocabulary words with flash cards. Feel free to skip this activity.

Gather six index cards. Have students create flash cards by writing each vocabulary word on the front of an index card and their own definition for each word on the back. Help students with spelling as necessary.

 If students are not ready to read and write on their own, skip this optional activity.

 **15 minutes**

Students will work online **independently** to complete activities on Vocabulary words. Help students locate the online activities, and provide support as needed.

Skills Update ••

Review Kitchen Words
Students will answer a few questions to refresh their Vocabulary knowledge.

Objectives
- Increase oral vocabulary.
- Increase concept vocabulary.

Learn ••

Introduce Travel Words
Students will be introduced to the words *atlas, driver, automobile, signal, avenue,* and *trip*.

Objectives
- Increase oral vocabulary.
- Increase reading vocabulary.
- Increase concept vocabulary.
- Identify and use new meanings for known words.

My Best Day and Travel Words (A)

Lesson Overview

Offline		**15** minutes
All About Me	My Best Day	

Online		**15** minutes
Practice	Travel Words	

Materials

Supplied
- *K¹² All About Me*, p. 18

Also Needed
- crayons

Offline **15** minutes

Work **together** with students to complete an offline All About Me activity.

All About Me

My Best Day

Students will begin page 18 in *K¹² All About Me*. They will complete this page over two lessons.

1. Ask students to think about the best day they've ever had. Prompt them with the following questions:

   ▶ When was it?
   ▶ Who was there?
   ▶ What happened that day? (Encourage students to think sequentially—what happened first, what happened next, what happened last.)
   ▶ Where did your best day take place?
   ▶ Why was it better than other days?

2. If time permits, have students begin illustrating their best day ever.

Objectives
- Write and/or draw narrative text.
- Generate ideas for writing and drawing through discussion.
- Draw a picture or write about an idea generated through discussion.
- Describe people, places, things, locations, actions, events, and/or feelings.

 **15 minutes**

Students will work online **independently** to complete activities on Vocabulary words. Help students locate the online activities, and provide support as needed.

Practice ....

Travel Words

Students will practice the travel words *atlas, driver, automobile, signal, avenue,* and *trip.*

Offline Alternative

No computer access? At any time, you can print a list of the unit Vocabulary words and their definitions from the online lesson. Use this list to review the words with students offline. In addition, if students made their own flash cards, these can be used for offline review.

Objectives
- Increase oral vocabulary.
- Increase reading vocabulary.
- Increase concept vocabulary.
- Identify and use new meanings for known words.

"Red at Night, Sailors Delight" and Travel Words

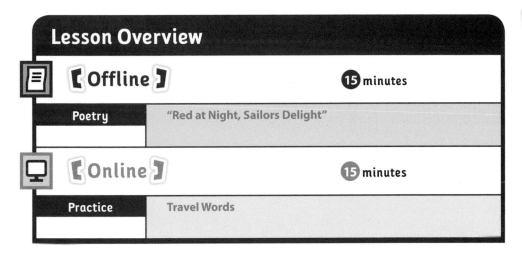

Lesson Overview

Offline   **15** minutes

| Poetry | "Red at Night, Sailors Delight" |

Online   **15** minutes

| Practice | Travel Words |

Materials

Supplied
- *The Rooster Crows*

Advance Preparation

Before reading today's poem, you will need to find the poem in *The Rooster Crows*. If your book has page numbers, turn to page 21. Otherwise, you will need to use a pencil to number the pages in the book. Mark the title page as page 1.

Offline   **15** minutes

Work **together** with students to complete an offline Poetry activity.

Poetry •••

"Red at Night, Sailors Delight"

It's time to read "Red at Night, Sailors Delight" from *The Rooster Crows*.

1. Remind students that some poems were written to help predict the weather. Explain to them that the poem they will hear predicts when the weather on the ocean will be good and when it will be bad.

2. Tell students that many poems have a steady **rhythm**. Rhythm is a repeated pattern of beats or sounds. Have students listen as you recite this rhyme, clapping with each beat to demonstrate rhythm: "Ring around the rosie, / A pocket full of posies. / Ashes, ashes, / We all fall down."

Objectives
- Listen to and discuss poetry.
- Recite short poems or rhymes.
- Identify rhyme and rhythm in poetry.
- Identify the purpose of a text.

3. Have students sit next to you so they can see the picture and words while you **read the entire poem aloud**, and then ask:

   ▸ Is a red night good or bad for sailors? good
   ▸ What word in the poem rhymes with *morning*: *night, sailors,* or *warning*? *warning*
   ▸ What does it mean to "take warning"? Answers will vary, but students should understand that it means something like "to be careful."
   ▸ If you were the sailor in the picture, would you want to sail after a red night or a red morning? a red night

4. Read aloud each line of the poem, having students repeat the lines. As you read, stress the beats to help students feel and hear the poem's rhythm. You may wish to clap with each beat (shown in boldface).

   Red at **night**,
   Sail-ors de-**light**.
   Red in the **morn**-ing,
   Sail-ors take **warn**-ing.

    If time permits, have students clap along to the rhythm of another short poem in *The Rooster Crows* as you read the poem aloud. For example, "Engine, Engine, Number Nine" has four beats per line.

 **[Online]** ⓕ **minutes**

Students will work online **independently** to complete activities on Vocabulary words. Help students locate the online activities, and provide support as needed.

Practice •

Travel Words
Students will practice the travel words *atlas, driver, automobile, signal, avenue,* and *trip*.

Objectives
• Increase oral vocabulary.
• Increase concept vocabulary.

Offline Alternative

No computer access? At any time, you can print a list of the unit Vocabulary words and their definitions from the online lesson. Use this list to review the words with students offline. In addition, if students made their own flash cards, these can be used for offline review.

Travel Words (B)

Lesson Overview

📖 【 Offline 】   ⏱ 15 minutes

Vocabulary	Introduce Travel Words
	⊕ OPTIONAL: Make Your Own Flash Cards

🖥 【 Online 】   ⏱ 15 minutes

Skills Update	Review Community Words
Learn	Introduce Travel Words

【 Materials 】

Supplied
- *K¹² Language Arts Activity Book*, p. LS 33

Also Needed
- scissors, round-end safety
- glue stick
- index cards (7) (optional)

【 Offline 】 ⏱ 15 minutes

Work **together** with students to complete an offline Vocabulary activity.

Vocabulary ··

Introduce Travel Words

Introduce students to more travel words.

airplane	ship	train
bus	taxi	truck
ferry		

⭐ **Objectives**
- Increase oral vocabulary.
- Increase concept vocabulary.

1. Turn to page LS 33 in *K¹² Language Arts Activity Book*. Point to each vehicle at the bottom of the page and name it for students. Ask them to repeat each word and, if they can, tell you what each vehicle is used for. If necessary, provide students with definitions or examples.

2. Have students cut out each vehicle and glue it where it might go in the scene.

3. Have students make the sound each vehicle makes. For example, students might make the sound of a foghorn for the ship, a train whistle for the train, and a car horn for the taxi.

⊕ OPTIONAL: Make Your Own Flash Cards

This activity is intended for students who have extra time and would benefit from practicing their vocabulary words with flash cards. Feel free to skip this activity.

Gather seven index cards. Have students create flash cards by writing each vocabulary word on the front of an index card and their own definition for each word on the back. Help students with spelling as necessary.

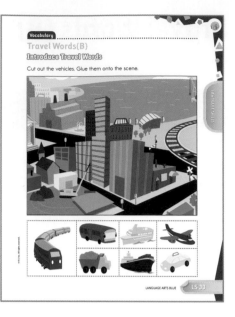

 **minutes**

Students will work online **independently** to complete activities on Vocabulary words. Help students locate the online activities, and provide support as needed.

Skills Update •

Review Community Words
Students will answer a few questions to refresh their Vocabulary knowledge.

Objectives
- Increase oral vocabulary.
- Increase concept vocabulary.

Learn •

Introduce Travel Words
Students will be introduced to the travel words *train, ship, airplane, ferry, bus, truck,* and *taxi*.

Objectives
- Increase oral vocabulary.
- Increase reading vocabulary.
- Increase concept vocabulary.

My Best Day and Travel Words (B)

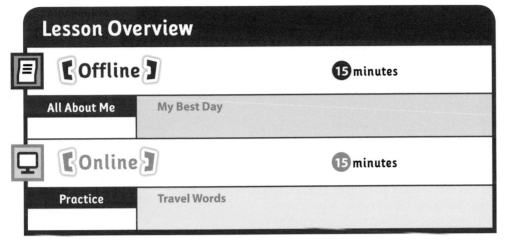

Lesson Overview

Offline		**15** minutes
All About Me	My Best Day	
Online		**15** minutes
Practice	Travel Words	

Materials

Supplied
- *K¹² All About Me*, p. 18

Also Needed
- crayons

Offline **15** minutes

Work **together** with students to complete an offline All About Me activity.

All About Me

My Best Day
Students will complete page 18 in *K¹² All About Me*.

1. Give students time to complete the illustration of their best day. Encourage them to add details to the picture as appropriate.

2. As necessary, help students label items in their picture.

3. Have students explain their drawing, using details of the picture to help them.

4. Encourage students to share their finished work with others.

Objectives
- Write and/or draw narrative text.
- Draw a picture or write about an idea generated through discussion.
- Add supporting details to written or drawn work.
- Discuss own drawing.
- Share finished written and drawn works.

 **Online** **15** minutes

Students will work online **independently** to complete activities on Vocabulary words. Help students locate the online activities, and provide support as needed.

Practice

• •

Travel Words

Students will practice the travel words *train, ship, airplane, ferry, bus, truck,* and *taxi.*

Offline Alternative

No computer access? At any time, you can print a list of the unit Vocabulary words and their definitions from the online lesson. Use this list to review the words with students offline. In addition, if students made their own flash cards, these can be used for offline review.

 Objectives

• Increase oral vocabulary.
• Increase reading vocabulary.
• Increase concept vocabulary.

"The Little Elf" and Travel Words

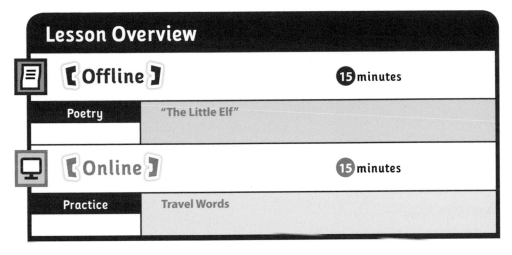

Lesson Overview

Offline		15 minutes
Poetry	"The Little Elf"	

Online		15 minutes
Practice	Travel Words	

Materials

Supplied
- *K¹² Read Aloud Treasury*, p. 93

Offline · 15 minutes

Work **together** with students to complete an offline Poetry activity.

Poetry

"The Little Elf"

It's time to read "The Little Elf" from *K¹² Read Aloud Treasury*.

1. Have students tell you what they know about elves. As necessary, tell them that elves are little make-believe people who are known for playing tricks. Answers to questions may vary.

   ▶ What would you do if you met an elf?
   ▶ What questions would you ask an elf?

2. Have students sit next to you so they can see the picture and words while you **read aloud the entire poem**, and then ask:

   ▶ What word in the poem rhymes with *blow*: *once, grow,* or *small*? *grow*
   ▶ What does the little girl in the poem ask the elf? why he is so small, and why he doesn't grow
   ▶ How does the elf feel about the person's questions? Answers will vary, but students should understand that the elf is unhappy or insulted.

> **Objectives**
> - Listen to and discuss poetry.
> - Recite short poems or rhymes.
> - Identify rhyme and rhythm in poetry.
> - Describe characters.

3. Talk with students about what it is like to be smaller than other people. Answers to questions may vary.

> ► What are some good things about being small?
> ► Are there any bad things about being small? What are they?

4. Tell students to think about what the elf says. Reread the line if necessary.

> ► Does the elf think that he is small? No. He thinks he is the proper size.
> ► Why is it good to be happy being whatever size you are? Answers will vary.

 **15 minutes**

Students will work online **independently** to complete activities on Vocabulary words. Help students locate the online activities, and provide support as needed.

Practice

Travel Words

Students will practice the travel words *train, ship, airplane, ferry, bus, truck,* and *taxi.*

 Objectives
- Increase oral vocabulary.
- Increase concept vocabulary.

Offline Alternative

No computer access? At any time, you can print a list of the unit Vocabulary words and their definitions from the online lesson. Use this list to review the words with students offline. In addition, if students made their own flash cards, these can be used for offline review.

Comparison Words (A)

Lesson Overview

Offline		**15** minutes
Vocabulary	Introduce Comparison Words	
	⊕ OPTIONAL: Make Your Own Flash Cards	

Online		**15** minutes
Skills Update	Review Body Part Words	
Learn	Introduce Comparison Words	

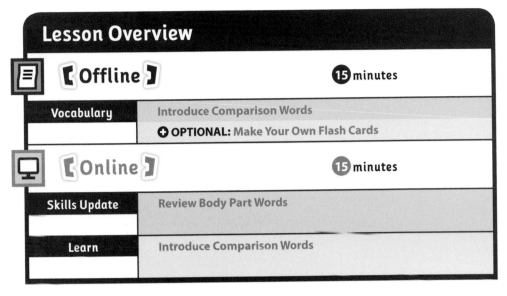

[Materials]

Supplied
- *K¹² Language Arts Activity Book*, p. LS 35

Also Needed
- index cards (6) (optional)

[Offline] **15** minutes

Work **together** with students to complete an offline Vocabulary activity.

Vocabulary

Introduce Comparison Words

Introduce students to the following comparison words:

good	**better**	**best**
bad	**worse**	**worst**

1. Turn to page LS 35 in *K¹² Language Arts Activity Book*.

   ▸ Point to the first set of pictures and read the labels *good*, *better*, and *best*.
   ▸ Point to the second set of pictures and read the labels *bad*, *worse*, and *worst*.

2. Discuss the pictures with students.

   ▸ Is it possible to describe the picture labeled "worse" without seeing the picture labeled "bad"? Why? Answers will vary.

3. Tell students that when you use words like *worse* or *better*, you need to have something with which to compare them—something else has to be *bad* or *good* for there to be a *worse* or *better*.

Objectives
- Increase oral vocabulary.
- Increase reading vocabulary.
- Increase concept vocabulary.
- Describe people places, things, locations, actions, events, and/or feelings.

4. Ask students to name a *good* food. Ask them to name a food that they think is *better* than the first food. Finally, ask them to name a food that they think is the *best*.

5. If time permits, repeat Step 4 using *bad*, *worse*, and *worst*.

➕ **OPTIONAL: Make Your Own Flash Cards**
This activity is intended for students who have extra time and would benefit from practicing their vocabulary words with flash cards. Feel free to skip this activity.

Gather six index cards. Have students create flash cards by writing each vocabulary word on the front of an index card and their own definition for each word on the back. Help students with spelling as necessary.

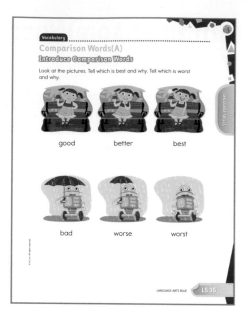

⟦ Online ⟧ minutes

Students will work online **independently** to complete activities on Vocabulary words. Help students locate the online activities, and provide support as needed.

Skills Update

Review Body Part Words
Students will answer a few questions to refresh their Vocabulary knowledge.

⭐ **Objectives**
- Increase oral vocabulary.
- Increase concept vocabulary.

Learn

Introduce Comparison Words
Students will be introduced to the comparison words *good*, *better*, *best*, *bad*, *worse*, and *worst*.

⭐ **Objectives**
- Increase oral vocabulary.
- Increase reading vocabulary.
- Increase concept vocabulary.
- Describe people, places, things, locations, actions, events, and/or feelings.

My Best Friend and Comparison Words (A)

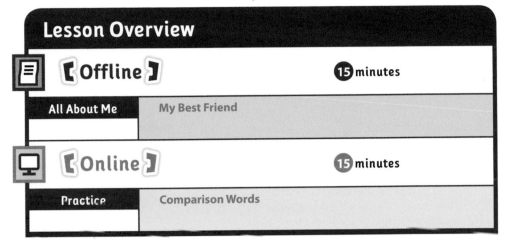

Lesson Overview

Offline — **15** minutes

| All About Me | My Best Friend |

Online — **15** minutes

| Practice | Comparison Words |

[Materials]

Supplied
- *K¹² All About Me*, p. 19

Also Needed
- crayons

Offline — **15** minutes

Work **together** with students to complete an offline All About Me activity.

All About Me

My Best Friend

Students will begin page 19 in *K¹² All About Me*. They will complete this page over two lessons.

1. Read aloud the first incomplete sentence to students, pointing to each word as you read.

2. Have students repeat the first part of the sentence and tell you the answer to write in the blank space. Read the complete sentence to students, pointing to each word.

3. Draw students' attention to the first letter of their friend's name. Explain that the first letter of a person's name is always a capital letter.

4. Have students repeat the complete sentence and point to the word *best* and the name of their friend.

5. Repeat Steps 2–4 for the second incomplete sentence.

6. If time permits, have students begin to illustrate the sentences.

 Objectives
- Dictate or write simple sentences describing experiences, stories, people, objects, or events.
- Write and/or draw narrative text.

 **15 minutes**

Students will work online **independently** to complete activities on Vocabulary words. Help students locate the online activities, and provide support as needed.

Practice

∙∙

Comparison Words

Students will practice the comparison words *good, better, best, bad, worse,* and *worst.*

Offline Alternative

No computer access? At any time, you can print a list of the unit Vocabulary words and their definitions from the online lesson. Use this list to review the words with students offline. In addition, if students made their own flash cards, these can be used for offline review.

Objectives
- Increase oral vocabulary.
- Increase reading vocabulary.
- Increase concept vocabulary.
- Describe people, places, things, locations, actions, events, and/or feelings.

"This Little Pig Goes to Market" and Vocabulary Unit Review

Lesson Overview

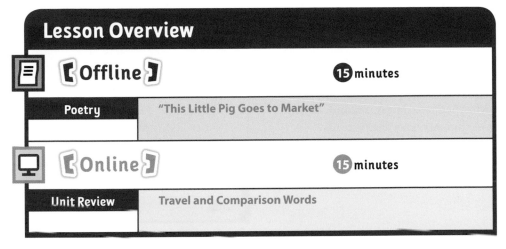

Offline		**15** minutes
Poetry	"This Little Pig Goes to Market"	

Online		**15** minutes
Unit Review	Travel and Comparison Words	

Materials

Supplied
- *The Rooster Crows*
- *K¹² Language Arts Activity Book,* p. LS 36

Also Needed
- crayons

Advance Preparation

Before reading today's poem, you will need to find the poem in *The Rooster Crows*. If your book has page numbers, turn to page 12. Otherwise, you will need to use a pencil to number the pages in the book. Mark the title page as page 1.

 **15** minutes

Work **together** with students to complete an offline Poetry activity.

Poetry ....

"This Little Pig Goes to Market"

It's time to read "This Little Pig Goes to Market" from *The Rooster Crows*.

1. Tell students that we say some poems while playing games with our fingers or our toes and adults say them while playing with babies. Then recite the following, touching your right index finger to your left thumb, touching your left index finger to your right thumb, and slowly twisting your hands to the rhythm of the poem:

> *The itsy bitsy spider went up the water spout.*
> *Down came the rain and washed the spider out.*
> *Out came the sun and dried up all the rain,*
> *And the itsy bitsy spider went up the spout again.*

Objectives
- Listen to and discuss poetry.
- Respond to text through art, writing, and/or drama.
- Sequence events from a text.

2. Have students sit next to you so they can see the picture and words while you **read the entire poem aloud**, and then ask:

   ▸ What does the first little pig do? goes to market
   ▸ How many little pigs are there? five
   ▸ What does the last little pig do? cries "wee, wee, wee!" all the way home

3. Turn to page LS 36 in *K¹² Language Arts Activity Book*. Help students recite the poem as they point to each pig. Then have students tell what happens in the poem in their own words. Have them use the pictures as prompts to help them remember what happened **first**, **second**, **third**, **next**, and **last**. If time permits, have students color the pictures.

[Online] ⓯ minutes

Students will work online **independently** to complete an activity on Vocabulary words. Help students locate the online activity, and provide support as needed.

Unit Review

• •

Travel and Comparison Words
Students will review all words from the unit to prepare for the Unit Checkpoint.

Offline Alternative

No computer access? At any time, you can print a list of the unit Vocabulary words and their definitions from the online lesson. Use this list to review the words with students offline. In addition, if students made their own flash cards, these can be used for offline review.

⭐ **Objectives**
- Increase oral vocabulary.
- Increase concept vocabulary.
- Identify and use new meanings for known words.
- Describe people, places, things, locations, actions, events, and/or feelings.

Unit Checkpoint

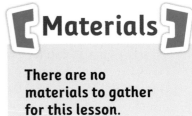

Lesson Overview

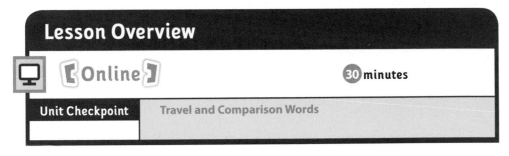

🖥	**〖Online〗**	③⓪ minutes
Unit Checkpoint	Travel and Comparison Words	

〖Materials〗

There are no materials to gather for this lesson.

〖Online〗 ③⓪ minutes

Students will work online to complete the Unit Checkpoint. Help students locate the Unit Checkpoint, and provide support as needed.

Travel and Comparison Words
Explain that students are going to show what they have learned about vocabulary words for travel and comparison.

Objectives
- Increase oral vocabulary.
- Increase reading vocabulary.
- Increase concept vocabulary.
- Identify and use new meanings for known words.
- Describe people, places, things, locations, actions, events, and/or feelings.

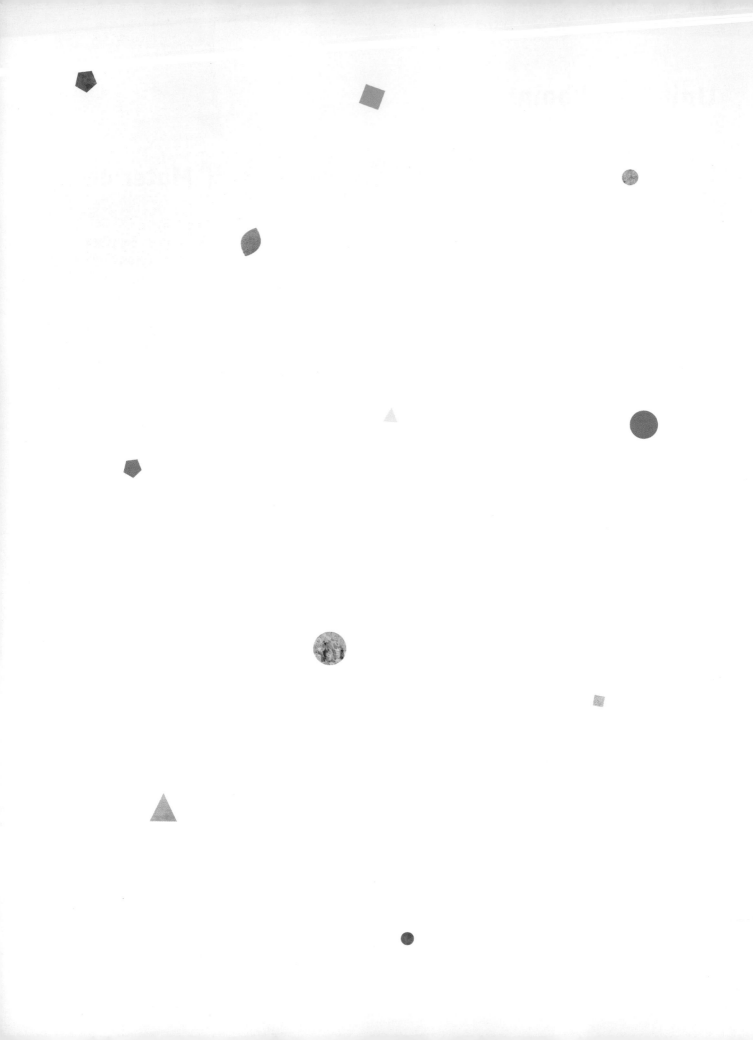

Literature &
Comprehension

Introduce "Little Red Riding Hood"

Unit Overview

In this unit, students will explore the theme of *Good Choices* through the following reading selections:

- ▶ "Little Red Riding Hood"
- ▶ "Healthy Snacks"
- ▶ "Jack and the Beanstalk"

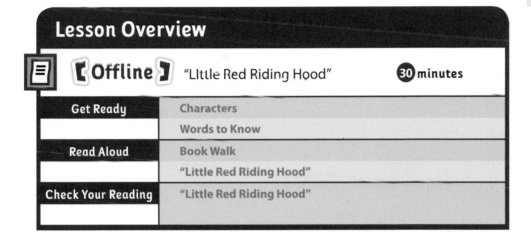

Lesson Overview

☰	[**Offline**] "LIttle Red Riding Hood"	**30** minutes
Get Ready	Characters	
	Words to Know	
Read Aloud	Book Walk	
	"Little Red Riding Hood"	
Check Your Reading	"Little Red Riding Hood"	

Advance Preparation

Read "Little Red Riding Hood" before beginning the Read Aloud activity, to locate the Words to Know within the text.

Big Ideas

- ▶ Comprehension requires an understanding of story structure.
- ▶ Early learners acquire vocabulary through active exposure (by talking and listening, being read to, and receiving explicit instruction).
- ▶ Books have a front cover, a back cover, and a spine.

[Materials]

Supplied

- • "Little Red Riding Hood," *K¹² Read Aloud Treasury,* pp. 2–7

Story Synopsis

In this adaptation of the well-known fairy tale, a girl encounters a sly wolf in the woods on the way to her grandmother's house.

In this updated version, the wolf is not killed; instead, the woodman reaches into the belly of the wolf to retrieve Little Red Riding Hood and her grandmother, and then the wolf runs away.

Keywords

character – a person or animal in a story

setting – when and where a story takes place

[Offline] ③⓪ minutes

"Little Red Riding Hood"

Work **together** with students to complete offline Get Ready, Read Aloud, and Check Your Reading activities.

Get Ready ··

Characters

Tell students that the people in a story are called **characters**. In fairy tales like "Little Red Riding Hood," animals can also be characters. Where the story takes place is called the **setting**.

_____

Words to Know

Before reading "Little Red Riding Hood,"

1. Have students say each word aloud.

2. Ask students if they know what each word means.

   ▸ If students know a word's meaning, have them define it and use it in a sentence.
   ▸ If students don't know a word's meaning, read them the definition and discuss the word with them.

cider – a drink made from apple juice
cottage – a small house
path – a trail for walking
wander – when you walk around without having an exact place to go
wood – a place where many trees grow; the forest

Objectives
- Identify character(s).
- Identify setting.
- Build vocabulary through listening, reading, and discussion.
- Use new vocabulary in written and spoken sentences.

Read Aloud

Book Walk

Prepare students by taking them on a Book Walk of "Little Red Riding Hood." Scan the story together and ask students to make predictions. Answers to questions may vary.

1. Point to the **front cover** of *K¹² Read Aloud Treasury.*
   Say: This is the front cover.

2. Point to the **back cover**.
   Say: This is the back cover.

3. Turn to the **table of contents**. Help students find today's selection, and turn to that page.

4. Point to and read aloud the **title of the story.**

5. Have students look at the **pictures** of the story.

   ▶ What do you think the story is about?
   ▶ Where do you think the story takes place?

Objectives

- Make predictions based on title, illustrations and/or context clues.
- Listen and respond to texts representing a variety of cultures, time periods, and traditions.
- Read and listen to a variety of texts for information and pleasure independently or as part of a group.

"Little Red Riding Hood"

Now it's time to read the story. Have students sit next to you so that they can see the pictures and words while you read the story aloud.

Read aloud the entire story. Emphasize Words to Know as you come to them. If appropriate, use the pictures to help show what each word means.

TIP Before reading today's story, tell students that long ago, hungry wolves roamed the woods near towns and villages, looking for food. This caused most people to fear these big-toothed animals.

Check Your Reading

"Little Red Riding Hood"

Have students retell the story in their own words to develop grammar, vocabulary, comprehension, and fluency skills. When finished, **ask students the following questions** to check comprehension and encourage discussion.

▶ Who is the story mostly about? Little Red Riding Hood
▶ Who is another person, or character, in the story? mother; wolf; Grandmother; woodman
▶ Who is Little Red Riding Hood going to visit? her grandmother
▶ Where does the beginning of the story take place? Little Red Riding Hood's house

Objectives

- Identify character(s).
- Identify the main character(s).
- Identify setting.

Explore "Little Red Riding Hood"

Lesson Overview

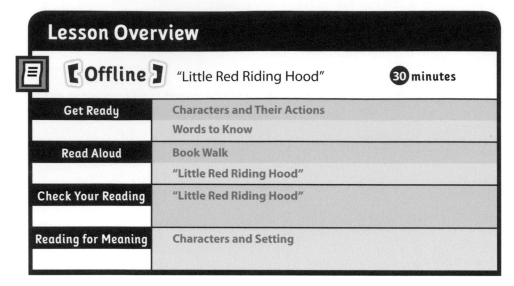

[Offline] "Little Red Riding Hood"　　**30** minutes

Get Ready	Characters and Their Actions
	Words to Know
Read Aloud	Book Walk
	"Little Red Riding Hood"
Check Your Reading	"Little Red Riding Hood"
Reading for Meaning	Characters and Setting

[Materials]

Supplied
- "Little Red Riding Hood," *K¹² Read Aloud Treasury,* pp. 2–7

Keywords

character – a person or animal in a story

setting – when and where a story takes place

Advance Preparation

Before working with students, spend a few minutes reviewing the Words to Know. Then read the Check Your Reading and Reading for Meaning activities to familiarize yourself with the questions and answers.

Big Ideas

► Comprehension requires an understanding of story structure.
► Comprehension entails asking and answering questions about the text.

[Offline] **30** minutes

"Little Red Riding Hood"

Work **together** with students to complete Get Ready, Read Aloud, Check Your Reading, and Reading for Meaning activities.

Get Ready ....

Characters and Their Actions

Remind students that the people in a story are called **characters**. In fairy tales like "Little Red Riding Hood," animals can also be characters.

Tell students that you will be discussing the characters and how they act. To better understand characters' actions, it's helpful to think about our own actions in different situations. Answers to questions may vary.

▶ Have you ever forgotten to do something that you promised you would do?
▶ Why do you think you forgot? Were you busy doing something else?

Remind students that in this story, Little Red Riding Hood forgets her promise to not leave the path. Tell students to listen for why Little Red Riding Hood forgets her promise.

Objectives
- Identify details that explain characters' actions.
- Build vocabulary through listening, reading, and discussion.
- Use new vocabulary in written and spoken sentences.

Words to Know

Before reading "Little Red Riding Hood,"

1. Have students say each word aloud.

2. Ask students if they know what each word means.

  ▶ If students know a word's meaning, have them define it and use it in a sentence.
  ▶ If students don't know a word's meaning, read them the definition and discuss the word with them.

cider – a drink made from apple juice
cottage – a small house
path – a trail for walking
wander – when you walk around without having an exact place to go
wood – a place where many trees grow; the forest

Read Aloud

Book Walk

Prepare students by taking them on a Book Walk of "Little Red Riding Hood." Scan the story together to revisit the characters and events. Answers to questions may vary.

1. Turn to today's selection. Point to and read aloud the **title of the story.**

2. Have students look at the **pictures** of the story.

   ▸ Which characters do you see in the pictures?
   ▸ Which picture is your favorite?
   ▸ Where is that part of the story taking place?

Objectives

- Listen and respond to texts representing a variety of cultures, time periods, and traditions.
- Read and listen to a variety of texts for information and pleasure independently or as part of a group.

"Little Red Riding Hood"

Now it's time to read the story. Have students sit next to you so that they can see the pictures and words while you read the story aloud.

   Read aloud the entire story. Emphasize Words to Know as you come to them. If appropriate, use the pictures to help show what each word means.

Check Your Reading

"Little Red Riding Hood"

Have students retell the story in their own words to develop grammar, vocabulary, comprehension, and fluency skills. When finished, **ask students the following questions** to check comprehension and encourage discussion.

   ▸ What does Little Red Riding Hood have in her basket? cake and a jug of cider
   ▸ Who does Little Red Riding Hood meet on the way to her grandmother's house? the wolf
   ▸ Why doesn't Little Red Riding Hood run away from the wolf? She doesn't know the wolf is a wicked creature.
   ▸ Where does the end of the story take place? Grandmother's cottage

Objectives

- Answer questions requiring literal recall of details.
- Identify details that explain characters' actions.
- Identify setting.

Reading for Meaning

Characters and Setting

Ask students the following questions to further check comprehension. If students have trouble answering a question, reread the part of the story that will help refresh their memory.

- What does Little Red Riding Hood promise her mother? not to leave the path
- Where is Little Red Riding Hood when she makes this promise? in her house
- Does Little Red Riding Hood keep her promise? No
- How does Little Red Riding Hood break her promise? She goes off the path.
- Why does Little Red Riding Hood go off the path? She wants to pick flowers in the wood.
- Do you think it was smart for Little Red Riding Hood to go off the path to pick flowers? Why or why not? Answers will vary.
- Where does the middle of the story take place? the path through the wood
- Who is your favorite character in the story? Describe this character in one or two words. Answers will vary.

Objectives

- Describe character(s).
- Identify details that explain characters' actions.
- Identify setting.

Review "Little Red Riding Hood"

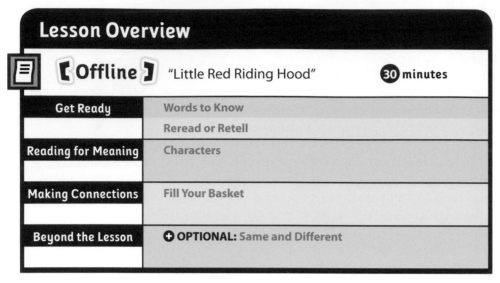

Lesson Overview

[Offline] "Little Red Riding Hood"   **30** minutes

Get Ready	Words to Know
	Reread or Retell
Reading for Meaning	Characters
Making Connections	Fill Your Basket
Beyond the Lesson	⊕ OPTIONAL: Same and Different

Materials

Supplied

- "Little Red Riding Hood," *K¹² Read Aloud Treasury*, pp. 2–7
- *K¹² Language Arts Activity Book*, p. LC 1

Also Needed

- crayons

Keywords

character – a person or animal in a story

Big Ideas

▶ Comprehension requires an understanding of story structure.
▶ Comprehension is facilitated when readers connect new information to information previously learned.

 **30** minutes

"Little Red Riding Hood"

Work **together** with students to complete offline Get Ready, Reading for Meaning, Making Connections, and Beyond the Lesson activities.

Get Ready

Words to Know

Ask students to define the following words and use them in a sentence:

cider   path   wood

cottage   wander

Correct any incorrect or vague definitions.

Objectives

- Build vocabulary through listening, reading, and discussion.
- Use new vocabulary in written and spoken sentences.

Reread or Retell

If you'd like to, reread the story to students. Otherwise, have students retell the story using the pictures as a guide, or move on to the next activity.

Reading for Meaning

Characters

Ask students the following questions to check comprehension.

Objectives
- Describe character(s).
- Identify details that explain characters' actions.

- ▶ Describe Little Red Riding Hood. Why do you describe her this way? Answers will vary.
- ▶ Do you think going off the path was a good choice or bad choice? Why? Answers will vary.
- ▶ Why does the wolf ask Little Red Riding Hood where her grandmother lives? He wants to eat her grandmother.
- ▶ Which words best describe the wolf? scary, mean, tricky
- ▶ What does the wolf do after he eats Grandmother and Little Red Riding Hood? He falls asleep.
- ▶ Why does the wolf run away when he wakes up? He sees the woodman's ax and is scared.
- ▶ What does Little Red Riding Hood promise herself at the end of the story? to never go off the path again

Making Connections

Fill Your Basket

Ask students what foods they would bring to a sick friend or family member. Have them draw these foods in the basket on page LC 1 in *K¹² Language Arts Activity Book*. Have students explain their choices.

Objectives

- Make connections with text: text-to-text, text-to-self, text-to-world.
- Respond to text through art, writing, and/or drama.

Beyond the Lesson

⊕ OPTIONAL: Same and Different

This activity is intended for students who have extra time and would benefit from reading another version of the story. Feel free to skip this activity.

1. Go to a library and get another version of "Little Red Riding Hood."

2. Lead a Book Walk, and read aloud the different version of the story.

3. Have students tell how the two books are alike and different.

4. Have students discuss the different endings and tell which they liked better.

5. Ask them to tell which book is their favorite and why.

Objectives

- Compare and contrast two texts on the same topic.

Introduce "Healthy Snacks"

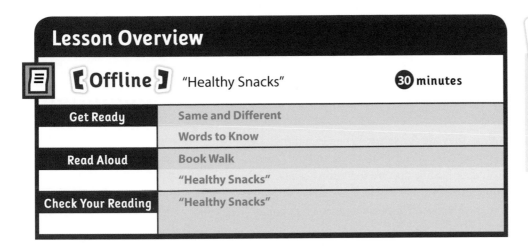

Lesson Overview

	Offline "Healthy Snacks"	30 minutes
Get Ready	Same and Different	
	Words to Know	
Read Aloud	Book Walk	
	"Healthy Snacks"	
Check Your Reading	"Healthy Snacks"	

Advance Preparation

Read "Healthy Snacks" before beginning the Read Aloud activity, to locate the Words to Know within the text.

Big Ideas

Comprehension entails asking and answering questions about the text.

Materials

Supplied
- "Healthy Snacks," *K¹² World: Taking Care of Ourselves and Our Earth,* pp. 2–9

Article Synopsis

Students learn that not all foods are created equal by comparing healthy, natural snacks with packaged, man-made ones.

Keywords

compare – to explain how two or more things are alike

contrast – to explain how two or more things are different

detail – a bit of information in a text

[Offline] 🕥 minutes

"Healthy Snacks"

Work **together** with students to complete offline Get Ready, Read Aloud, and Check Your Reading activities.

Get Ready ....

Same and Different

Tell students that when two things are alike, they are the **same**. When two things are not alike, they are **different**. Explain that two things can be the same, and they can also be different. For example, an apple and a pudding cup are the same because both are sweet snacks. They're also different because an apple is a natural snack that grows on a tree, and a pudding cup is a snack that isn't natural because it's made by people.

Ask the following questions:

▶ What is your favorite fruit to eat as a snack? Answers will vary.
▶ What is your favorite kind of cookie? Answers will vary.
▶ How are these two foods the same? They're both sweet; they're both snacks.
▶ How are they different? Fruit comes from a tree or vine, and cookies are made by people.

Objectives

- Compare and contrast elements within a text.
- Increase concept and content vocabulary.
- Use new vocabulary in written and spoken sentences.

Words to Know

Before reading "Healthy Snacks,"

1. Have students say each word aloud.

2. Ask students if they know what each word means.

   ▶ If students know a word's meaning, have them define it and use it in a sentence.
   ▶ If students don't know a word's meaning, read them the definition and discuss the word with them.

compare – to see how two or more things are alike
healthy – when you are not sick
ingredient – what a food item is made out of
natural – made by nature, not people

Read Aloud

Book Walk

Prepare students by taking them on a Book Walk of "Healthy Snacks." Scan the magazine article together and ask students to make predictions about the text. Answers to questions will vary.

1. Turn to the **table of contents**. Help students find today's selection, and turn to that page.

2. Point to and read aloud the **title of the article**.

3. Have students look at the **pictures** in the article.

   ▸ What do you think the article is about?
   ▸ What does the phrase "healthy snacks" mean to you?

4. Point to and read aloud any **headers, captions, or other features** that stand out.

   ▸ What do you think the article might tell us about healthy snacks?

Objectives

- Make predictions based on title, illustrations, and/or context clues.
- Read and listen to a variety of texts for information and pleasure independently or as part of a group.

"Healthy Snacks"

Now it's time to read the article. Have students sit next to you so that they can see the pictures and words while you read the article aloud.

Read aloud the entire article. Emphasize Words to Know as you come to them. If appropriate, use the pictures to help show what each word means.

Check Your Reading

"Healthy Snacks"

Have students retell the article in their own words to develop grammar, vocabulary, comprehension, and fluency skills. When finished, **ask students the following questions** to check comprehension and encourage discussion.

▸ Name a healthy snack from the article. oranges; bananas; almonds; carrots
▸ Can you tell if a snack is healthy just by tasting it? No   Why not? Both healthy and unhealthy snacks can taste good.
▸ What is a good way to tell if a snack food is healthy? Read the ingredients on the label.

Objectives

- State the details of a text.

Explore "Healthy Snacks"

Lesson Overview

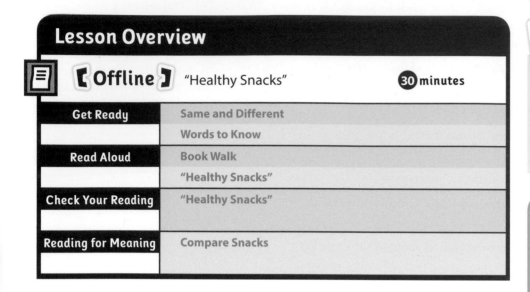

Offline	"Healthy Snacks"	30 minutes
Get Ready	Same and Different	
	Words to Know	
Read Aloud	Book Walk	
	"Healthy Snacks"	
Check Your Reading	"Healthy Snacks"	
Reading for Meaning	Compare Snacks	

[Materials]

Supplied

- "Healthy Snacks,"
  *K¹² World: Taking Care of
  Ourselves and Our Earth,*
  pp. 2–9

Keywords

compare – to explain how
two or more things are alike

contrast – to explain how two
or more things are different

detail – a bit of information
in a text

Advance Preparation

Before working with students, spend a few minutes reviewing the Words to Know.
Then read the Check Your Reading and Reading for Meaning activities to familiarize
yourself with the questions and answers.

Big Ideas

▶ Comprehension entails asking and answering questions about the text.
▶ Comprehension is facilitated when readers connect new information to
information previously learned.

[Offline]   30 minutes

"Healthy Snacks"

Work **together** with students to complete offline Get Ready, Read Aloud, Check Your Reading, and Reading for Meaning activities.

Get Ready

Same and Different

Remind student that when two things are alike, they have something in common, so they are the **same**. When two things are not alike, they are **different**.

- ▶ Can two things be both the same and different? Yes
- ▶ Name two snacks that are both the same and different. Answers will vary; remind students of the example of the apple and the pudding cup if they have trouble responding.

Tell students that as you read the article, they should listen to hear how some snack foods are natural, healthy, and good for you, and how others are made in factories, out of unhealthy ingredients.

> **Objectives**
> - Compare and contrast elements within a text.
> - Increase concept and content vocabulary.
> - Use new vocabulary in written and spoken sentences.

Words to Know

Before reading "Healthy Snacks,"

1. Have students say each word aloud.

2. Ask students if they know what each word means.

   - ▶ If students know a word's meaning, have them define it and use it in a sentence.
   - ▶ If students don't know a word's meaning, read them the definition and discuss the word with them.

compare – to see how two or more things are alike
healthy – when you are not sick
ingredient – what a food item is made out of
natural – made by nature, not people

Read Aloud

Book Walk

Prepare students by taking them on a Book Walk of "Healthy Snacks." Scan the magazine article together to revisit the text. Answers to questions may vary.

1. Turn to today's selection.

2. Point to and read aloud the **title of the article**.

3. Have students look at the **pictures** in the article.

   ▸ Which picture shows a snack food that you like?
   ▸ Do you think this snack is healthy or unhealthy?

"Healthy Snacks"

Now it's time to read the article. Have students sit next to you so that they can see the pictures and words while you read the article aloud.

Read aloud the entire article. To emphasize the concept of **same and different**, discuss the banana and the chocolate candy example when you come to those paragraphs.

TIP Ask students if they've ever heard the expression "You are what you eat." Explain that this expression means that what you eat affects how well your body works and how good you feel.

Check Your Reading

"Healthy Snacks"

Have students retell the article in their own words to develop grammar, vocabulary, comprehension, and fluency skills. When finished, **ask students the following questions** to check comprehension and encourage discussion.

▸ Name a snack food from the article that is made by people. chocolate candy; cookies; potato chips; doughnut
▸ Where does a banana come from? a tree; from nature
▸ How is the snack food from the article the same as the banana? How is it different? Answers will vary.
▸ Name something that can happen if you eat too many unhealthy snacks. They can make you less fit; you may feel sick.

 TIP Encourage students to use Words to Know and other words from the article when they retell the article and answer questions.

Reading for Meaning

Compare Snacks

Ask students the following questions to further check comprehension. **Reread parts of the article** if they have trouble answering a question. **Use previous examples of snacks** as needed to help students recall the concepts of same and different.

▶ What is your favorite snack? Answers will vary.

▶ Is your favorite snack good for you? Why or why not? Answers will vary.

▶ How are a banana and a cookie the same? Both taste sweet and give you energy.

▶ How are a banana and a cookie different? A banana is a natural snack, and a cookie is made by people.

▶ The story asks, "What if you had to pick between an orange and a bag of potato chips?" Which would you choose, and why? Answers will vary.

▶ Which snack is healthier, an orange or a bag of potato chips? an orange Why? An orange is natural, and potato chips are made in a factory.

Objectives

- Compare and contrast elements within a text.
- Identify important details in informational text.
- Make connections with text: text-to-text, text-to-self, text-to-world.

Review "Healthy Snacks"

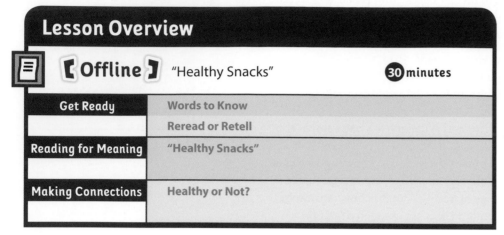

Lesson Overview

[Offline] "Healthy Snacks"		30 minutes
Get Ready	Words to Know	
	Reread or Retell	
Reading for Meaning	"Healthy Snacks"	
Making Connections	Healthy or Not?	

Materials

Supplied
- "Healthy Snacks," *K¹² World: Taking Care of Ourselves and Our Earth*, pp. 2–9
- *K¹² Language Arts Activity Book*, p. LC 2

Also Needed
- crayons

Keywords

compare – to explain how two or more things are alike
contrast – to explain how two or more things are different
detail – a bit of information in a text

Big Ideas

▶ Comprehension entails asking and answering questions about the text.
▶ Comprehension is facilitated when readers connect new information to information previously learned.

 **30** minutes

"Healthy Snacks"

Work **together** with students to complete offline Get Ready, Reading for Meaning, and Making Connections activities.

Get Ready ....

Words to Know

Ask students to define the following words and use them in a sentence:

compare   ingredient
healthy   natural

Correct any incorrect or vague definitions.

 Tell students that some snacks that are made in factories have *both* healthy and unhealthy ingredients in them. Use chocolate-covered raisins as an example.

Objectives

- Increase concept and content vocabulary.
- Use new vocabulary in written and spoken sentences.

Reread or Retell

If you'd like to, reread the article to students. Otherwise, have students retell the article using the pictures as a guide, or move on to the next activity.

Reading for Meaning ....

"Healthy Snacks"

Ask students the following questions to check comprehension. **Reread parts of the article** if they have trouble answering a question.

▸ How are almonds and a doughnut alike? Both are snacks that taste good and give you energy.
▸ How are almonds and a doughnut different? Almonds are natural, and a doughnut is made by people.
▸ Do you think eating *any* kind of fresh fruit will help keep you fit? Why or why not? Answers will vary; tell students that too much of *any* sweet food can make a person feel ill.
▸ Is a candy bar a natural food? No   Why not? It's made by people.
▸ Why is it important to read the ingredients listed on a snack food package? to see if it's healthy or not
▸ Now that you know more about snack foods, will you change what you snack on? Why or why not? Answers will vary.

Objectives

- Compare and contrast elements within a text.
- Identify important details in informational text.
- Make connections with text: text-to-text, text-to-self, text-to-world.

Making Connections

Healthy or Not?

Have students color the snack foods on page LC 2 in *K¹² Language Arts Activity Book*. Then have them circle only the pictures of healthy snacks. When done,

- ▶ Point out any overlooked healthy snacks, or unhealthy snacks mistakenly circled because students think they are healthy.
- ▶ Review how all the snacks are the same in one way (sweet), and how they are also different (natural vs. man-made).

Objectives

- Compare and contrast elements within a text.
- Make connections with text: text-to-text, text-to-self, text-to-world.

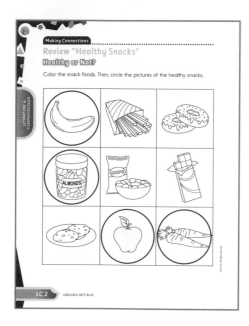

Introduce "Jack and the Beanstalk"

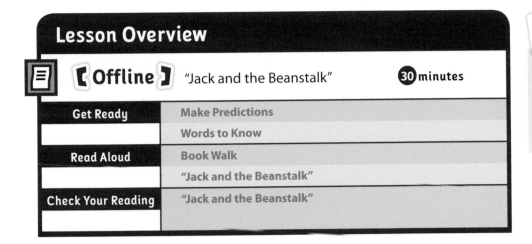

Lesson Overview

	Offline "Jack and the Beanstalk"	30 minutes
Get Ready	Make Predictions	
	Words to Know	
Read Aloud	Book Walk	
	"Jack and the Beanstalk"	
Check Your Reading	"Jack and the Beanstalk"	

Advance Preparation

Read "Jack and the Beanstalk" before beginning the Read Aloud activity, to locate Words to Know within the text.

Big Ideas

Comprehension entails actively thinking about what is being read.

[Materials]

Supplied

- "Jack and the Beanstalk," *K¹² Read Aloud Treasury,* pp. 10–21

Story Synopsis

A young man redeems himself after trading his mother's cow for a handful of what looks like worthless beans.

Keywords

prediction – a guess about what might happen that is based on information in a story and what you already know

 **30** minutes

"Jack and the Beanstalk"

Work **together** with students to complete offline Get Ready, Read Aloud, and Check Your Reading activities.

Get Ready

Make Predictions

Explain to students that **a prediction is a guess** about what might happen in a story. We make guesses, or predictions, about things in our daily lives, too.

▸ If you see big, dark clouds in the sky, what would you predict is going to happen? It's going to rain.

Sometimes we think we know what's going to happen in a story. Then we're surprised because something different occurs, which can make reading fun and exciting. It can also make us want to continue reading a story to see if our predictions happen. Tell students they will make predictions while they listen to the story of "Jack and the Beanstalk."

 Objectives
- Make predictions before and during reading.
- Build vocabulary through listening, reading, and discussion.
- Use new vocabulary in written and spoken sentences.

Words to Know

Before reading "Jack and the Beanstalk,"

1. Have students say each word aloud.

2. Ask students if they know what each word means.

   ▸ If students know a word's meaning, have them define it and use it in a sentence.
   ▸ If students don't know a word's meaning, read them the definition and discuss the word with them.

cross – angry
giant – a very, very tall person
harp – a musical instrument with many strings
hatchet – a small ax
hen – a chicken that lays eggs
rent – an amount of money paid regularly to live in a home

Read Aloud

Book Walk

Prepare students by taking them on a Book Walk of "Jack and the Beanstalk." Scan the story together and ask students to make predictions about the text. Answers to questions may vary.

1. Point to the **front cover** of *K¹² Read Aloud Treasury*.
   Say: This is the front cover.

2. Point to the **back cover**.
   Say: This is the back cover.

3. Turn to the **table of contents**. Help students find today's selection, and turn to that page.

4. Point to and read aloud the **title of the story**.

5. Have students look at the **pictures** of the story.
   ▸ What do you think the story is about?
   ▸ Where do you think the story takes place?

"Jack and the Beanstalk"

Now it's time to read the story. Have students sit next to you so that they can see the pictures and words while you read the story aloud.

Read aloud the entire story. Emphasize Words to Know as you come to them. If appropriate, use the pictures to help show what each word means. Throughout the story, **pause and ask, "What do you think will happen next?"** Jot down students' predictions so you will have them at hand for the next activity. The following are suggested points for making predictions:

▸ Page 12: Jack gets to the top of the beanstalk.
▸ Page 15: The giant thinks he smells something.
▸ Page 18: Jack climbs the beanstalk a second time.
▸ Page 21: The giant chases Jack down the beanstalk.

Check Your Reading

"Jack and the Beanstalk"

Have students retell the story in their own words to develop grammar, vocabulary, comprehension, and fluency skills. When finished, **ask students the following questions** to check comprehension and encourage discussion. Answers to questions may vary.

▸ What did you predict would happen when Jack climbed to the top of the beanstalk?
▸ Were you surprised that the giant didn't find Jack in the oven? Why or why not?
▸ Were you surprised by what happened when Jack climbed the beanstalk a second time?
▸ What did you think would happen when the giant chased Jack down the beanstalk? What really happened?

Explore "Jack and the Beanstalk"

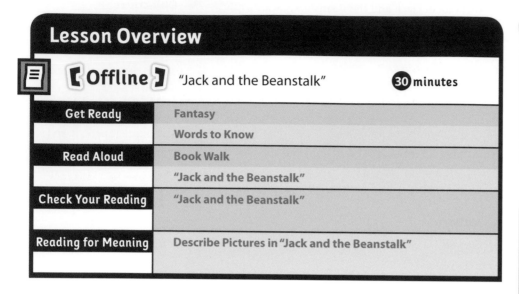

Lesson Overview

[Offline] "Jack and the Beanstalk"		**30** minutes
Get Ready	Fantasy	
	Words to Know	
Read Aloud	Book Walk	
	"Jack and the Beanstalk"	
Check Your Reading	"Jack and the Beanstalk"	
Reading for Meaning	Describe Pictures in "Jack and the Beanstalk"	

[Materials]

Supplied

- "Jack and the Beanstalk,"
  K¹² Read Aloud Treasury,
  pp. 10–21

Keywords

fantasy – a story with
characters, settings, or
other elements that could
not really exist

sequence – order

Advance Preparation

Before working with students, spend a few minutes reviewing Words to Know.
Then read the Check Your Reading and Reading for Meaning activities to familiarize
yourself with the questions and answers.

Big Ideas

- ▸ Comprehension requires an understanding of story structure.
- ▸ Comprehension entails asking and answering questions about the text.

 **30** minutes

"Jack and the Beanstalk"

Work **together** with students to complete offline Get Ready, Read Aloud, Check Your Reading, and Reading for Meaning activities.

Get Ready ••

Fantasy

Tell students that fairy tales often have characters that don't exist in real life, or events that could not happen in real life.

> ► Is there is a character in "Jack and the Beanstalk" that doesn't exist in real life? Yes, the giant

Explain that we use the word *fantasy* to describe these types of things.

Objectives
- Identify and define fantasy.
- Build vocabulary through listening, reading, and discussion.
- Use new vocabulary in written and spoken sentences.

Words to Know

Before reading "Jack and the Beanstalk,"

1. Have students say each word aloud.

2. Ask students if they know what each word means.

> ► If students know a word's meaning, have them define it and use it in a sentence.
> ► If students don't know a word's meaning, read them the definition and discuss the word with them.

cross – angry
giant – a very, very tall person
harp – a musical instrument with many strings
hatchet – a small ax
hen – a chicken that lays eggs
rent – an amount of money paid regularly to live in a home

Read Aloud

Book Walk

Prepare students by taking them on a Book Walk of "Jack and the Beanstalk." Scan the story together to revisit the characters and events. Answers to questions may vary.

1. Turn to today's selection. Point to and read aloud the **title of the story**.

2. Have students look at the **pictures** of the story.

   ▸ Which picture is your favorite?
   ▸ Which part of the story does your favorite picture show?
   ▸ Does it show something make-believe or real?

Objectives

- Describe illustrations and their relationship to story events.
- Listen and respond to texts representing a variety of cultures, time periods, and traditions.
- Identify and define fantasy.

"Jack and the Beanstalk"

Now it's time to read the story. Have students sit next to you so that they can see the pictures and words while you read the story aloud.

    Read aloud the entire story. Tell students to listen for examples of fantasy, or things that could not happen in real life, as you read the story.

Check Your Reading

"Jack and the Beanstalk"

Have students retell the story in their own words to develop grammar, vocabulary, comprehension, and fluency skills. When finished, **ask students the following questions** to check comprehension and encourage discussion.

▸ Why does Jack's mother ask him to sell the cow? She needs money to pay the rent.
▸ What does Jack trade the cow for? five beans
▸ What happens to the beans after Jack's mother throws them out the window? They grow into a giant beanstalk.
▸ What does Jack do after he sees the beanstalk? He climbs it.
▸ Is a beanstalk that reaches up to the sky fantasy? Why or why not? It's fantasy because it could not happen in real life.
▸ Is there anything else in the story that does not exist in real life? Possible answers: the giant; the hen that lays golden eggs; the magic harp

Objectives

- Answer questions requiring literal recall of details.
- Sequence events from a text.
- Identify and define fantasy.

Reading for Meaning

Describe Pictures in "Jack and the Beanstalk"

Ask students the following questions to further check comprehension. **Reread parts of the story** if they have trouble answering a question.

Explain to students that looking at **a story's pictures can help them remember the order** of the story's events.

Point to a picture from the **beginning** of the story.

▸ What is happening in this picture? Answers will vary. If students cannot describe what is happening in the picture, reread the appropriate part of the story.

▸ Which part of the story does this picture show? Guide students to understand that it shows an event from the beginning of the story.

Point to a picture from the **middle** of the story.

▸ What is happening in this picture? Answers will vary. If students cannot describe what is happening in the picture, reread the appropriate part of the story.

▸ Which part of the story does this picture show? Guide students to understand that it shows an event from the middle of the story.

Point to a picture from the **end** of the story.

▸ What is happening in this picture? Answers will vary. If students cannot describe what is happening in the picture, reread the appropriate part of the story.

▸ Which part of the story does this picture show? Guide students to understand that it shows an event from the end of the story.

Objectives

- Describe illustrations and their relationship to story events.
- Sequence events from a text.

Review "Jack and the Beanstalk"

Lesson Overview

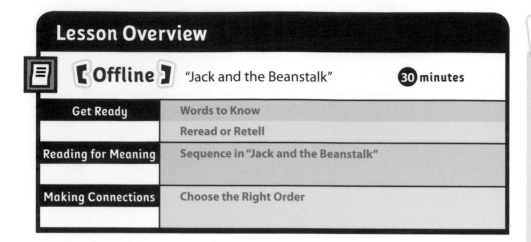

	Offline	"Jack and the Beanstalk"	30 minutes
Get Ready		Words to Know	
		Reread or Retell	
Reading for Meaning		Sequence in "Jack and the Beanstalk"	
Making Connections		Choose the Right Order	

Big Ideas

Comprehension requires an understanding of story structure.

Materials

Supplied
- "Jack and the Beanstalk," *K¹² Read Aloud Treasury,* pp. 10–21
- *K¹² Language Arts Activity Book,* p. LC 3

Also Needed
- scissors, round-end safety
- glue stick

Keywords
retelling – using your own words to tell a story that you have listened to or read
sequence – order

 **[Offline] 30 minutes**

"Jack and the Beanstalk"

Work **together** with students to complete offline Get Ready, Reading for Meaning, and Making Connections activities.

Get Ready ···

Words to Know

Ask students to define the following words and use them in a sentence:

cross	**harp**	**hen**
giant	**hatchet**	**rent**

Correct any incorrect or vague definitions.

Objectives
- Build vocabulary through listening, reading, and discussion.
- Use new vocabulary in written and spoken sentences.

Reread or Retell

If you'd like to, reread the story to students. Otherwise, have students retell the story using the pictures as a guide, or move on to the next activity.

Reading for Meaning ·····························

Sequence in "Jack and the Beanstalk"

Ask students the following questions to check comprehension. Tell them that when they name the order of things that happen in a story, they are describing the **sequence**.

Objectives
- Sequence events from a text.
- Make connections with text: text-to-text, text-to-self, text-to-world.

- ▸ What does Jack's mother ask him to do at the beginning of the story? sell the cow
- ▸ What happens when Jack takes the cow to sell in town? He trades her for five beans.
- ▸ What happens after Jack climbs the beanstalk the first time? Possible answers: goes into the giant's house; meets the giant's wife; takes the hen that lays gold eggs
- ▸ What happens after Jack climbs the beanstalk the second time? Possible answers: goes into the giant's house; hides in the breadbox; takes the magic harp
- ▸ Do you think that Jack made a good choice when he climbed the beanstalk the second time? Why or why not? Answers will vary.
- ▸ What does Jack do while the giant is climbing down the beanstalk? He chops down the beanstalk.

Making Connections

Choose the Right Order

Have students complete page LC 3 in *K¹² Language Arts Activity Book*.

1. Have students cut out the pictures and put them in the order in which the story happens.

2. Have students glue the pictures in the correct order onto a blank piece of paper.

3. Have students retell the story of "Jack and the Beanstalk," using the pictures as a guide.

Objectives

- Sequence pictures illustrating story events.
- Retell a story using illustrations from the text as a guide.

Introduce "Everyday Exercises"

Unit Overview

In this unit, students will explore the theme of *Get Moving* through the following reading selections:

- ▸ "Everyday Exercises"
- ▸ "The Gingerbread Man"
- ▸ "Lousy Litter"

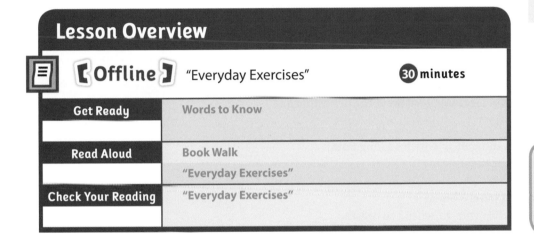

Lesson Overview

[Offline] "Everyday Exercises"		30 minutes
Get Ready	Words to Know	
Read Aloud	Book Walk	
	"Everyday Exercises"	
Check Your Reading	"Everyday Exercises"	

Advance Preparation

Read "Everyday Exercises" before beginning the Read Aloud activity, to locate Words to Know within the text.

Big Ideas

Comprehension entails asking and answering questions about the text.

Materials

Supplied
- ● "Everyday Exercises," *K¹² World: Taking Care of Ourselves and Our Earth,* pp. 10–15

Article Synopsis

Everyday exercises—such as running, climbing, and swimming—are fun to do and good for you.

Keywords

cause – the reason something happens
effect – the result of a cause

 **30 minutes**

"Everyday Exercises"

Work **together** with students to complete offline Get Ready, Read Aloud, and Check Your Reading activities.

Get Ready ··

Words to Know

Before reading "Everyday Exercises,"

1. Have students say each word aloud.

2. Ask students if they know what each word means.

   ▸ If students know a word's meaning, have them define it and use it in a sentence.
   ▸ If students don't know a word's meaning, read them the definition and discuss the word with them.

endurance – when you're able to do a difficult activity for a long time
exercise – a way to use muscles to make them strong
flexible – easy to bend
heart – an organ inside your body that pumps blood
lung – an organ inside your body that fills with air when you breathe
muscle – the part of the body that makes a bone move

Objectives
- Increase concept and content vocabulary.
- Use new vocabulary in written and spoken sentences.

Read Aloud ··

Book Walk

Prepare students by taking them on a Book Walk of "Everyday Exercises." Scan the magazine article together and ask students to make predictions about the text. Answers to questions may vary.

1. Turn to the **table of contents**. Help students find today's selection, and turn to that page.

2. Point to and read aloud the **title of the article**.

3. Have students look at the **pictures** in the article.

   ▸ What do you think the article is about?
   ▸ What is your favorite way to get exercise?

4. Point to and read aloud any **headers, captions, or other features** that stand out.

   ▸ What do you think the article might tell us about exercising?

Objectives
- Make predictions based on title, illustrations and/or context clues.
- Read and listen to a variety of texts for information and pleasure independently or as part of a group.

"Everyday Exercises"

Now it's time to read the article. Have students sit next to you so that they can see the pictures and words while you read the article aloud.

Read aloud the entire article. Emphasize Words to Know as you come to them. If appropriate, use the pictures to help show what each word means. Tell students to listen to the article carefully to hear how everyday exercises can cause good things to happen to your body.

Check Your Reading

"Everyday Exercises"

Have students retell the article in their own words to develop grammar, vocabulary, comprehension, and fluency skills. When finished, **ask students the following questions** to check comprehension and encourage discussion.

- ▶ What is the article mostly about? how exercises we do every day are good for us
- ▶ What is it called when you are moving your body? exercising
- ▶ Name an everyday exercise that's mentioned in the article. running; climbing; dancing; playing tag; playing soccer; swimming
- ▶ What does the article say will happen if you climb a lot? Your muscles will work hard; your muscles will get stronger.

Objectives
- Describe cause-and-effect relationships in text.
- Identify important details in informational text.

Explore "Everyday Exercises"

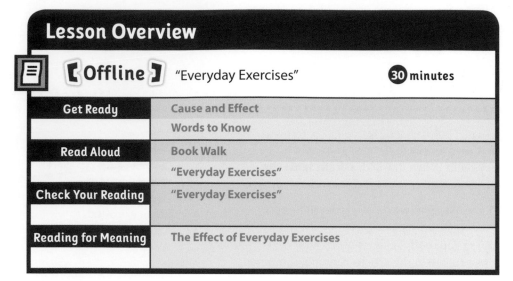

Lesson Overview

Offline	"Everyday Exercises"	**30** minutes
Get Ready	Cause and Effect	
	Words to Know	
Read Aloud	Book Walk	
	"Everyday Exercises"	
Check Your Reading	"Everyday Exercises"	
Reading for Meaning	The Effect of Everyday Exercises	

Materials

Supplied

- "Everyday Exercises,"
  *K¹² World: Taking Care of
  Ourselves and Our Earth,*
  pp. 10–15

Keywords

cause – the reason something
happens

effect – the result of a cause

Advance Preparation

Before working with students, spend a few minutes reviewing the Words to Know.
Then read the Check Your Reading and Reading for Meaning activities to familiarize
yourself with the questions and answers.

Big Ideas

- ▶ Comprehension entails asking and answering questions about the text.
- ▶ Comprehension entails an understanding of the organizational patterns
  of text.

❲ Offline ❳ ⏱ 30 minutes

"Everyday Exercises"

Work **together** with students to complete offline Get Ready, Read Aloud, Check Your Reading, and Reading for Meaning activities.

Get Ready

Cause and Effect

Tell students that doing one thing can make another thing happen. The thing that you do is called the **cause** and the thing that happens is called the **effect**. Examples of cause and effect are all around us.

▸ **Cause:** You stand outside in the rain.
  Effect: You get wet.
▸ **Cause:** You drop a glass.
  Effect: The glass breaks.

Say: As we read "Everyday Exercises," we will hear more examples of cause and effect, such as the following:

▸ Doing jumping jacks will *cause* your heart to beat faster.
▸ Strong arm muscles are the *effect* of swimming every day.

Objectives
- Describe cause-and-effect relationships in text.
- Increase concept and content vocabulary.
- Use new vocabulary in written and spoken sentences.

Words to Know

Before reading "Everyday Exercises,"

1. Have students say each word aloud.

2. Ask students if they know what each word means.

   ▸ If students know a word's meaning, have them define it and use it in a sentence.
   ▸ If students don't know a word's meaning, read them the definition and discuss the word with them.

endurance – when you're able to do a difficult activity for a long time
exercise – a way to use muscles to make them strong
flexible – easy to bend
heart – an organ inside your body that pumps blood
lung – an organ inside your body that fills with air when you breathe
muscle – the part of the body that makes a bone move

Read Aloud

Book Walk

Prepare students by taking them on a Book Walk of "Everyday Exercises." Scan the magazine article together to revisit the text. Answers to questions may vary.

1. Turn to today's selection.

2. Point to and read aloud the **title of the article**.

3. Have students look at the **pictures** in the article.

   ▸ Which picture shows your favorite exercise?
   ▸ How do you think this exercise helps your body?

Objectives
- Describe cause-and-effect relationships in text.
- Read and listen to a variety of texts for information and pleasure independently or as part of a group.

"Everyday Exercises"

Now it's time to read the article. Have students sit next to you so that they can see the pictures and words while you read the article aloud.

   Read aloud the entire article. Tell students to listen for examples of how exercise helps different parts of your body, or the **effects** of exercise.

Check Your Reading

"Everyday Exercises"

Have students retell the article in their own words to develop grammar, vocabulary, comprehension, and fluency skills. When appropriate, **help students correctly use the words** *cause* **and** *effect* as they retell the article. When finished, **ask students the following questions** to check comprehension and encourage discussion.

Objectives
- Identify important details in informational text.
- Describe cause and effect relationships in text.

   ▸ Name two everyday exercises that are mentioned in the article. running; climbing; dancing; playing tag; playing soccer; swimming
   ▸ What is the effect on your heart when you run? The effect is that it beats faster; the effect is that it pumps more blood to your muscles.
   ▸ What will running every day do to your legs? It will cause them to get stronger.

Reading for Meaning

The Effect of Everyday Exercises

Ask students the following questions to further check comprehension and focus on cause-and-effect relationships. **Reread parts of the article** if they have trouble answering a question. **Repeat the examples in the Get Ready** to refresh their memory about what a cause and an effect are.

- ▶ What is the effect of dancing every day? It will cause your muscles to become more flexible.
- ▶ What can you do if you have flexible muscles? You can stretch and bend your body easily.
- ▶ What will be the effect on your body if you run every day? It will cause your leg muscles, heart, and lungs to get stronger; it will cause you to run farther before you get tired.
- ▶ Which kind of exercise can cause your back muscles to get stronger? climbing a tree or a jungle gym
- ▶ What is your favorite everyday exercise? What do you like about it? What effect do you think it would have on your body if you did it every day? Answers will vary.

TIP Ask students if they've ever heard the expression "Use it or lose it." Tell them this expression can mean that if you don't use your muscles every day, they will slowly lose their strength.

Objectives

- Describe cause-and-effect relationships in text.
- Make connections with text: text-to-text, text-to-self, text-to-world.
- Increase concept and content vocabulary.

Review "Everyday Exercises"

Lesson Overview

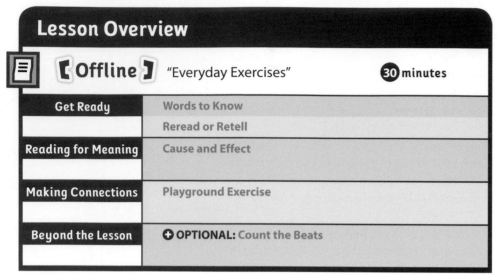

Offline	"Everyday Exercises"	**30** minutes
Get Ready	Words to Know	
	Reread or Retell	
Reading for Meaning	Cause and Effect	
Making Connections	Playground Exercise	
Beyond the Lesson	⊕ **OPTIONAL:** Count the Beats	

Big Ideas

▶ Comprehension entails asking and answering questions about the text.
▶ Comprehension entails an understanding of the organizational patterns of text.

[Materials]

Supplied
- "Everyday Exercises," *K¹² World: Taking Care of Ourselves and Our Earth*, pp. 10–15
- *K¹² Language Arts Activity Book*, p. LC 5

Also Needed
- crayons

Keywords
cause – the reason something happens
effect – the result of a cause

[Offline] 🕥 minutes

"Everyday Exercises"

Work **together** with students to complete offline Get Ready, Reading for Meaning, Making Connections, and Beyond the Lesson activities.

Get Ready ·

Words to Know

Ask students to define the following words and use them in a sentence:

endurance	**flexible**	**lung**
exercise	**heart**	**muscle**

Correct any incorrect or vague definitions.

Objectives
- Increase concept and content vocabulary.
- Use new vocabulary in written and spoken sentences.

Reread or Retell

If you'd like to, reread the article to students. Otherwise, have students retell the article using the pictures as a guide, or move on to the next activity.

Reading for Meaning ·

Cause and Effect

Ask students the following questions to check comprehension. **Reread parts of the article or point to pictures** if they have trouble answering a question. Remind students that **every cause creates an effect**.

Objectives
- Describe cause and effect relationships in text.
- Identify important details in informational text.
- Make connections with text: text-to-text, text-to-self, text-to-world.

- ► What is an effect of your heart working hard? It pumps more blood; it gets stronger.
- ► What causes your muscles to get and stay strong? Exercising every day.
- ► Is playing a game of tag exercise? Yes   How can you tell? You run around when you play tag, and running is exercise.
- ► Is watching TV exercise? No   How can you tell? You don't move around when you sit and watch TV.
- ► How does everyday exercise help you stay healthy? Answers will vary; responses should include how exercise makes parts of your body strong.

Making Connections

Playground Exercise

Have students color the picture on page LC 5 in *K¹² Language Arts Activity Book*. When done, ask students to describe what everyday exercise each child is doing and what effect it will have on his or her body.

Objectives

- Make connections with text: text-to-text, text-to-self, text-to-world.
- Describe cause and effect relationships in text.

Beyond the Lesson

⊕ OPTIONAL: Count the Beats

This activity is intended for students who have extra time and would benefit from learning how to measure their heart rate. Feel free to skip this activity.

If students are in good health, have them compare their heart rate when relaxed to their heart rate after doing jumping jacks for a few minutes. Doing so will show students how exercise increases heartbeats per minute and strengthens the heart muscle.

Go to the following website for instructions on how to take your pulse: http://www.cyh.com/HealthTopics/HealthTopicDetailsKids.aspx?p=335&np=285&id=1467.

Objectives

- Make connections with text: text-to-text, text-to-self, text-to-world.

Introduce "The Gingerbread Man"

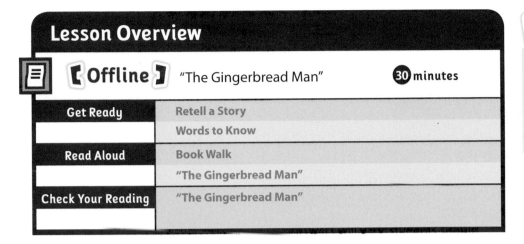

Lesson Overview

📋 [Offline] "The Gingerbread Man"		30 minutes
Get Ready	Retell a Story	
	Words to Know	
Read Aloud	Book Walk	
	"The Gingerbread Man"	
Check Your Reading	"The Gingerbread Man"	

Advance Preparation

Read "The Gingerbread Man" before beginning the Read Aloud activity, to locate Words to Know within the text.

Big Ideas

- ▸ Comprehension is the reason for reading.
- ▸ Comprehension requires an understanding of story structure.
- ▸ Comprehension entails asking and answering questions about the text.

Materials

Supplied

- "The Gingerbread Man," *K¹² Read Aloud Treasury*, pp. 24–28

Story Synopsis

A cookie comes to life, hops out of the oven, and runs down the road while shouting, "You can't catch me, I'm the Gingerbread Man!"

Ultimately, someone *does* catch the Gingerbread Man and gobbles him up.

Keywords

detail – a piece of information in a text

retelling – using your own words to tell a story that you have listened to or read

 **Offline** **30** minutes

"The Gingerbread Man"

Work **together** with students to complete offline Get Ready, Read Aloud, and Check Your Reading activities.

Get Ready

Retell a Story

Tell students that one way we can check that we understand a story is by telling the story in our own words. We call this **retelling**.

1. **Say:** When we retell a story, we use our own words to tell the important things that happen in order. For example, imagine that you spent a special day at the zoo. Now you want to tell your friend about it.

   ▸ Would you begin by saying that you got to stay up late, or would you say that you woke up early? Why? woke up early, because that happened first and staying up late happened at the end of the day

   ▸ Would you then say that you went to the zoo in the morning or that you had spaghetti for dinner after you got home from the zoo? Why? went to the zoo, because that happened before dinner

2. Tell students to listen carefully to the story so they can retell what happens in order.

> **Objectives**
> - Retell read aloud stories.
> - Build vocabulary through listening, reading, and discussion.
> - Use new vocabulary in written and spoken sentences.

Words to Know

Before reading "The Gingerbread Man,"

1. Have students say each word aloud.

2. Ask students if they know what each word means.

   ▸ If students know a word's meaning, have them define it and use it in a sentence.

   ▸ If students don't know a word's meaning, read them the definition and discuss the word with them.

burn – to bake or cook something too long
fox – a wild animal that looks like a small dog with a thick tail
outrun – when you run faster than somebody else
oven – something used for cooking that looks like a box with a door; you heat it up and cook food inside

Read Aloud

Book Walk

Prepare students by taking them on a Book Walk of "The Gingerbread Man." Scan the story together, and ask students to make predictions. Answers to questions may vary.

1. Point to the **front cover** of *K¹² Read Aloud Treasury*.
   Say: This is the front cover.

2. Point to the **back cover**.
   Say: This is the back cover.

3. Turn to the **table of contents**. Help students find today's selection, and turn to that page.

4. Point to and read aloud the **title of the story**.

5. Have students look at the **pictures** of the story.

   ▸ What do you think the story is about?
   ▸ Where do you think the story takes place?

Objectives
- Make predictions based on title, illustrations and/or context clues.
- Listen and respond to texts representing a variety of cultures, time periods, and traditions.

"The Gingerbread Man"

Now it's time to read the story. Have students sit next to you so that they can see the pictures and words while you read the story aloud.

   Read aloud the entire story. Emphasize Words to Know as you come to them. If appropriate, use the pictures to help show what each word means. If students have never seen a gingerbread man, explain that it is a type of cookie that is shaped and decorated to look like a little man.

Check Your Reading

"The Gingerbread Man"

Have students retell the story in their own words to develop grammar, vocabulary, comprehension, and fluency skills. When finished, **ask students the following questions** to check comprehension and encourage discussion.

▸ What is the story mostly about? how the Gingerbread Man jumps out of the oven and runs away
▸ Where does the beginning of the story take place? in the old woman's kitchen (or house)
▸ What does the old woman use for eyes for the Gingerbread Man? raisins
▸ Who does the old woman ask to watch the oven? her little boy

Objectives
- Retell read aloud stories.
- State the details of a text.

Explore "The Gingerbread Man"

Lesson Overview

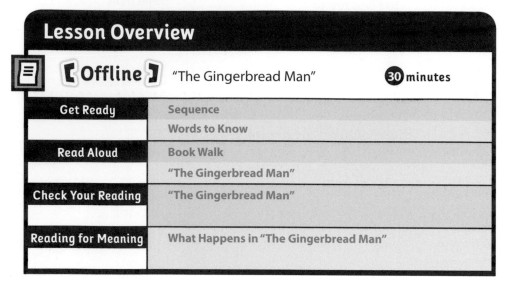

[Offline] "The Gingerbread Man"	**30 minutes**
Get Ready	Sequence
	Words to Know
Read Aloud	Book Walk
	"The Gingerbread Man"
Check Your Reading	"The Gingerbread Man"
Reading for Meaning	What Happens in "The Gingerbread Man"

Materials

Supplied
- "The Gingerbread Man," *K¹² Read Aloud Treasury,* pp. 24–28

Keywords

sequence – order

Advance Preparation

Before working with students, spend a few minutes reviewing Words to Know. Then read the Check Your Reading and Reading for Meaning activities to familiarize yourself with the questions and answers.

Big Ideas

- ► Comprehension requires an understanding of story structure.
- ► Comprehension entails asking and answering questions about the text.

 **[Offline]** **30** minutes

"The Gingerbread Man"
Work **together** with students to complete offline Get Ready, Read Aloud, Check Your Reading, and Reading for Meaning activities.

Get Ready ·

Sequence

Tell students that the order in which things happen in a story is called the **sequence**. Sequence is what happens first, second, third, and so on.

▸ Listen for the sequence of things that happen to Jack and Jill:

> *Jack and Jill went up the hill*
> *To fetch a pail of water.*
> *Jack fell down and broke his crown,*
> *And Jill came tumbling after.*

▸ There are four things in the sequence. Let's repeat them in order.

1. Jack and Jill went up the hill.
2. Jack fell down.
3. Jack broke his crown.
4. Jill came tumbling after.

Tell students to listen carefully for the sequence of today's story.

Words to Know

Before reading "The Gingerbread Man,"

1. Have students say each word aloud.

2. Ask students if they know what each word means.

   ▸ If students know a word's meaning, have them define it and use it in a sentence.
   ▸ If students don't know a word's meaning, read them the definition and discuss the word with them.

burn – to bake or cook something too long
fox – a wild animal that looks like a small dog with a thick tail
outrun – when you run faster than somebody else
oven – something used for cooking that looks like a box with a door; you heat it up and cook food inside

Objectives
- Sequence events from a text.
- Build vocabulary through listening, reading, and discussion.
- Use new vocabulary in written and spoken sentences.

Read Aloud

Book Walk

Prepare students by taking them on a Book Walk of "The Gingerbread Man." Scan the story together to revisit the characters and events. Answers to questions may vary.

1. Turn to today's selection. Point to and read aloud the **title of the story.**

2. Have students look at the **pictures** of the story.

   ▸ Which is your favorite picture? Why?
   ▸ Which part of the story does the picture show?
   ▸ Use your own words to describe what's happening in the picture.

Objectives

- Describe illustrations and their relationship to story events.
- Listen and respond to texts representing a variety of cultures, time periods, and traditions.

"The Gingerbread Man"

Now it's time to read the story. Have students sit next to you so that they can see the pictures and words while you read the story aloud.

Read aloud the entire story. Emphasize Words to Know as you come to them. To engage students' interest, have them **repeat the Gingerbread Man's rhyme with you** each time it appears in the story. Remind students to listen for the sequence, or order, of events in the story.

Check Your Reading

"The Gingerbread Man"

Have students retell the story in their own words to develop grammar, vocabulary, comprehension, and fluency skills. When finished, **ask students the following questions** to check comprehension and encourage discussion.

▸ Who runs after the Gingerbread Man first? the boy
▸ Name the animals that chase the Gingerbread Man but can't catch him. the puppies
▸ First the puppies meet the Gingerbread Man. What do they do next? They sniff him.
▸ Why do the puppies think the Gingerbread Man would be good to eat? He smells good.

Objectives

- State the details of a text.
- Sequence events from a text.

Reading for Meaning

What Happens in "The Gingerbread Man"

Ask students the following questions to further check comprehension and focus on sequence.

When appropriate, **reread parts of the story and point to pictures** to help them remember the sequence of events. Remind students that sequence is the order in which things happen in a story. Tell students that words like *first*, *next*, *after*, and *then* are sequence words. They help tell the order of things that happen.

If you think it might be helpful, repeat the example of *Jack and Jill* in the Get Ready to reinforce the concept of sequence as the order of events.

Objectives
- Sequence events from a text.
- Identify repetitive text.
- State the details of a text.

- What does the boy do after watching the oven for a while? He gets a drink of water.
- What happens right after the boy goes to get a drink of water? The Gingerbread Man jumps out of the oven.
- Who runs after the Gingerbread Man with the little boy? the old woman and the old man
- Who runs after the Gingerbread Man next? the farmers
- Say what comes after the first two lines of the rhyme:

  Run, run, as fast as you can.
  You can't catch me,
  I'm the Gingerbread Man!

- Describe where you think the Gingerbread Man was running, and why he was running there. Answers will vary.

Review "The Gingerbread Man"

Lesson Overview

Materials

Offline	"The Gingerbread Man"	**30** minutes

Get Ready	Words to Know
	Reread or Retell
Reading for Meaning	The End of "The Gingerbread Man"
Making Connections	Color and Retell
Beyond the Lesson	✚ OPTIONAL: Gingerbread and Pancakes

Supplied

- "The Gingerbread Man," *K¹² Read Aloud Treasury*, pp. 24–28
- *K¹² Language Arts Activity Book*, p. LC 7

Also Needed

- crayons
- scissors, round-end safety

Keywords

retelling – using your own words to tell a story that you have listened to or read

sequence – order

Big Ideas

▸ Comprehension requires an understanding of story structure.
▸ Comprehension entails asking and answering questions about the text.

 **30 minutes**

"The Gingerbread Man"

Work **together** with students to complete offline Get Ready, Reading for Meaning, Making Connections, and Beyond the Lesson activities.

Get Ready

Words to Know

Ask students to define the following words and use them in a sentence:

burn   outrun
fox   oven

Correct any incorrect or vague definitions.

Objectives
- Build vocabulary through listening, reading, and discussion.
- Use new vocabulary in written and spoken sentences.

Reread or Retell

If you'd like to, reread the story to students. Otherwise, have students retell the story using the pictures as a guide, or move on to the next activity.

Reading for Meaning

The End of "The Gingerbread Man"

Ask students the following questions to check comprehension.

▶ Who was the first person to run after the Gingerbread Man? the little boy
▶ What happens after the Gingerbread Man outruns the two puppies? He meets the fox.
▶ What does the Gingerbread Man do when the fox speaks to him? He stops running.
▶ Why does the fox tell the Gingerbread Man to come closer? to trick him so he could get close enough to eat him
▶ What happens last in the story? The fox jumps up and eats the Gingerbread Man.
▶ What would *you* do to catch the Gingerbread Man? Answers will vary. What would you do next if you caught him? Answers will vary.

Objectives
- Sequence events from a text.
- State the details of a text.
- Make connections with text: text-to-text, text-to-self, text-to-world.

Making Connections

Color and Retell

Have students color the picture of the Gingerbread Man on page LC 7 in K^{12} *Language Arts Activity Book*. When done, help them cut out the figure. Next, have students retell the story using the Gingerbread Man as a prop. Remind students to tell the story in the correct sequence. Allow them to change the ending of the story if it suits them.

Objectives
- Retell read aloud stories using various media.

Beyond the Lesson

⊕ OPTIONAL: Gingerbread and Pancakes

This activity is intended for students who have extra time and would benefit from hearing a variation of "The Gingerbread Man" story. Feel free to skip this activity.

Objectives
- Compare and contrast two texts on the same topic.

1. Go to a library and look for a copy of *Marsupial Sue Presents "The Runaway Pancake"* by John Lithgow.

2. Have a Book Walk, and then read aloud the story or play the included audio CD of the author telling the story to a live audience.

   ▶ If you play the CD, follow along in the book so that students can look at the pictures.

3. Have students repeat the Runaway Pancake rhyme whenever it appears in the text or is heard on the CD.

4. When finished, have students discuss what is the same and what is different in the two stories.

5. Ask them to tell which story is their favorite and why.

Introduce "Lousy Litter"

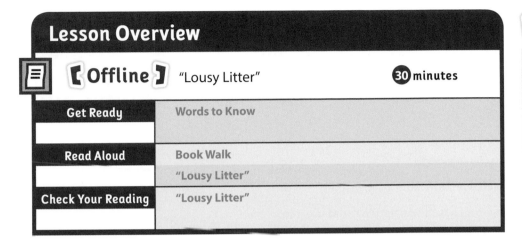

Lesson Overview

Offline	"Lousy Litter"	**30** minutes

Get Ready	Words to Know
Read Aloud	Book Walk
	"Lousy Litter"
Check Your Reading	"Lousy Litter"

Advance Preparation

Read "Lousy Litter" before beginning the Read Aloud activity, to locate the Words to Know within the text.

Materials

Supplied

● "Lousy Litter," *K¹² World: Taking Care of Ourselves and Our Earth,* pp. 16–21

Article Synopsis

Litter is an unnecessary eyesore that can have many nasty consequences.

Keywords

detail – a piece of information in a text

 **Offline** **30** minutes

"Lousy Litter"

Work **together** with students to complete offline Get Ready, Read Aloud, and Check Your Reading activities.

Get Ready

Words to Know

Before reading "Lousy Litter,"

1. Have students say each word and phrase aloud.

2. Ask students if they know what each word and phrase means.

   ▸ If students know a word's meaning, have them define it and use it in a sentence.
   ▸ If students don't know a word's meaning, read them the definition and discuss the word with them.

get tangled – to get caught or trapped in something
litter – trash or garbage lying on the ground
recycle – to turn something old into something new
waste – trash or garbage

 Objectives
- Increase concept and content vocabulary.
- Use new vocabulary in written and spoken sentences.

Read Aloud

Book Walk

Prepare students by taking them on a Book Walk of "Lousy Litter." Scan the magazine article together, and ask students to make predictions about the text. Answers to questions may vary.

1. Turn to the **table of contents**. Help students find today's selection, and turn to that page.

2. Point to and read aloud the **title of the article**.

3. Have students look at the **pictures** in the article.

   ▸ What do you think the article is about?
   ▸ Have you ever seen trash lying on the ground?
   ▸ How do you think the trash got there?

4. Point to and read aloud any **headers, captions, or other features** that stand out.

   ▸ What do you think the article might tell us about litter?

 Objectives
- Make predictions based on title, illustrations and/or context clues.
- Read and listen to a variety of texts for information and pleasure independently or as part of a group.

"Lousy Litter"

Now it's time to read the article. Have students sit next to you so that they can see the pictures and words while you read the article aloud.

Read aloud the entire article. Emphasize Words to Know as you come to them. If appropriate, use the pictures to help show what each word means.

Check Your Reading

"Lousy Litter"

Have students retell the article in their own words to develop grammar, vocabulary, comprehension, and fluency skills. When finished, **ask students the following questions** to check comprehension and encourage discussion.

▶ What do you call trash that is on the ground? litter

▶ Name something bad about litter. It's ugly; it's dirty; it's smelly; it can hurt animals.

▶ What is the best thing to do with a snack wrapper when you're done with it? throw it in a trash can

Objectives

- Identify important details in informational text.

Explore "Lousy Litter"

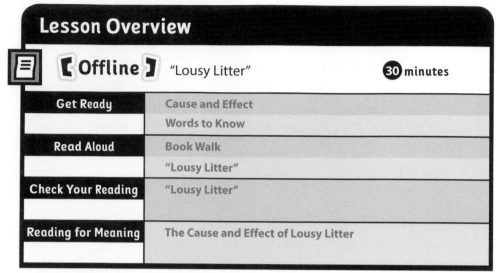

Lesson Overview

⬛ 【 Offline 】 "Lousy Litter"   ⬛ **30** minutes

Get Ready	Cause and Effect
	Words to Know
Read Aloud	Book Walk
	"Lousy Litter"
Check Your Reading	"Lousy Litter"
Reading for Meaning	The Cause and Effect of Lousy Litter

【 Materials 】

Supplied
- "Lousy Litter," *K¹² World: Taking Care of Ourselves and Our Earth,* pp. 16–21

Keywords
cause – the reason something happens
effect – the result of a cause

Advance Preparation

Before working with students, spend a few minutes reviewing Words to Know. Then read the Check Your Reading and Reading for Meaning activities to familiarize yourself with the questions and answers.

Big Ideas

Comprehension entails an understanding of the organizational patterns of text.

[Offline] 30 minutes

"Lousy Litter"

Work **together** with students to complete offline Get Ready, Read Aloud, Check Your Reading, and Reading for Meaning activities.

Get Ready

Cause and Effect

Tell students that doing one thing can make another thing happen. The thing that you do is called the **cause**, and the thing that happens is called the **effect**. Examples of cause and effect are all around us.

- **Cause:** You bump into a tower of blocks.
  Effect: The blocks fall down.
- **Cause:** You turn off the light.
  Effect: The room gets dark.

Tell students that they will hear more examples of cause and effect in the article "Lousy Litter."

Objectives

- Describe cause-and-effect relationships in text.
- Increase concept and content vocabulary.
- Use new vocabulary in written and spoken sentences.

Words to Know

Before reading "Lousy Litter,"

1. Have students say each word and phrase aloud.

2. Ask students if they know what each word and phrase means.

   - If students know a word's meaning, have them define it and use it in a sentence.
   - If students don't know a word's meaning, read them the definition and discuss the word with them.

get tangled – to get caught or trapped in something
litter – trash or garbage lying on the ground
recycle – to turn something old into something new
waste – trash or garbage

Read Aloud

Book Walk

Prepare students by taking them on a Book Walk of "Lousy Litter." Scan the magazine article together to revisit the text. Answers to questions may vary.

1. Turn to today's selection.

2. Point to and read aloud the **title of the article**.

3. Have students look at the **pictures** in the article.

4. Point to the **picture of the park with litter scattered around**.

   ▸ When and where have you seen litter?
   ▸ What kind of litter did you see?
   ▸ How did looking at the litter make you feel?

Objectives

- Use prior knowledge to aid understanding of text.
- Read and listen to a variety of texts for information and pleasure independently or as part of a group.

"Lousy Litter"

Now it's time to read the article. Have students sit next to you so that they can see the pictures and words while you read the article aloud.

　　Read aloud the entire article. Tell students to listen carefully to hear how trash left on the ground can cause bad things to happen. **Remember: Doing one thing can make another thing happen.** The thing that you do is the **cause**, and the thing that happens is the **effect**.

Check Your Reading

"Lousy Litter"

Have students retell the article in their own words to develop grammar, vocabulary, comprehension, and fluency skills. **Help students correctly use the words *cause* and *effect*** when they retell the article, whenever necessary. When finished, **ask students the following questions** to check comprehension and encourage discussion.

▸ How does litter make our world look? ugly
▸ What is another name, or word, for litter? trash; garbage; waste
▸ What causes litter? people throwing their trash on the ground

Objectives

- Identify important details in informational text.
- Describe cause-and-effect relationships in text.
- Increase concept and content vocabulary.

Reading for Meaning

The Cause and Effect of Lousy Litter

Ask students the following questions to further check comprehension and focus on cause-and-effect relationships. **Reread parts of the article** if they have trouble answering a question. **Repeat the definitions in the Read Aloud** to refresh their memories about what is a cause and what is an effect.

▸ Name something from the article that is a piece of litter. empty bottle; plastic bag; snack wrapper

▸ What causes litter to move from one place to another? The wind blows it around; the rain washes it into rivers.

▸ Tell how litter like a snack wrapper in a river can have a bad effect on a fish. If the fish eats the wrapper, it will get sick.

▸ What would people probably do if a park was full of litter? They would stop coming to the park.

▸ What would be a good thing to do if you see a friend throw a wrapper on the ground? help that person look for a trash can; pick up the wrapper and put it in the trash yourself

Objectives

- Describe cause-and-effect relationships in text.
- Make connections with text: text-to-text, text-to-self, text-to-world.

Review "Lousy Litter"

Lesson Overview

 【 Offline 】 "Lousy Litter"　　30 minutes

Get Ready	**Words to Know**
	Reread or Retell
Reading for Meaning	**The Cause and Effect of Litter**
Making Connections	**Don't Be a Litterbug!**
Beyond the Lesson	⊕ **OPTIONAL:** Every Litter Bit Helps

Big Ideas

Comprehension entails an understanding of the organizational patterns of text.

【 **Materials** 】

Supplied

- "Lousy Litter," *K¹² World: Taking Care of Ourselves and Our Earth*, pp. 16–21
- *K¹² Language Arts Activity Book*, p. LC 9

Also Needed

- crayons

Keywords

cause – the reason something happens
effect – the result of a cause

 **30** minutes

"Lousy Litter"

Work **together** with students to complete offline Get Ready, Reading for Meaning, Making Connections, and Beyond the Lesson activities.

Get Ready ....

Words to Know

Ask students to define the following words and use them in a sentence:

get tangled	**recycle**
litter	**waste**

Correct any incorrect or vague definitions.

Objectives
- Increase concept and content vocabulary.
- Use new vocabulary in written and spoken sentences.

Reread or Retell

If you'd like to, reread the article to students. Otherwise, have students retell the article using the pictures as a guide, or move on to the next activity.

Reading for Meaning ....

The Cause and Effect of Litter

Ask students the following questions to check comprehension. **Reread parts of the article or point to pictures** if they have trouble answering a question. Remind students that **litter always has some sort of effect**.

Objectives
- Describe cause-and-effect relationships in text.
- Identify important details in informational text.
- Make connections with text: text-to-text, text-to-self, text-to-world.

- ▶ Who or what causes litter? people who throw their trash on the ground
- ▶ What was the effect of the plastic bag in the article blowing into a tree? It caused a bird to get tangled up in it.
- ▶ What can cause litter to end up in a river? Rain can wash litter into a river.
- ▶ What is a dangerous effect of litter on roads? It might cause an accident when it blows in the way of cars.
- ▶ How do we get rid of litter once it's on the ground? Someone has to pick it up.
- ▶ What would be the effect of everyone putting their garbage in trash cans? There would be no more litter.

Making Connections

Don't Be a Litterbug!

Have students color the poster of a litterbug on page LC 9 in *K¹² Language Arts Activity Book*. Explain that the poster can be used to remind people to put their trash in garbage cans. Have students identify what is in each of the litterbug's "hands." Discuss how dropping each of these items on the ground can cause trouble for animals and make our world ugly. When done, tear out the poster, and help students find a place to post it, such as on a refrigerator, cabinet, or bedroom door.

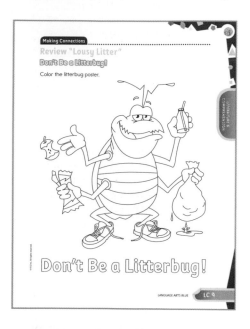

Objectives

- Make connections with text: text-to-text, text-to-self, text-to-world.
- Respond to text through art, writing, and/or drama.
- Identify purpose of environmental print.
- Identify and comprehend environmental print.

Beyond the Lesson

⊕ OPTIONAL: Every Litter Bit Helps

This activity is intended for students who have extra time and would benefit from applying what they've learned about litter to a real-life experience and gaining a sense of achievement. Feel free to skip this activity.

Help students decorate a paper bag to use as a litter bag in a place where they spend time, such as the family car, the living room, or their bedroom. Tell students that it's their responsibility to empty the contents of the litter bag into a trash can when the litter bag gets full.

Objectives

- Make connections with text: text-to-text, text-to-self, text-to-world.
- Respond to text through art, writing, and/or drama.

Introduce "Recycling Is Smart"

Unit Overview

In this unit, students will explore the theme of *House and Home* through the following reading selections:

► "Recycling Is Smart"
► *A Chair for My Mother*
► "Their Castles Were Their Homes"

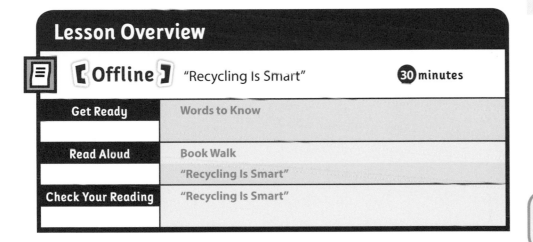

Lesson Overview

[Offline] "Recycling Is Smart"   **30** minutes

Get Ready	Words to Know
Read Aloud	Book Walk
	"Recycling Is Smart"
Check Your Reading	"Recycling Is Smart"

Advance Preparation

Read "Recycling Is Smart" before beginning the Read Aloud activity, to locate Words to Know within the text.

Big Ideas

Comprehension entails an understanding of the organizational patterns of text.

[Materials]

Supplied

● "Recycling Is Smart,"
  *K¹² World: Taking Care of
  Ourselves and Our Earth,*
  pp. 22–27

Article Synopsis

Everyday household items—paper, glass bottles, and metal cans—can be easily recycled and thereby help preserve our precious resources. The article follows a juice bottle through each step of the recycling process.

Keywords

sequence – order

[Offline] (30) minutes

"Recycling Is Smart"

Work **together** with students to complete offline Get Ready, Read Aloud, and Check Your Reading activities.

Get Ready

Words to Know

Before reading "Recycling Is Smart,"

1. Have students say each word aloud.

2. Ask students if they know what each word means.

   ▶ If students know a word's meaning, have them define it and use it in a sentence.
   ▶ If students don't know a word's meaning, read them the definition and discuss the word with them.

furnace – like a big oven; it holds a very hot fire
liquid – something wet, like water
recycle – to turn old items into new ones
solid – hard and firm
waste – trash or garbage

Objectives
- Increase concept and content vocabulary.
- Use new vocabulary in written and spoken sentences.

Read Aloud

Book Walk

Prepare students by taking them on a Book Walk of "Recycling Is Smart." Scan the magazine article together and ask students to make predictions about the text. Answers to questions may vary.

1. Turn to the **table of contents**. Help students find today's selection, and turn to that page.

2. Point to and read aloud the **title of the article**.

Objectives
- Make predictions based on title, illustrations and/or context clues.
- Read and listen to a variety of texts for information and pleasure independently or as part of a group.

3. Have students study the **pictures** in the article.

   ▸ What do you think the article is about?
   ▸ What do you already know about recycling?
   ▸ Have you or a family member ever recycled anything?

4. Point to and read aloud any **headers, captions, or other features** that stand out.

   ▸ What do you think the article will tell us about recycling?

"Recycling Is Smart"

Now it's time to read the article. Have students sit next to you so that they can see the pictures and words while you read the article aloud. Ask students to listen carefully so they can learn the steps in recycling a bottle.

Read aloud the entire article. Emphasize Words to Know as you come to them. If appropriate, use the pictures to help show what a word means.

Check Your Reading

"Recycling Is Smart"

Have students retell the article in their own words to develop grammar, vocabulary, comprehension, and fluency skills. When finished, **ask students the following questions** to check comprehension and encourage discussion.

▸ What is the article mostly about? Answers will vary.
▸ What are some things (besides a glass bottle) the article says can be recycled? paper; plastic; newspaper; soda cans; metal
▸ Where can you take items to be recycled? a recycling center
▸ What is the first thing that happens to a bottle at a recycling plant? It's washed.
▸ After a bottle is washed, what happens next? It's sorted by its color.

Objectives
- State the details of a text.
- Sequence events from a text.

Explore "Recycling Is Smart"

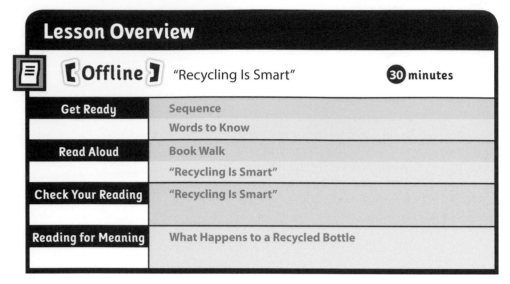

Lesson Overview

[Offline] "Recycling Is Smart" **30** minutes

Get Ready	Sequence
	Words to Know
Read Aloud	Book Walk
	"Recycling Is Smart"
Check Your Reading	"Recycling Is Smart"
Reading for Meaning	What Happens to a Recycled Bottle

[Materials]

Supplied

- "Recycling Is Smart,"
  *K¹² World: Taking Care of
  Ourselves and Our Earth,*
  pp. 22–27

Keywords

sequence – order

Advance Preparation

Before working with students, spend a few minutes reviewing Words to Know.
Then read the Check Your Reading and Reading for Meaning activities to familiarize
yourself with the questions and answers.

Big Ideas

Comprehension entails an understanding of the organizational patterns of text.

 **30 minutes**

"Recycling Is Smart"

Work **together** with students to complete offline Get Ready, Read Aloud, Check Your Reading, and Reading for Meaning activities.

Get Ready

Sequence

Tell students that the order in which things happen in a story or article is called the **sequence**. Words like *first, next, before, after, then,* and *finally* help tell the sequence, or the order in which things happen.

Say: Listen for words that tell the sequence, or order: First, I poured a glass of juice. Then, I saw that the juice bottle was empty. Next, I put the juice bottle in the recycling bin. Finally, I drank my juice.

▸ How many things did you hear in the sequence? four
▸ What happened first? I poured a glass of juice.
▸ What happened last? I drank my juice.

Objectives
- Sequence events from a text.
- Increase concept and content vocabulary.
- Use new vocabulary in written and spoken sentences.

Words to Know

Before reading "Recycling Is Smart,"

1. Have students say each word aloud.

2. Ask students if they know what each word means.

   ▸ If students know a word's meaning, have them define it and use it in a sentence.
   ▸ If students don't know a word's meaning, read them the definition and discuss the word with them.

furnace – like a big oven; it holds a very hot fire
liquid – something wet, like water
recycle – to turn old items into new ones
solid – hard and firm
waste – trash or garbage

Read Aloud

Book Walk

Prepare students by taking them on a Book Walk of "Recycling Is Smart." Scan the magazine article together to revisit the text. Answers to questions may vary.

1. Turn to today's selection.

2. Point to and read aloud the **title of the article**.

3. Have students study the **pictures** in the article.

   ► Have you ever seen a recycling bin? Did you put anything in it?

"Recycling Is Smart"

Now it's time to read the article. Have students sit next to you so that they can see the pictures and words while you read the article aloud. Remind students that the order in which things happen in a story or article is called the **sequence**. Words like *first, next, before, after, then,* and *finally* help tell the sequence, or the order in which things happen.

   Read aloud the entire article. Emphasize Words to Know as you come to them. If appropriate, use the pictures to help show what a word means. Remind students to listen carefully to hear the order in which things happen to a bottle in a recycling plant.

Objectives

- Read and listen to a variety of texts for information and pleasure independently or as part of a group.

Check Your Reading

"Recycling Is Smart"

Have students retell the article in their own words to develop grammar, vocabulary, comprehension, and fluency skills. When finished, **ask students the following questions** to check comprehension and encourage discussion.

► What happens to a bottle after it's taken to a recycling center? It gets taken to a recycling plant.

► What is a recycling plant? the place where people use machines to change things like glass bottles so they can be used again

► What happens after a bottle is sorted by color? It gets crushed into small pieces.

Objectives

- Sequence events from a text.
- Build vocabulary through listening, reading, and discussion.

Reading for Meaning

What Happens to a Recycled Bottle

Ask students the following questions to further check comprehension and focus on sequence. When appropriate, **reread parts of the article and point to pictures** to help students remember the sequence of events.

Remind students that words like *first, next, after,* and *then* are sequence words. They help tell the order of things that happen. If you think it might be helpful, reread example about the juice bottle in the Read Aloud to reinforce the concept of **sequence**.

Objectives
- Sequence events from a text.
- Identify important details in informational text.

▸ What happens after the glass is crushed? It goes into the furnace, where it turns into a liquid.

▸ What happens next to the liquid glass? It gets poured into molds.

▸ What happens after the liquid glass is poured into the molds? The liquid glass cools and becomes new bottles.

▸ Can a metal can be recycled? Yes   What might a metal can be turned into at a recycling plant? Answers will vary; if necessary, suggest it will become another can.

Review "Recycling Is Smart"

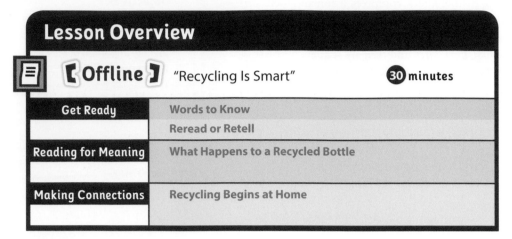

Lesson Overview

[Offline] "Recycling Is Smart"　　　**30** minutes

Get Ready	Words to Know
	Reread or Retell
Reading for Meaning	What Happens to a Recycled Bottle
Making Connections	Recycling Begins at Home

Big Ideas

Comprehension entails an understanding of the organizational patterns of text.

[Materials]

Supplied

- "Recycling Is Smart," *K¹² World: Taking Care of Ourselves and Our Earth*, pp. 22–27
- *K¹² Language Arts Activity Book*, p. LC 11

Also Needed

- crayons
- tape, masking

Keywords

sequence – order

 **30 minutes**

"Recycling Is Smart"

Work **together** with students to complete offline Get Ready, Reading for Meaning, and Making Connections activities.

Get Ready

Words to Know
Ask students to define the following words and use them in a sentence:

furnace	**recycle**	**waste**
liquid	**solid**	

Correct any incorrect or vague definitions.

Objectives
- Increase concept and content vocabulary.
- Use new vocabulary in written and spoken sentences.

Reread or Retell
If you'd like to, reread the article to students. Otherwise, have students retell the article using the pictures as a guide, or move on to the next activity.

Reading for Meaning

What Happens to a Recycled Bottle
Ask students the following questions to check comprehension.

- ▶ Name the first two things that happen to a bottle after it gets to a recycling plant. First it gets washed, and then it gets sorted.
- ▶ Which happens first? A bottle is crushed, or a bottle is put in the furnace. A bottle is crushed.
- ▶ What happens to the crushed glass in the furnace? It melts into a liquid.
- ▶ What happens to the liquid glass? It's poured into bottle-shaped molds.
- ▶ What's the last thing that happens at a glass recycling plant? The new bottles are taken out of their molds.
- ▶ Why is it smart to recycle things like bottles and cans? It cuts down on waste; they won't become trash.

Objectives
- Sequence events from a text.
- Identify important details in informational text.
- Make connections with text: text-to-text, text-to-self, text-to-world.

Making Connections

Recycling Begins at Home

Have students color the poster on page LC 11 in *K¹² Language Arts Activity Book*. When done, tear out and tape the poster to a small trash can or box.

Objectives

- Comprehend environmental print.
- Make connections with text: text-to-text, text-to-self, text-to-world.

Introduce *A Chair for My Mother*

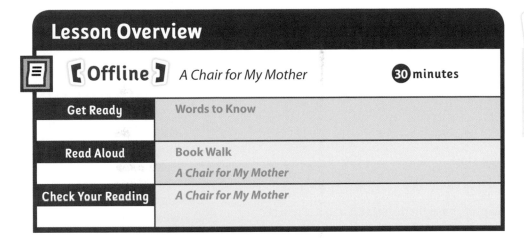

Lesson Overview

[Offline] *A Chair for My Mother* — **30** minutes

Get Ready	Words to Know
Read Aloud	Book Walk
	A Chair for My Mother
Check Your Reading	*A Chair for My Mother*

Advance Preparation

Read *A Chair for My Mother* before beginning the Read Aloud activity, to locate Words to Know within the story.

[Materials]

Supplied
- *A Chair for My Mother* by Vera B. Williams

Story Synopsis

All Rosa's mother wants is a comfortable, overstuffed chair to relax in after a hard day's work because her old one burned in a house fire. Everyone in the family helps out by saving dimes and nickels in a big jar until they can afford to buy one.

Keywords

first-person point of view – the telling of a story by a character in that story, using pronouns such as *I*, *me*, and *we*

 **30** minutes

A Chair for My Mother

Work **together** with students to complete offline Get Ready, Read Aloud, and Check Your Reading activities.

Get Ready

Words to Know

Before reading *A Chair for My Mother*,

1. Have students say each word aloud.

2. Ask students if they know what each word means.

   ▸ If students know a word's meaning, have them define it and use it in a sentence.
   ▸ If students don't know a word's meaning, read them the definition and discuss the word with them.

change – loose coins
sofa – a couch
spoil – to ruin
tip – money given to servers in a restaurant to thank them for their service
waitress – a woman who serves food at a restaurant

Objectives
- Build vocabulary through listening, reading, and discussion.
- Use new vocabulary in written and spoken sentences.

Read Aloud

Book Walk

Prepare students by taking them on a Book Walk of *A Chair for My Mother*. Scan the book together and ask students to make predictions about the story. Answers to questions may vary.

1. Point to the **front cover** of the book.
   Say: This is the front cover.

2. Point to the **back cover**.
   Say: This is the back cover.

3. Point to and read aloud the **book title**.

   ▸ What do you think the book is about?

4. Read the name of the **author**. Explain what it means to be an author.

5. Turn to the **title page**. Explain that the title page repeats the book title and author's name.

6. Look through the book. Have students describe what they see in the **pictures**.

   ▸ Where do you think the story takes place?
   ▸ What do you think might happen in the story?
   ▸ Have you ever saved money to buy something special?

Objectives
- Make predictions based on title, illustrations and/or context clues.
- Read and listen to a variety of texts for information and pleasure independently or as part of a group.

A Chair for My Mother

Now it's time to read the story. Have students sit next to you so that they can see the pictures and words while you read the story aloud.

Read aloud the entire story. Emphasize Words to Know as you come to them. If appropriate, use the pictures to help show what a word means.

Check Your Reading

A Chair for My Mother

Have students retell the story in their own words to develop grammar, vocabulary, comprehension, and fluency skills. When finished, **ask students the following questions** to check comprehension and encourage discussion.

- ▶ Who is telling the story? a little girl
- ▶ How can you tell who is telling the story? Answers will vary; students should mention that the person telling the story uses words like *I, we,* and *my.*
- ▶ What does the title of the book mean? The family is saving up to buy a new chair for the mother.
- ▶ What happened to the mother's first chair? It burned in a fire.
- ▶ What is the mother's job? She is a waitress.

Objectives
- Identify first-person point of view.
- Answer questions requiring literal recall of details.

Explore *A Chair for My Mother*

Lesson Overview

[Offline] *A Chair for My Mother*   **30** minutes

Get Ready	Words That Paint a Picture
	Words to Know
Read Aloud	Book Walk
	A Chair for My Mother
Check Your Reading	*A Chair for My Mother*
Reading for Meaning	Paint a Picture with Words

[Materials]

Supplied
- *A Chair for My Mother* by Vera B. Williams

Keywords

imagery – language that helps readers imagine how something looks, sounds, smells, feels, or tastes

Advance Preparation

Before working with students, spend a few minutes reviewing Words to Know. Then read the Check Your Reading and Reading for Meaning activities to familiarize yourself with the questions and answers.

Big Ideas

▸ Comprehension entails actively thinking about what is being read.
▸ An author writes a story.
▸ Readers who visualize, or form mental pictures, while they read have better recall of text than those who do not.

 **Offline** **30** minutes

A Chair for My Mother

Work **together** with students to complete offline Get Ready, Read Aloud, Check Your Reading, and Reading for Meaning activities.

Get Ready ....

Words That Paint a Picture

Tell students that authors often use words that paint a picture in readers' head. They do this to help readers see the story in their head, and to make the story more interesting. **Read aloud the following two sentences.** Tell students to listen carefully to hear the difference between the two sentences.

Flames came out of the roof.

Tall orange flames came out of the roof.

> ▸ Which sentence is more interesting and helps paint a picture in your head? the second one   Why? Answers will vary.
> ▸ What words in the second sentence help you see a picture in your head?
> *tall orange flames*

 When authors use words that paint a picture in the reader's head, it is called using **imagery**.

 Objectives
- Identify words that create mental imagery.
- Build vocabulary through listening, reading, and discussion.
- Use new vocabulary in written and spoken sentences.

Words to Know

Before reading *A Chair for My Mother*,

1. Have students say each word aloud.

2. Ask students if they know what each word means.

> ▸ If students know a word's meaning, have them define it and use it in a sentence.
> ▸ If students don't know a word's meaning, read them the definition and discuss the word with them.

change – loose coins
sofa – a couch
spoil – to ruin
tip – money given to servers in a restaurant to thank them for their service
waitress – a woman who serves food at a restaurant

Read Aloud

Book Walk

Prepare students by taking them on a Book Walk of *A Chair for My Mother*. Scan the book together to revisit the characters and events. Answers to questions may vary.

1. Point to the **front cover** of the book.
   Say: This is the front cover.

2. Point to the **back cover**.
   Say: This is the back cover.

3. Point to and read aloud the **book title**.

4. Read the name of the **author**.

   ▸ What does it mean to be an author?

5. Look through the book. Have students describe what they see in the **pictures**.

   ▸ What do you notice about the colorful borders?

Objectives

- Describe role of author and/or illustrator.
- Read and listen to a variety of texts for information and pleasure independently or as a group.

A Chair for My Mother

Now it's time to read the story. Have students sit next to you so that they can see the pictures and words while you read the story aloud.

   Read aloud the entire story. Ask students to listen for descriptive words that help create pictures in their head.

Check Your Reading

A Chair for My Mother

Have students retell the story in their own words to develop grammar, vocabulary, comprehension, and fluency skills. When finished, **ask students the following questions** to check comprehension and encourage discussion.

▸ What kind of job does the mother have? waitress
▸ What did the neighbors bring to fill the family's new apartment? Answers may include: table; chairs; bed
▸ Which words in this sentence from the story help paint a picture in your head? "My mother's other sister, Sally, made us red and white curtains." *red and white curtains* Describe what you see in your head. Are they striped? Do they have polka dots or flowers? Answers will vary.

Objectives

- Answer questions requiring literal recall of details.
- Identify words that create mental imagery.

Reading for Meaning

Paint a Picture with Words

Ask students the following questions to further check comprehension and identify words that create mental imagery.

Objectives
- Identify words that create mental imagery.

1. **Say:** Listen to this sentence from the story:

    "A wonderful, beautiful, fat, soft armchair."

    ▸ Which words in the sentence help paint a picture in your head? *wonderful; fat; beautiful; soft*
    ▸ Describe the chair you see in your head. Answers will vary.

2. **Say:** Listen to these two sentences:

    "All the neighbors stood in a bunch across the street."
    "People stood across the street."

    ▸ Which of the two sentences has words in it that help you see a picture in your head? the first one
    ▸ Which words in the first sentence help you see a picture in your head? *all; neighbors; bunch*

3. **Say:** Listen to this sentence:

    "Mamma brought home a jar."

    ▸ What words would you use to describe the word *jar* to help readers see a picture in their head? Answers will vary; students should use adjectives such as *big, giant, old, glass.*

Review *A Chair for My Mother*

Lesson Overview

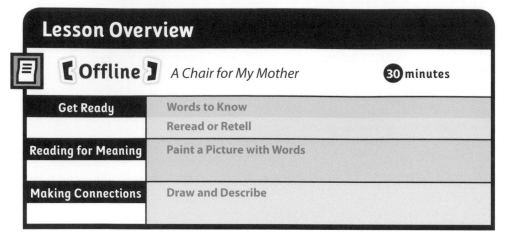

Offline	*A Chair for My Mother*	**30** minutes
Get Ready	Words to Know	
	Reread or Retell	
Reading for Meaning	Paint a Picture with Words	
Making Connections	Draw and Describe	

Materials

Supplied
- *A Chair for My Mother* by Vera B. Williams
- *K¹² Language Arts Activity Book*, p. LC 13

Also Needed
- crayons

Keywords

imagery – language that helps readers imagine how something looks, sounds, smells, feels, or tastes

Big Ideas

▸ Comprehension entails actively thinking about what is being read.
▸ Readers who visualize, or form mental pictures, while they read have better recall of text than those who do not.

 **30 minutes**

A Chair for My Mother

Work **together** with students to complete offline Get Ready, Reading for Meaning, and Making Connections activities.

Get Ready

Words to Know

Ask students to define the following words and use them in a sentence:

change	**spoil**	**waitress**
sofa	**tip**	

Correct any incorrect or vague definitions.

 Objectives
- Build vocabulary through listening, reading, and discussion.
- Use new vocabulary in written and spoken sentences.

Reread or Retell

If you'd like to, reread the story to students. Otherwise, have students retell the story using the pictures as a guide, or move on to the next activity.

Reading for Meaning

Painting a Picture with Words

Ask students the following questions to check comprehension.

 Objectives
- Identify words that create mental imagery.

1. **Say:** Listen to this sentence from the story:

   "What was left of the house was charcoal and ashes."

   ▸ Which words in the sentence help paint a picture in your head? *charcoal and ashes*
   ▸ Describe what you see in your head. Answers will vary.

2. **Say:** Listen to these two sentences:

   "We will get a chair."
   "We will get a chair covered in velvet with roses all over it."

   ▸ Which of the two sentences better helps you paint a picture in your head? the second one
   ▸ Which words in that sentence help you see a picture in your head? *velvet; roses*

3. **Say:** Listen to this sentence:

   "We painted the walls."

   ▸ What words could you use to help readers picture the walls in their head? Answers will vary.

Making Connections

Draw and Describe

Have students think of something they would like to save up to buy. Then have them draw a picture of their item on page LC 13 in *K¹² Language Arts Activity Book*. Ask students to describe their item with words that would help readers see the item in their heads. Write the words students dictate around the picture.

Objectives

- Identify words that create mental imagery.

Introduce "Their Homes Were Their Castles"

Lesson Overview

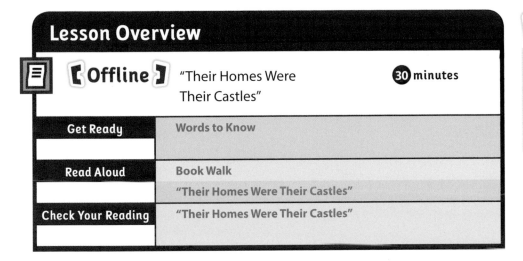

Offline	"Their Homes Were Their Castles"	30 minutes
Get Ready	Words to Know	
Read Aloud	Book Walk	
	"Their Homes Were Their Castles"	
Check Your Reading	"Their Homes Were Their Castles"	

Advance Preparation

Read "Their Homes Were Their Castles" before beginning the Read Aloud activity, to locate Words to Know within the text.

Materials

Supplied

- "Their Homes Were Their Castles," *K¹² World: Amazing Places,* pp. 2–11

Article Synopsis

Students take a step back in time and visit an old European castle. They learn about such things as the moat, towers, courtyard, and chapel.

Note that there is a brief reference to the dungeon and the criminals that were locked inside.

Keywords

detail – a piece of information in a text

 **30 minutes**

"Their Homes Were Their Castles"

Work **together** with students to complete offline Get Ready, Read Aloud, and Check Your Reading activities.

Get Ready

Words to Know

Before reading "Their Homes Were Their Castles,"

1. Have students say each word aloud.

2. Ask students if they know what each word means.

    ▸ If students know a word's meaning, have them define it and use it in a sentence.

    ▸ If students don't know a word's meaning, read them the definition and discuss the word with them.

chapel – a room or building used for worship or private prayer
courtyard – an open space that has walls or buildings around it
drawbridge – a heavy bridge that can be pulled up to keep someone from crossing
dungeon – a dark underground room used as a prison
gate – a door in an outside wall or fence
keep – the main tower of a castle, usually the best-protected part of the castle
moat – a deep ditch around a castle, usually filled with water
tower – a tall, narrow structure that stands alone or is part of another building

> **Objectives**
> - Increase concept and content vocabulary.
> - Use new vocabulary in written and spoken sentences.

Read Aloud

Book Walk

Prepare students by taking them on a Book Walk of "Their Homes Were Their Castles." Scan the magazine article together and ask students to make predictions about the text. Answers to questions may vary.

1. Turn to the **table of contents**. Help students find today's selection, and turn to that page.

2. Point to and read aloud the **title of the article**.

3. Have students study the **pictures** in the article.

    ▸ What do you think the article is about?
    ▸ What do you know about castles?

4. Point to and read aloud any **headers, captions, or other features** that stand out.

    ▸ What do you think the article might tell us about castles?

> **Objectives**
> - Make predictions based on title, illustrations and/or context clues.
> - Listen and respond to texts representing a variety of cultures, time periods, and traditions.

"Their Homes Were Their Castles"

Now it's time to read the article. Have students sit next to you so that they can see the pictures and words while you read the article aloud. Tell students to listen carefully to the descriptions of parts of the castle to learn what things are called and what they are used for.

Read aloud the entire article. Emphasize Words to Know as you come to them. If appropriate, use the pictures to help show what a word means.

Check Your Reading

"Their Homes Were Their Castles"

Have students retell the article in their own words to develop grammar, vocabulary, comprehension, and fluency skills. When finished, **ask students the following questions** to check comprehension and encourage discussion.

- What is something that you learned about castles? Answers will vary.
- Who used to live in castles? kings and queens
- What are the castle walls made of? stone
- What is the moat filled with? water
- How do you get across the moat? by using the drawbridge

Objectives
- Answer questions requiring literal recall of details.

Explore "Their Homes Were Their Castles"

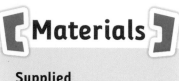

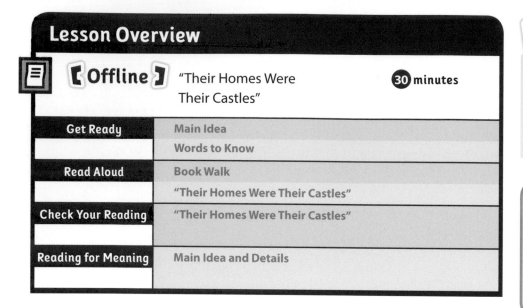

Lesson Overview

[Offline]	"Their Homes Were Their Castles"	30 minutes

Get Ready	Main Idea
	Words to Know
Read Aloud	Book Walk
	"Their Homes Were Their Castles"
Check Your Reading	"Their Homes Were Their Castles"
Reading for Meaning	Main Idea and Details

[Materials]

Supplied

- "Their Homes Were Their Castles," *K¹² World: Amazing Places,* pp. 2–11

Keywords

main idea – the most important idea in a paragraph or text

supporting detail – a detail that gives more information about a main idea

Advance Preparation

Before working with students, spend a few minutes reviewing Words to Know. Then read the Check Your Reading and Reading for Meaning activities to familiarize yourself with the questions and answers.

Big Ideas

Comprehension entails an understanding of the organizational patterns of text.

[Offline] **30** minutes

"Their Homes Were Their Castles"

Work **together** with students to complete offline Get Ready, Read Aloud, Check Your Reading, and Reading for Meaning activities.

Get Ready ·

Main Idea

Tell students that every paragraph in an article has a **main idea**. It's what a paragraph is mostly about. The other sentences in a paragraph tell other things, or **details** about the main idea.

1. Read aloud the following paragraph:

   Sweet Pea is a cat. She has white fur and a pink nose. Sweet Pea is four years old.

2. Tell students that this paragraph is about a cat named Sweet Pea. That is the main idea of the paragraph.

3. Ask the following question:

   ► What is the paragraph mostly about? a cat named Sweet Pea

   If students have trouble answering, ask them to name some things about Sweet Pea. Tell students those things are called *details*. The details are: white fur; pink nose; four years old.

> **Objectives**
> - Identify the main idea.
> - Increase concept and content vocabulary.
> - Use new vocabulary in written and spoken sentences.

Words to Know

Before reading "Their Homes Were Their Castles,"

1. Have students say each word aloud.

2. Ask students if they know what each word means.

   ► If students know a word's meaning, have them define it and use it in a sentence.

   ► If students don't know a word's meaning, read them the definition and discuss the word with them.

chapel – a room or building used for worship or private prayer
courtyard – an open space that has walls or buildings around it
drawbridge – a heavy bridge that can be pulled up to keep someone from crossing
dungeon – a dark underground room used as a prison
gate – a door in an outside wall or fence
keep – the main tower of a castle, usually the best-protected part of the castle
moat – a deep ditch around a castle, usually filled with water
tower – a tall, narrow structure that stands alone or is part of another building

Read Aloud

Book Walk

Prepare students by taking them on a Book Walk of "Their Homes Were Their Castles." Scan the magazine article together to revisit the text. Answers to questions may vary.

1. Turn to today's selection.

2. Point to and read aloud the **title of the article**.

3. Have students look at the **pictures** in the article.

   ▶ What is the article mostly about?
   ▶ Which picture of the castle do you like best?
   ▶ Which part of the castle does it show?

"Their Homes Were Their Castles"

Now it's time to read the article. Have students sit next to you so that they can see the pictures and words while you read the article aloud.

   Read aloud the entire article. Pause after some of the paragraphs to discuss what the paragraph is mostly about.

Objectives
- Listen and respond to texts representing a variety of cultures, time periods, and traditions.

Check Your Reading

"Their Homes Were Their Castles"

Have students retell the article in their own words to develop grammar, vocabulary, comprehension, and fluency skills. When finished, **ask students the following questions** to check comprehension and encourage discussion. **Read the following excerpt:**

> "This castle's walls are stone. Stone walls are strong and thick. The stone walls of this castle are still standing after many hundreds of years."

   ▶ The main idea is what the paragraph talks about the most. What is the main idea of this paragraph? the castle walls
   ▶ What are the castle walls made out of? stone
   ▶ What other information, or details, did you learn about the castle walls? They are thick; they are strong; they are still standing.

Objectives
- Identify the main idea.
- Identify supporting details.

Reading for Meaning ....

Main Idea and Details

Ask students the following questions to further check comprehension and focus on the main idea. Read aloud paragraphs from the article as directed.

1. **Read the following excerpt:**

   "Around the outside of the castle walls runs a **moat**. A moat is a ditch filled with water. The moat goes all the way around the castle."

   ▸ What is the main idea of this paragraph? the moat
   ▸ Where would you find the moat? around the castle
   ▸ What is another name for a moat? ditch
   ▸ What is a moat filled with? water

2. **Read the following excerpt:**

   "Here is the castle's **chapel**. A chapel is another name for a church. This chapel is very small—it was only for the king and queen."

   ▸ What is the main idea of this paragraph? the chapel
   ▸ What is another name for a chapel? church
   ▸ Name a detail that tells who used the chapel. the king and queen
   ▸ Name another detail about the chapel. This chapel is very small.

TIP If students have trouble identifying what the paragraph is mostly about, use a single sentence from the article as an example. The main idea of a sentence is the subject.

Review "Their Homes Were Their Castles"

Lesson Overview

[Offline]	"Their Homes Were Their Castles"	**30** minutes

Get Ready	Words to Know	
	Reread or Retell	
Reading for Meaning	Main Idea and Details	
Making Connections	Color a Castle	
Beyond the Lesson	⊕ OPTIONAL: More About Castles	

Big Ideas

Comprehension entails an understanding of the organizational patterns of text.

[Materials]

Supplied
- "Their Homes Were Their Castles," *K¹² World: Amazing Places*, pp. 2–11
- *K¹² Language Arts Activity Book*, p. LC 14

Also Needed
- crayons

Keywords
main idea – the most important idea in a paragraph or text
supporting detail – a detail that gives more information about a main idea

[Offline] ⏱ 30 minutes

"Their Homes Were Their Castles"

Work **together** with students to complete Get Ready, Reading for Meaning, Making Connections, and Beyond the Lesson activities.

Get Ready ....

Words to Know
Ask students to define the following words and use them in a sentence:

chapel	dungeon	moat
courtyard	gate	tower
drawbridge	keep	

Correct any incorrect or vague definitions.

⭐ **Objectives**
- Increase concept and content vocabulary.
- Use new vocabulary in written and spoken sentences.

Reread or Retell
If you'd like to, reread the article to students. Otherwise, have students retell the article using the pictures as a guide, or move on to the next activity.

Reading for Meaning ....

Main Idea and Details
Read aloud paragraphs from the article as directed, and then ask students the questions that follow to check comprehension.

⭐ **Objectives**
- Identify the main idea.
- Identify supporting details.

1. **Read aloud this paragraph:**

   "You can find many castles in Europe. Many of these castles are more than a thousand years old. Some of these castles were the homes of kings and queens."

   ▸ The main idea is what the paragraph is mostly about. What is the main idea of this paragraph? Possible answers: castles; castles in Europe
   ▸ Name two details about the castles. Many are more than a thousand years old; some were the homes of kings and queens.

2. **Read aloud this paragraph:**

   "We are in the **courtyard** of the castle. The courtyard is an open space inside the castle walls. In the old days, the courtyard buzzed with activity. People talked and laughed and worked here."

   ▸ What is the main idea of this paragraph? the courtyard
   ▸ Name two details, or things, about the courtyard. It's an open space; it's inside the castle walls; it would buzz with activity; people laughed and worked there.

Making Connections

Color a Castle

Have students color the castle on page LC 14 in *K¹² Language Arts Activity Book*. When done, point to the parts of the castle (such as the moat and towers), one by one. Label the parts of the castle as students name them.

Objectives
- State the details of a text.

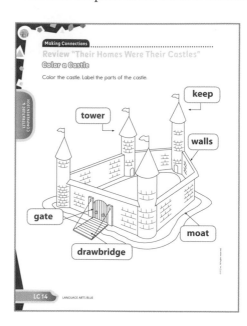

Beyond the Lesson

✚ OPTIONAL: More About Castles

This activity is intended for students who have extra time and would benefit from building a castle or exploring these medieval buildings further. Feel free to skip this activity.

1. Help students build their own cardboard-box castle. See the following website for a list of materials and instructions: http://www.enchantedlearning.com/crafts/Boxcastle.shtml.

2. If students would like to learn more about castles, go to the following website: http://history.howstuffworks.com/middle-ages/castle.htm.

Objectives
- Respond to text through art, writing, and/or drama.
- Listen and respond to texts representing a variety of cultures, time periods, and traditions.

Introduce "Cinderella"

Unit Overview

In this unit, students will explore three classic fairy tales through the following reading selections:

► "Cinderella"
► "Sleeping Beauty"
► "Rapunzel"

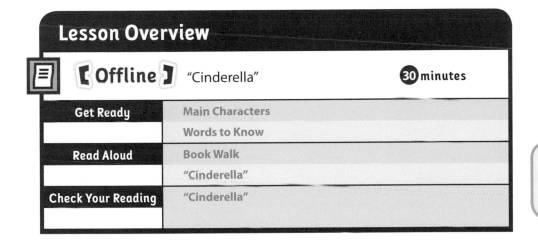

Lesson Overview

☰	[Offline] "Cinderella"	30 minutes
Get Ready	Main Characters	
	Words to Know	
Read Aloud	Book Walk	
	"Cinderella"	
Check Your Reading	"Cinderella"	

Advance Preparation

Read "Cinderella" before beginning the Read Aloud activity, to locate Words to Know within the text.

Big Ideas

Comprehension requires an understanding of story structure.

Materials

Supplied
• "Cinderella," *K¹² Read Aloud Treasury,* pp. 34–43

Story Synopsis

Cinderella lives a life of drudgery until one astonishing day when her fairy godmother shows up. There are elements of magic in this story.

Keywords

character – a person or animal in a story

 **30 minutes**

"Cinderella"

Work **together** with students to complete offline Get Ready, Read Aloud, and Check Your Reading activities.

Get Ready

Main Characters

Tell students they will read a story called "Cinderella." Explain that the people in the story are called **characters**. There can be many characters in a story. Tell students to listen carefully to learn who the most important characters in the story are. The most important characters are called the **main characters**.

Objectives

- Identify character(s).
- Identify the main character(s).
- Build vocabulary through listening, reading, and discussion.
- Use new vocabulary in written and spoken sentences.

Words to Know

Before reading "Cinderella,"

1. Have students say each word aloud.

2. Ask students if they know what each word means.

   ▶ If students know a word's meaning, have them define it and use it in a sentence.

   ▶ If students don't know a word's meaning, read them the definition and discuss the word with them.

ball – a kind of party where people dance
carriage – an old-fashioned vehicle pulled by horses; sometimes called a coach
cinder – a small piece of wood or coal that has been partly burned
delicate – small and beautifully shaped; easy to damage or break
fair – beautiful
frock – a woman's dress
proud – thinking highly of oneself

Read Aloud

Book Walk

Prepare students by taking them on a Book Walk of "Cinderella." Scan the story together.

1. Turn to the **table of contents**. Help students find today's selection, and turn to that page.

2. Point to and read aloud the **title of the story**.

3. Have students look at the **pictures** of the story. Answers to questions may vary.

   ► What do you think the story is about?
   ► Where do you think the story takes place?
   ► Do you think it's fair to make children do chores around the house?

Objectives

- Make predictions based on title, illustrations, and/or context clues.
- Activate prior knowledge by previewing text and/or discussing topic.
- Listen and respond to texts representing a variety of cultures, time periods, and traditions.

"Cinderella"

Now it's time to read the story. Have students sit next to you so that they can see the pictures and words while you read the story aloud.

Read aloud the entire story. Emphasize Words to Know as you come to them. If appropriate, use the pictures to help show what each word means.

Check Your Reading

"Cinderella"

Have students retell the story in their own words to develop grammar, vocabulary, comprehension, and fluency skills. When finished, **ask students the following questions** to check comprehension and encourage discussion.

Objectives

- Identify character(s).
- Identify the main character(s).

► Name some of the characters in the story. Cinderella; father; stepmother; two stepsisters; fairy godmother; the Prince
► Who helps Cinderella? her fairy godmother
► Who is the most important character in the story? Cinderella
► Is Cinderella's father a main character? Why or why not? No, because he's hardly in the story at all and he's not an important character.
► Is Cinderella a main character? Yes

Explore "Cinderella"

Lesson Overview

	[Offline] "Cinderella"	**30** minutes
Get Ready	Fairy Tales and Characters	
	Words to Know	
Read Aloud	Book Walk	
	"Cinderella"	
Check Your Reading	"Cinderella"	
Reading for Meaning	Characters and What They Do	

[Materials]

Supplied
- "Cinderella," *K¹² Read Aloud Treasury,* pp. 34–43

Keywords

character – a person or animal in a story

fairy tale – a folk tale with magical elements

Advance Preparation

Before working with students, spend a few minutes reviewing Words to Know. Then read the Check Your Reading and Reading for Meaning activities to familiarize yourself with the questions and answers.

Big Ideas

Comprehension requires an understanding of story structure.

[Offline] **30** minutes

"Cinderella"

Work **together** with students to complete offline Get Ready, Read Aloud, Check Your Reading, and Reading for Meaning activities.

Get Ready

Fairy Tales and Characters

Tell students that "Cinderella" is a fairy tale. A **fairy tale** is a folk story with magical parts, such as a talking wolf or a giant who lives at the top of a beanstalk. Magical characters don't exist in real life.

Tell students that you will be discussing the characters and how they act. To better understand characters' actions, it's helpful to think about our own actions in different situations. Answers to questions may vary.

▸ Do you ever complain about doing chores? Why or why not?

▸ Has anyone ever treated you badly? What did you do?

> **Objectives**
> - Identify genre.
> - Describe character(s).
> - Build vocabulary through listening, reading, and discussion.
> - Use new vocabulary in written and spoken sentences.

Words to Know

Before reading "Cinderella,"

1. Have students say each word aloud.

2. Ask students if they know what each word means.

   ▸ If students know a word's meaning, have them define it and use it in a sentence.

   ▸ If students don't know a word's meaning, read them the definition and discuss the word with them.

ball – a kind of party where people dance
carriage – an old-fashioned vehicle pulled by horses; sometimes called a coach
cinder – a small piece of wood or coal that has been partly burned
delicate – small and beautifully shaped; easy to damage or break
fair – beautiful
frock – a woman's dress
proud – thinking highly of oneself

Read Aloud

Book Walk

Prepare students by taking them on a Book Walk of "Cinderella." Scan the story together to revisit the characters and events.

1. Turn to today's selection. Point to and read aloud the **title of the story**.

2. Have students look at the **pictures** of the story. Answers to questions may vary.

    ▸ Do any of the pictures show something magical? What do they show?
    ▸ Describe the characters you see in the pictures.

Objectives
- Identify genre.
- Activate prior knowledge by previewing text and/or discussing topic.
- Listen and respond to texts representing a variety of cultures, time periods, and traditions.

"Cinderella"

Now it's time to read the story. Have students sit next to you so that they can see the pictures and words while you read the story aloud.

Read aloud the entire story. Tell students to listen for parts of the story that couldn't happen in real life, and think about why the characters act the way they do.

Check Your Reading

"Cinderella"

Have students retell the story in their own words to develop grammar, vocabulary, comprehension, and fluency skills. When finished, **ask students the following questions** to check comprehension and encourage discussion.

▸ What kind of story is "Cinderella"? a fairy tale
▸ Name something in the story that tells you "Cinderella" is a fairy tale. Answers will vary.   Could this happen in real life? No
▸ What kind of person is Cinderella? Answers will vary.   What words would you use to describe her? If students have trouble coming up with words, ask if Cinderella is selfish or kind.
▸ How do Cinderella's stepsisters treat her? They are mean to her.
▸ How does Cinderella treat her stepsisters? She is nice to them and does what they tell her to do without complaining.

Objectives
- Identify genre.
- Describe character(s).
- Compare and contrast actions of characters in a text.

Reading for Meaning

Characters and What They Do

Ask students the following questions to further check comprehension. **Help them find answers in the story** if they have trouble responding to a question.

   Reread the information on fairy tales and characters in the Get Ready as needed to help students better understand how characters' actions tell us what kind of people they are.

► Why do you think Cinderella's stepsisters make her do all the chores? Answers will vary.

► How do the stepsisters act when they first hear about the ball? They go wild with delight; they imagine what they will wear.

► Why do you think the stepsisters act this way? Answers will vary.

► What do the stepsisters do when they talk about who will be the most beautiful girl at the ball? They quarrel.

► What does Cinderella do when the stepsisters quarrel? She makes peace between them.

► Why do you think Cinderella helps her stepsisters stop quarreling? Answers will vary.   What does this tell us about Cinderella? Steer students to understand that this shows us that Cinderella is kind.

Objectives

- Seek information in provided sources to answer questions.
- Compare and contrast actions of characters in a text.
- Identify details that explain characters' actions.

Review "Cinderella"

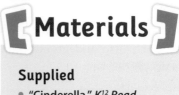

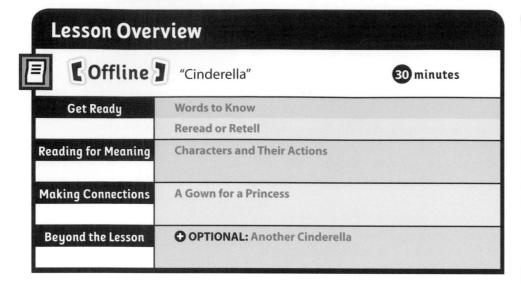

Lesson Overview

Offline	"Cinderella"	30 minutes

Get Ready	Words to Know
	Reread or Retell
Reading for Meaning	Characters and Their Actions
Making Connections	A Gown for a Princess
Beyond the Lesson	⊕ OPTIONAL: Another Cinderella

Materials

Supplied
- "Cinderella," *K¹² Read Aloud Treasury*, pp. 34–43
- *K¹² Language Arts Activity Book*, p. LC 15

Also Needed
- crayons

Keywords

character – a person or animal in a story

 **30** minutes

"Cinderella"

Work **together** with students to complete offline Get Ready, Reading for Meaning, Making Connections, and Beyond the Lesson activities.

Get Ready ....

Words to Know

Ask students to define the following words and use them in a sentence:

ball	cinder	fair	proud
carriage	delicate	frock	

Correct any incorrect or vague definitions.

 Objectives
- Build vocabulary through listening, reading, and discussion.
- Use new vocabulary in written and spoken sentences.

Reread or Retell

If you'd like to, reread the story to students. Otherwise, have students retell the story using the pictures as a guide, or move on to the next activity.

Reading for Meaning ....

Characters and Their Actions

Ask students the following questions to check comprehension. Tell them that *why* characters do something is just as important as *what* they do. How characters think and act tells us what kind of people they are.

 Objectives
- Compare and contrast actions of characters in a text.
- Identify details that explain characters' actions.

- ▶ What do the stepsisters do when the messenger arrives with the glass slipper? They argue about who should try it on first.
- ▶ What do the stepsisters do when Cinderella asks to try on the slipper? They say her foot could never fit such a delicate thing.
- ▶ Why do you think they act like that? Answers will vary.
- ▶ What does Cinderella do for her stepsisters after she and the Prince are married? She gives them rooms in the palace.
- ▶ Why do you think she does this? Answers will vary.
- ▶ What words would you use to describe Cinderella? Answers will vary. Possible answers: *fair; happy; good; beautiful; kind; generous*
- ▶ What words would you use to describe the stepsisters? Answers will vary. Possible answers: *cross; unkind; idle; selfish; proud*

Making Connections

A Gown for a Princess

Turn to page LC 15 in *K¹² Language Arts Activity Book.*

1. Have students connect the dots and then color the picture.

2. Ask students to describe Cinderella. Have them find examples in the story to support their descriptions.

3. Write the words students say around the picture.

Beyond the Lesson

➕ OPTIONAL: Another Cinderella

This activity is intended for students who have extra time and would benefit from hearing a variation of the story. Feel free to skip this activity.

1. Go to a library and look for a copy of *Yeh-Shen: A Cinderella Story from China,* retold by Ai-Ling Louie.

2. Lead a Book Walk, and read aloud *Yeh-Shen.*

3. Discuss how the two stories are alike and different.

4. Ask students which story they like better, and why.

TIP The ending of *Yeh-Shen* involves the sudden death of two unkind characters.

Objectives
- Compare and contrast two texts on the same topic.

Introduce "Sleeping Beauty"

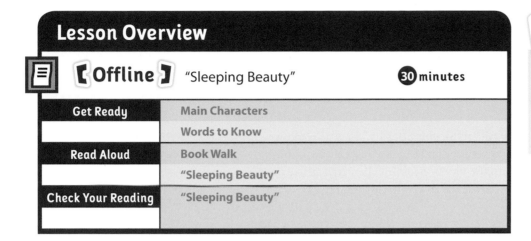

Lesson Overview

【Offline 】 "Sleeping Beauty" **30** minutes

Get Ready	Main Characters
	Words to Know
Read Aloud	Book Walk
	"Sleeping Beauty"
Check Your Reading	"Sleeping Beauty"

Advance Preparation

Read "Sleeping Beauty" before beginning the Read Aloud activity, to locate Words to Know within the text.

Big Ideas

Comprehension requires an understanding of story structure.

【 Materials 】

Supplied

- "Sleeping Beauty,"
  K¹² Read Aloud Treasury,
  pp. 44–51

Story Synopsis

Beautiful Briar-Rose falls into a deep sleep on her 15th birthday after being cursed by a scorned fairy. And so she becomes and remains a "sleeping beauty" for a hundred years until she is rescued by a determined prince. This story contains elements of revenge and magic.

Keywords

character – a person or animal in a story

setting – when and where a story takes place

 **30 minutes**

"Sleeping Beauty"

Work **together** with students to complete offline Get Ready, Read Aloud, and Check Your Reading activities.

Get Ready

Main Characters

Tell students that they will read a story called "Sleeping Beauty." Explain that the people in the story are called **characters**. There can be many characters in a story. Tell them to listen carefully to learn who the most important characters in the story are. The most important characters are called the **main characters**.

Words to Know

Before reading "Sleeping Beauty,"

1. Have students say each word aloud.

2. Ask students if they know what each word means.

   ▸ If students know a word's meaning, have them define it and use it in a sentence.
   ▸ If students don't know a word's meaning, read them the definition and discuss the word with them.

canopy – a cover above a bed
feast – a large, fancy meal attended by many people
hedge – a thick row of bushes
passage – a long, thin space that you can use to get from one place to another
prick – to poke a small hole with something sharp like a pin
spindle – the round stick on a spinning wheel that holds and winds the thread

Objectives

- Identify the main character(s).
- Build vocabulary through listening, reading, and discussion.
- Use new vocabulary in written and spoken sentences.

Read Aloud

Book Walk

Prepare students by taking them on a Book Walk of "Sleeping Beauty." Scan the story together.

1. Turn to the **table of contents**. Help students find today's selection, and turn to that page.

2. Point to and read aloud the **title of the story.**

3. Have students look at the **pictures** of the story. Answers to questions may vary.

   ▸ What do you think the story is about?
   ▸ Where do you think the story takes place?

4. Tell students that if they listen carefully, they will figure out the **setting** of the story. The setting is when and where a story takes place.

> **Objectives**
> - Make predictions based on title, illustrations, and/or context clues.
> - Identify setting.
> - Listen and respond to texts representing a variety of cultures, time periods, and traditions.
> - Use prior knowledge to aid understanding of text.

"Sleeping Beauty"

Now it's time to read the story. Have students sit next to you so that they can see the pictures and words while you read the story aloud.

Read aloud the entire story. Emphasize Words to Know as you come to them. If appropriate, use the pictures to help show what each word means.

TIP Students might benefit from reviewing the pictures in the article "Their Homes Were Their Castles" in the *K¹² World: Amazing Places* magazine.

Check Your Reading

"Sleeping Beauty"

Have students retell the story in their own words to develop grammar, vocabulary, comprehension, and fluency skills. When finished, **ask students the following questions** to check comprehension and encourage discussion. If students have trouble responding to a question, **help them locate the answer in the story**.

▸ Where does the story take place? a peaceful kingdom; a castle
▸ When does the story happen? Answers will vary. Students should understand that the story happens long ago.
▸ Who are the most important, or main, characters in this story? Answers will vary; guide students to mention Briar-Rose and the prince.
▸ Do you think the fairy who casts an evil spell over Briar-Rose is a main character? Why or why not? Answers will vary; have students support their answers with events in the story.
▸ Who is the "sleeping beauty"? Briar-Rose

> **Objectives**
> - Identify setting.
> - Identify the main character(s).
> - Seek information in provided sources to answer questions.

Explore "Sleeping Beauty"

Lesson Overview

[Offline] "Sleeping Beauty" **30** minutes

Get Ready	What Is a Fairy Tale?
	Words to Know
Read Aloud	Book Walk
	"Sleeping Beauty"
Check Your Reading	"Sleeping Beauty"
Reading for Meaning	Fairy-Tale Characters

[Materials]

Supplied

- "Sleeping Beauty,"
  K¹² Read Aloud Treasury,
  pp. 44–51

Keywords

character – a person or
animal in a story

fairy tale – a folk tale with
magical elements

Advance Preparation

Before working with students, spend a few minutes reviewing the Words to Know.
Then review the Check Your Reading and Reading for Meaning activities to familiarize
yourself with the questions and answers.

Big Ideas

Comprehension requires an understanding of story structure.

[Offline] 30 minutes

"Sleeping Beauty"

Work **together** with students to complete offline Get Ready, Read Aloud, Check Your Reading, and Reading for Meaning activities.

Get Ready ....

What Is a Fairy Tale?

Tell students that "Sleeping Beauty" is a fairy tale. A **fairy tale** is a folk story with magical parts, such as a fairy godmother who can turn a pumpkin into a carriage with her wand. Magical characters don't exist in real life. Tell students to listen for parts of the story that could not happen in real life.

Words to Know

Before reading "Sleeping Beauty,"

1. Have students say each word aloud.

2. Ask students if they know what each word means.

   ▸ If students know a word's meaning, have them define it and use it in a sentence.
   ▸ If students don't know a word's meaning, read them the definition and discuss the word with them.

canopy – a cover above a bed
feast – a large, fancy meal attended by many people
hedge – a thick row of bushes
passage – a long, thin space that you can use to get from one place to another
prick – to poke a small hole with something sharp like a pin
spindle – the round stick on a spinning wheel that holds and winds the thread

> **Objectives**
> • Identify genre.
> • Build vocabulary through listening, reading, and discussion.
> • Use new vocabulary in written and spoken sentences.

Read Aloud ....

Book Walk

Prepare students by taking them on a Book Walk of "Sleeping Beauty." Scan the story together to revisit the characters and events.

1. Turn to today's selection. Point to and read aloud the **title of the story**.

2. Have students look at the **pictures** of the story. Answers to questions may vary.

   ▸ What is your favorite picture in the story? Why?
   ▸ Does it show something that can only happen in a fairy tale, or could it happen in real life? How can you tell?

>
> **Objectives**
> • Activate prior knowledge by previewing text and/or discussing topic.
> • Listen and respond to texts representing a variety of cultures, time periods, and traditions.

"Sleeping Beauty"

Now it's time to read the story. Have students sit next to you so that they can see the pictures and words while you read the story aloud.

Read aloud the entire story. Tell students to listen carefully for the parts of the story that are magical and couldn't happen in real life.

Check Your Reading

"Sleeping Beauty"

Have students retell the story in their own words to develop grammar, vocabulary, comprehension, and fluency skills. When finished, **ask students the following questions** to check comprehension and encourage discussion. If students have trouble responding to a question, **help them locate the answer in the story**.

► What kind of story is "Sleeping Beauty?" a fairy tale
► Name something in the story that tells you "Sleeping Beauty" is a fairy tale.
  Answers will vary.   Could this happen in real life? No
► Who casts a spell on Briar-Rose at the feast? the evil fairy
► Do fairies exist in real life? No

Objectives
• Identify genre.

Reading for Meaning

Fairy-Tale Characters

Tell students that fairy tales usually have certain kinds of characters. There is usually a good character such as a fairy. There is usually an evil, or bad, character such as a witch.

Many fairy tales have royal characters. Royal characters are people such as a king, queen, prince, or princess. Royal characters usually live in a castle.

Ask students the following questions to further check comprehension of fairy-tale characters and events. **Help them find answers in the story** if they have trouble responding to a question.

► Name the royal characters in "Sleeping Beauty." the king; the queen; the princess, Briar-Rose; the prince
► Think of another fairy tale you've heard. Does that story have a character that is also in "Sleeping Beauty"? Answers will vary. Characters could be any of the royalty mentioned above, a witch or evil fairy, or a good fairy.
► Can someone really go to a great feast? Yes
► Can someone really cast an evil spell? No
► Can someone really prick their finger on a spindle? Yes
► Can someone really fall asleep for a hundred years? No
► Who is the evil character in "Sleeping Beauty"? the fairy who wasn't invited to the feast
► Which royal character helps Briar-Rose at the end of the story? the prince

Objectives
• Identify genre.
• Identify recurring characters in folk and fairy tales.

Review "Sleeping Beauty"

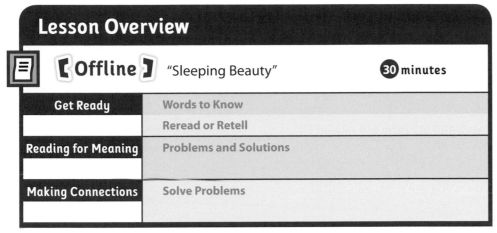

Lesson Overview

[Offline] "Sleeping Beauty"   **30** minutes

Get Ready	Words to Know
	Reread or Retell
Reading for Meaning	Problems and Solutions
Making Connections	Solve Problems

Big Ideas

Comprehension requires an understanding of story structure.

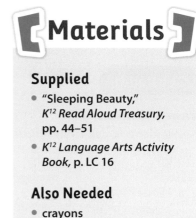

[Materials]

Supplied
- "Sleeping Beauty," *K¹² Read Aloud Treasury,* pp. 44–51
- *K¹² Language Arts Activity Book,* p. LC 16

Also Needed
- crayons

Keywords

problem – an issue a character must solve in a story

solution – how a character solves a problem in a story

 **30 minutes**

"Sleeping Beauty"

Work **together** with students to complete offline Get Ready, Reading for Meaning, and Making Connections activities.

Get Ready ....

Words to Know

Ask students to define the following words and use them in a sentence:

canopy	hedge	prick
feast	passage	spindle

Correct any incorrect or vague definitions.

 Objectives
- Build vocabulary through listening, reading, and discussion.
- Use new vocabulary in written and spoken sentences.

Reread or Retell

If you'd like to, reread the story to students. Otherwise, have students retell the story using the pictures in the book as a guide.

Reading for Meaning ....

Problems and Solutions

Fairy tales usually have a problem that a main character needs to solve. For example, a character might be lost and need to find the way home. Or a character might want to go to a ball but not have a gown or a way to get there. A story can have more than one problem to solve.

Ask students the following questions to check comprehension.

 Objectives
- Identify story structure elements—problem and solution.

▸ What problem does the evil fairy create for the baby Briar-Rose? She casts a spell on the baby that will cause her die on her 15th birthday.

▸ How is the problem of the curse solved? Another fairy changes the spell so Briar-Rose will fall asleep instead of die.

▸ The king's problem is to keep Briar-Rose away from a spinning wheel. How does the king try to solve this problem? He burns all the spinning wheels in the kingdom.

▸ What problem does Briar-Rose have after she pricks her finger on the spindle? She falls into a deep sleep and can't wake up.

▸ How is Briar-Rose's problem solved? The prince kisses Briar-Rose and wakes her up.

Making Connections

Solve Problems

Turn to page LC 16 in *K¹² Language Arts Activity Book*.

1. Have students look at the pictures.

2. Have them describe the problems from "Sleeping Beauty" shown in the pictures on the left.

3. Have students match each problem with its solution on the right.

4. When done, have students color the pictures.

Objectives

- Identify story structure elements—problem and solution.

Introduce "Rapunzel"

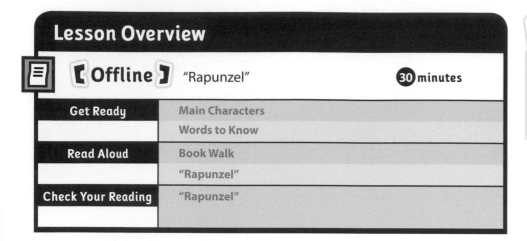

Lesson Overview

[Offline] "Rapunzel"		**30** minutes
Get Ready	Main Characters	
	Words to Know	
Read Aloud	Book Walk	
	"Rapunzel"	
Check Your Reading	"Rapunzel"	

Advance Preparation

Read "Rapunzel" before beginning the Read Aloud activity, to locate Words to Know within the text.

Big Ideas

Comprehension requires an understanding of story structure.

[Materials]

Supplied

- "Rapunzel," *K¹² Read Aloud Treasury,* pp. 52–60

Story Synopsis

Rapunzel—a lovely girl with long golden hair—is locked in a tower by a wicked old witch. How will Rapunzel make her escape?

Keywords

character – a person or animal in a story

 **30 minutes**

"Rapunzel"

Work **together** with students to complete offline Get Ready, Read Aloud, and Check Your Reading activities.

Get Ready

Main Characters

There can be many characters in a story. Tell student to listen carefully to learn who the most important characters in the story are. The most important characters are called the **main characters**.

Words to Know

Before reading "Rapunzel,"

1. Have students say each word aloud.

2. Ask students if they know what each word means.

   ▸ If students know a word's meaning, have them define it and use it in a sentence.
   ▸ If students don't know a word's meaning, read them the definition and discuss the word with them.

braid – hair that has been woven together
fasten – to tie firmly
grasp – to hold on to something tightly
longing – when you want something very much
weep – to cry because you feel very sad
wilderness – an area of land where nobody lives, like a forest or desert

 Objectives

- Identify the main character(s).
- Build vocabulary through listening, reading, and discussion.
- Use new vocabulary in written and spoken sentences.

Read Aloud

Book Walk

Prepare students by taking them on a Book Walk of "Rapunzel." Scan the story together.

1. Turn to the **table of contents.** Help students find today's selection, and turn to that page.

2. Point to and read aloud the **title of the story**.

3. Have students look at the **pictures** of the story. Answers to questions may vary.

   ▸ What do you think the story is about?
   ▸ Where do you think the story takes place?
   ▸ In this story, a character takes plants from someone's garden without permission. Do you think there's ever a time when that would be okay?

Objectives

- Use prior knowledge to aid understanding of text.
- Listen and respond to texts representing a variety of cultures, time periods, and traditions.

"Rapunzel"

Now it's time to read the story. Have students sit next to you so that they can see the pictures and words while you read the story aloud.

Read aloud the entire story. Emphasize Words to Know as you come to them. If appropriate, use the pictures to help show what each word means.

 Students might benefit from reviewing the picture of the towers in the article "Their Homes Were Their Castles" in the *K¹² World: Amazing Places* magazine.

Check Your Reading ....

"Rapunzel"

Have students retell the story in their own words to develop grammar, vocabulary, comprehension, and fluency skills. When finished, **ask students the following questions** to check comprehension and encourage discussion.

- ▶ Who are the most important, or main, characters in this story? Answers will vary; guide students to mention Rapunzel, the witch, and the prince.
- ▶ Why does the witch take the baby? The husband agrees to give the baby to the witch when she catches him stealing rapunzel from her garden.
- ▶ What does the witch do when Rapunzel turns 12 years old? She locks her in a tower.
- ▶ How does the witch enter the tower? She climbs up Rapunzel's long braids.

Objectives
- Identify the main character(s).
- Answer questions requiring literal recall of details.

Explore "Rapunzel"

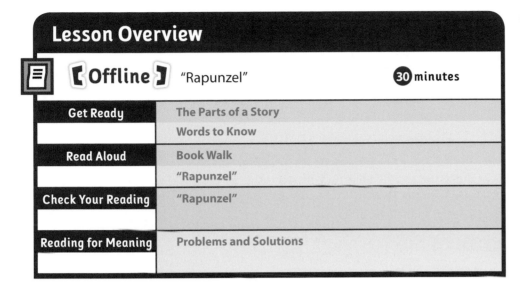

Materials

Supplied
- "Rapunzel," *K¹² Read Aloud Treasury*, pp. 52–60

Keywords

problem – an issue a character must solve in a story

retelling – using your own words to tell a story that you have listened to or read

solution – how a character solves a problem in a story

Advance Preparation

Before working with students, spend a few minutes reviewing Words to Know. Then review the Check Your Reading and Reading for Meaning activities to familiarize yourself with the questions and answers.

Big Ideas

Comprehension requires an understanding of story structure.

[Offline] 30 minutes

"Rapunzel"

Work **together** with students to complete offline Get Ready, Read Aloud, Check Your Reading, and Reading for Meaning activities.

Get Ready ....

The Parts of a Story

Tell students that a story has three main parts: the beginning, the middle, and the end.

> ▶ The **beginning** of a story introduces the characters. Readers find out who they are and where they live.
> ▶ In the **middle** of the story, readers usually learn that one of the main characters has a problem and he or she tries to solve the problem.
> ▶ The **end** of the story tells how the problem is solved, and how everything turns out.

Ask students if they remember the beginning of the story "Rapunzel." Let them retell the beginning if they remember it. If they do not remember, tell them that they will get to hear it again.

Objectives

- Retell the beginning, middle, and end of a story.
- Build vocabulary through listening, reading, and discussion.
- Use new vocabulary in written and spoken sentences.

Words to Know

Before reading "Rapunzel,"

1. Have students say each word aloud.

2. Ask students if they know what each word means.

   > ▶ If students know a word's meaning, have them define it and use it in a sentence.
   > ▶ If students don't know a word's meaning, read them the definition and discuss the word with them.

braid – hair that has been woven together
fasten – to tie firmly
grasp – to hold on to something tightly
longing – when you want something very much
weep – to cry because you feel very sad
wilderness – an area of land where nobody lives, like a forest or desert

Read Aloud

Book Walk

Prepare students by taking them on a Book Walk of "Rapunzel." Scan the story together to revisit the characters and events.

1. Turn to today's selection. Point to and read aloud the **title of the story.**

2. Have students look at the **pictures** of the story.

   ► Can you think of another fairy tale that has a witch? Answers will vary. If students can't recall another story with a witch, remind them of one you know they've heard before.
   ► What did the witch do in that fairy tale? Answers will vary.

Objectives
- Use prior knowledge to aid understanding of text.
- Listen and respond to texts representing a variety of cultures, time periods, and traditions.

"Rapunzel"

Now it's time to read the story. Have students sit next to you so that they can see the pictures and words while you read the story aloud.

Tell students to listen to the story carefully because they will be retelling each main part in their own words. **Read aloud the entire story.** Point to pictures to reinforce main events from the beginning, middle, and end of the story.

Check Your Reading

"Rapunzel"

Ask students the following questions to check comprehension and encourage discussion. Students should retell the beginning, middle, and end of the story in their own words. If students have trouble recalling parts of the story, **have them look at the pictures to guide their retelling.**

Objectives
- Retell the beginning, middle, and end of a story.

► What happens at the beginning of "Rapunzel"? Answers will vary.
► Why does the husband sneak into the witch's garden? His wife is craving the plant called "rapunzel."
► What happens in the middle of "Rapunzel"? Answers will vary.
► How does the prince learn how to enter the tower? He sees the witch call out to Rapunzel and climb her braid.
► What happens at the end of "Rapunzel"? Answers will vary.
► What happens to the prince after he falls out of the tower? Possible answers: He can't see; he wanders in the forest; he finds Rapunzel.

Reading for Meaning

Problems and Solutions

Fairy tales usually have a problem that a main character needs to solve. There can be more than one problem to solve in a story.

Ask students the following questions to further check comprehension. If students have trouble identifying a character's problem, **have them look at the pictures to refresh their memory**.

Objectives

• Identify story structure elements—problem and solution.

▶ What is Rapunzel's problem? She is locked in a tower.
▶ How do Rapunzel and the prince try to solve her problem? They plan to weave a ladder so she can climb down.
▶ When the witch finds out that Rapunzel has met the prince, what is the witch's problem? She needs to keep Rapunzel away from the prince.
▶ How does the witch solve her problem? First she cuts off Rapunzel's braids and drags her to the wilderness. Then she causes the prince to fall out of the tower.
▶ Why can't the prince find Rapunzel right away? He is blinded by thorns.
▶ How does the blinded prince find Rapunzel again? He hears Rapunzel singing in the wilderness and follows the song until he finds her.

Review "Rapunzel"

Lesson Overview

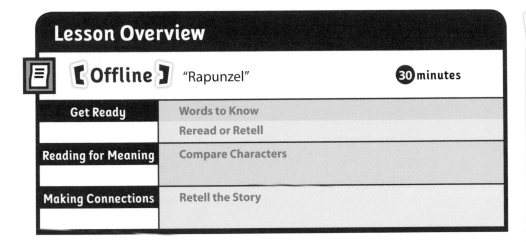

Offline "Rapunzel"	**30** minutes

Get Ready	Words to Know
	Reread or Retell
Reading for Meaning	Compare Characters
Making Connections	Retell the Story

Big Ideas

Comprehension requires an understanding of story structure.

Materials

Supplied
- "Rapunzel," *K¹² Read Aloud Treasury,* pp. 52–60
- *K¹² Language Arts Activity Book,* p. LC 17

Also Needed
- crayons
- scissors, round-end safety
- glue stick

Keywords

character – a person or animal in a story

retelling – using your own words to tell a story that you have listened to or read

sequence – order

[Offline] 30 minutes

"Rapunzel"

Work **together** with students to complete offline Get Ready, Reading for Meaning, and Making Connections activities.

Get Ready ·

Words to Know

Ask students to define the following words and use them in a sentence:

braid	**grasp**	**weep**
fasten	**longing**	**wilderness**

Correct any incorrect or vague definitions.

Objectives

- Build vocabulary through listening, reading, and discussion.
- Use new vocabulary in written and spoken sentences.

Reread or Retell

If you'd like to, reread the story to students. Otherwise, have students retell the story using the pictures in the book as a guide.

Reading for Meaning ·

Compare Characters

Tell students that being familiar with characters from one story can help us understand the characters in another story. The characters are very much alike and do the same kinds of things. We know what to expect of certain characters because we've met similar characters in other stories.

Ask students the following questions to check comprehension.

Objectives

- Describe character(s).
- Compare and contrast actions of characters in a text.
- Make connections with text: text-to-text, text-to-self, text-to-world.

▶ What words would you use to describe the witch? Answers will vary. If students have trouble answering, ask if she is good or evil.

▶ Think of the fairy that casts a spell on Briar-Rose in "Sleeping Beauty" or an evil character from another fairy tale. How are the witch in "Rapunzel" and the evil character from the other story alike? Answers will vary.

▶ What words would you use to describe the prince? Answers will vary. If students have trouble answering, ask if he is brave or scared.

▶ Think of the prince from "Sleeping Beauty" or a prince from another fairy tale. How are the prince in "Rapunzel" and the prince in the other story alike? Answers will vary.

Making Connections

Retell the Story

Turn to page LC 17 in *K¹² Language Arts Activity Book*.

1. Have students color the pictures.

2. Help them cut out the pictures.

3. Have them put the pictures in sequential order.

4. Help students glue the pictures to another sheet of paper.

5. Have them retell "Rapunzel," using the pictures as a guide.

Objectives

- Sequence pictures illustrating story events.
- Retell a story using illustrations from the text as a guide.

Introduce "The Grand Canyon"

Unit Overview

In this unit, students will explore the theme of *Dig Deep* through the following reading selections:
- ► "The Grand Canyon"
- ► *Mike Mulligan and His Steam Shovel*

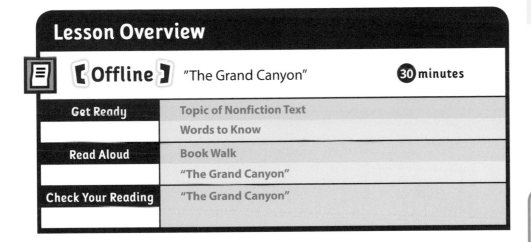

Lesson Overview

☰	【 Offline 】 "The Grand Canyon"	30 minutes
Get Ready	Topic of Nonfiction Text	
	Words to Know	
Read Aloud	Book Walk	
	"The Grand Canyon"	
Check Your Reading	"The Grand Canyon"	

Advance Preparation

Read "The Grand Canyon" before beginning the Read Aloud activity, to locate Words to Know within the text.

【 Materials 】

Supplied
- "The Grand Canyon," *K¹² World: Amazing Places,* pp. 12–19

Story Synopsis

From above, the Grand Canyon looks like a giant rip in the state of Arizona. Its overall size and the colorful layers of rock in its steep walls make it one of the world's seven natural wonders.

Keywords

nonfiction – writings about true things

topic – the subject of a text

 **30** minutes

"The Grand Canyon"

Work **together** with students to complete offline Get Ready, Read Aloud, and Check Your Reading activities.

Get Ready

Topic of Nonfiction Text

Tell students that they are going to hear an article called "The Grand Canyon." Point out that everything in this article is true. This kind of writing is called **nonfiction**. Nonfiction text is writing that is true and about real things.

Tell students that what a nonfiction text is mostly about is called the **topic**. Tell them to listen to the article carefully to figure out the topic.

 Objectives
- Identify different types of text.
- Identify topic.
- Increase concept and content vocabulary.
- Use new vocabulary in written and spoken sentences.

Words to Know

Before reading "The Grand Canyon,"

1. Have students say each word aloud.

2. Ask students if they know what each word means.

   ► If students know a word's meaning, have them define it and use it in a sentence.
   ► If students don't know a word's meaning, read them the definition and discuss the word with them.

canyon – a deep valley with steep sides
edge – a rim, like the rim of a bowl
soil – dirt

Read Aloud

Book Walk

Prepare students by taking them on a Book Walk of "The Grand Canyon." Scan the magazine article together and ask students to make predictions about the text.

1. Turn to the **table of contents.** Help students find today's selection, and turn to that page.

2. Point to and read aloud the **title of the article.**

3. Have students look at the **pictures** in the article. Answers to questions may vary.

    ▸ What do you think the article is about?
    ▸ Have you ever heard of the Grand Canyon? Have you ever seen pictures of it?

4. Point to and read aloud any **headers, captions, or other features** that stand out. Answers to questions may vary.

    ▸ What do you think the article might tell us about the Grand Canyon?

Objectives
- Make predictions based on title, illustrations, and/or context clues.
- Read and listen to a variety of texts for information and pleasure independently or as part of a group.

"The Grand Canyon"

Now it's time to read the article. Have students sit next to you so that they can see the pictures and words while you read the article aloud.

Read aloud the entire article. Emphasize Words to Know as you come to them. If appropriate, use the pictures to help show what each word means.

Check Your Reading

"The Grand Canyon"

Have students retell the article in their own words to develop grammar, vocabulary, comprehension, and fluency skills. When finished, **ask students the following questions** to check comprehension and encourage discussion. If students have trouble recalling facts, **help them locate the answer in the article.**

- ▸ What is the article mostly about? the Grand Canyon
- ▸ What is the topic of this article? the Grand Canyon
- ▸ Is the Grand Canyon real? Yes
- ▸ What does it mean if something is real? It means it's true and not made up.
- ▸ Everything in this article is true. What kind of writing is this? nonfiction
- ▸ Where is the Grand Canyon? Arizona
- ▸ How deep is the Grand Canyon? 1 mile

Objectives
- Identify topic.
- Identify and define reality.
- Identify different types of text.
- Answer questions requiring literal recall of details.

Explore "The Grand Canyon"

Materials

Lesson Overview

Offline	"The Grand Canyon"	30 minutes

Get Ready	What Is a Fact?
	Words to Know
Read Aloud	Book Walk
	"The Grand Canyon"
Check Your Reading	"The Grand Canyon"
Reading for Meaning	Facts About the Grand Canyon

Supplied
- "The Grand Canyon," *K¹² World: Amazing Places,* pp. 12–19

Keywords
fact – something that can be proven true
nonfiction – writings about true things
topic – the subject of a text

Advance Preparation

Before working with students, spend a few minutes reviewing Words to Know. Then review the Check Your Reading and Reading for Meaning activities to familiarize yourself with the questions and answers.

 **30 minutes**

"The Grand Canyon"

Work **together** with students to complete offline Get Ready, Read Aloud, Check Your Reading, and Reading for Meaning activities.

Get Ready

What Is a Fact?

Tell students that nonfiction articles are filled with **facts**. A fact is something that you can prove is true.

- ▸ What is your name? Answers will vary.
  Say: Your name is a fact. You can prove what your name is.
- ▸ How old are you? Answers will vary.
  Say: Your age is a fact. You can prove how old you are.
- ▸ Does an apple grow on a tree? Yes
  Say: This is a fact. You can prove that an apple grows on a tree.
- ▸ Does a horse have four legs? Yes
  Say: This is a fact. You can prove that a horse has four legs.

Remind students that they have heard an article called "The Grand Canyon." Ask students to tell you a fact about the Grand Canyon. If they cannot name a fact, tell them that they will have a chance to hear facts about the Grand Canyon when you reread the article.

Objectives

- Identify facts in informational text.
- Increase concept and content vocabulary.
- Use new vocabulary in written and spoken sentences.

Words to Know

Before reading "The Grand Canyon,"

1. Have students say each word aloud.

2. Ask students if they know what each word means.

   - ▸ If students know a word's meaning, have them define it and use it in a sentence.
   - ▸ If students don't know a word's meaning, read them the definition and discuss the word with them.

canyon – a deep valley with steep sides
edge – a rim, like the rim of a bowl
soil – dirt

Read Aloud

Book Walk

Prepare students by taking them on a Book Walk of "The Grand Canyon." Scan the magazine article together to revisit the text.

1. Turn to today's selection.

2. Point to and read aloud the **title of the article.**

3. Have students look at the **pictures** in the article.

   ▶ What do all the pictures in the article show? things about the Grand Canyon

   ▶ Why are all the pictures about the Grand Canyon? The article is about the Grand Canyon.

   ▶ What is the topic of the article? the Grand Canyon

Objectives

- Identify topic.
- Read and listen to a variety of texts for information and pleasure, independently or as part of a group.

"The Grand Canyon"

Now it's time to read the article. Have students sit next to you so that they can see the pictures and words while you read the article aloud.

Read aloud the entire article. Remind students to listen for facts about the Grand Canyon.

Check Your Reading

"The Grand Canyon"

Have students retell the article in their own words to develop grammar, vocabulary, comprehension, and fluency skills. When finished, **ask students the following questions** to check comprehension and encourage discussion. If students have trouble recalling facts, **help them locate the answer in the article.**

▶ The article about the Grand Canyon is filled with facts. What is this kind of writing called? nonfiction

▶ What is special about a fact? It is true.

▶ The article says astronauts can see the Grand Canyon from outer space. Is this a fact? Yes

▶ How do you know this is a fact? You can prove it.

▶ Who comes to visit the Grand Canyon? people from all over the world

▶ How wide is the Grand Canyon? 18 miles

Objectives

- Identify different types of text.
- Identify facts in informational text.
- Answer questions requiring literal recall of details.

Reading for Meaning

Facts About the Grand Canyon

Ask students the following questions to further check comprehension. If students have trouble recalling a fact, **help them locate the answer in the article**.

- ► If you were standing on one edge of the Grand Canyon at its widest point and your best friend was on the other edge, would you be able to see each other? No Why not? The canyon is too wide to see someone on the other side.
- ► If you could walk across the Grand Canyon, how long would it take? six hours
- ► What made the Grand Canyon so wide and deep? water; the Colorado River
- ► How did the Colorado River make the Grand Canyon deeper and deeper? It carried away the soil.
- ► How long did it take to make the Grand Canyon? many thousands of years
- ► What is something you can do when you visit the Grand Canyon? Answers will vary. Possible answers: *hike; camp; ride a raft*

Review "The Grand Canyon"

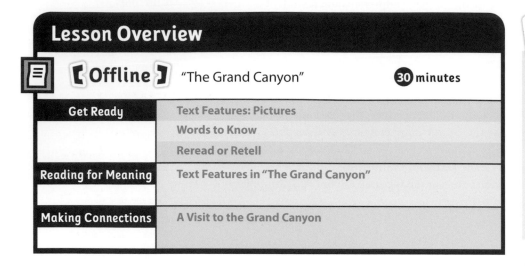

Lesson Overview	
[Offline] "The Grand Canyon"	**30** minutes

Get Ready	Text Features: Pictures
	Words to Know
	Reread or Retell
Reading for Meaning	Text Features in "The Grand Canyon"
Making Connections	A Visit to the Grand Canyon

Materials

Supplied

- "The Grand Canyon,"
  K¹² World: Amazing Places,
  pp. 12–19
- *K¹² Language Arts Activity
  Book,* p. LC 19

Also Needed

- crayons

Keywords

text feature – part of a text
that helps a reader locate
information and determine
what is most important; some
examples are the title, table of
contents, headings, pictures,
and glossary

Big Ideas

▸ Comprehension is facilitated by an understanding of physical presentation
(headings, subheads, graphics, and other features).
▸ Comprehension is enhanced when information is presented through more
than one learning modality; learning modalities are visual (seeing), auditory
(hearing), and kinesthetic (touching).

[Offline] 30 minutes

"The Grand Canyon"

Work **together** with students to complete offline Get Ready, Reading for Meaning, and Making Connections activities.

Get Ready

Text Features: Pictures

Tell students that **pictures are an important part of magazine articles.** Sometimes the ideas in an article can be hard to understand. Seeing **pictures can make it easier to understand those ideas.**

Tell students that they should also pay attention to the words found on or below a picture. Those words tell us what the picture is about and give extra information that can help us better understand the ideas in an article.

Words to Know

Ask students to define the following words and use them in a sentence:

canyon   **edge**   **soil**

Correct any incorrect or vague definitions.

Reread or Retell

If you'd like to, reread the article to students. Otherwise, have students retell the article using the pictures as a guide, or move on to the next activity.

> **Objectives**
> - Use visual text features to aid understanding of text.
> - Increase concept and content vocabulary.
> - Use new vocabulary in written and spoken sentences.

Reading for Meaning

Text Features in "The Grand Canyon"

Ask students the following questions to check comprehension.

Objectives
- Use visual text features to aid understanding of text.
- Identify purpose of environmental print.

1. Point to the picture of the football field on page 15.

   ▸ Why is there a picture of a football field on this page? to help readers understand how wide the Grand Canyon is

2. Point to the picture of the bridge on page 15.

   ▸ What do the picture of the bridge and the text below it help readers understand? how long it would take to walk across the Grand Canyon

3. Point to the picture on page 16.

   ▸ Why is there a building at the bottom of the Grand Canyon? to show how deep the canyon is
   ▸ What does the white arrow tell readers? that the Grand Canyon is a mile deep

4. Point to the picture on page 17.

   ▸ What do the white arrows on the picture tell readers? how wide, deep, and long the Grand Canyon is

5. Point to the picture of the trail sign at the bottom of page 18.

   ▸ What does this picture show? a trail sign
   ▸ What does the trail sign tell us? It shows where you can go hiking in the Grand Canyon.

Making Connections

A Visit to the Grand Canyon

Turn to page LC 19 in *K¹² Language Arts Activity Book*.

1. Have students draw a picture of what they would enjoy doing if they were to visit the Grand Canyon.

2. When they have finished drawing, ask students to explain their picture.

3. Help them complete the sentence at the bottom of the page by writing the words that they dictate.

Objectives

- Respond to text through art, writing, and/or drama.
- Create illustrations that represent personal connections to text.

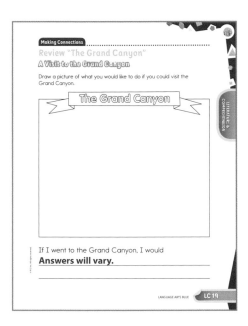

Introduce *Mike Mulligan and His Steam Shovel*

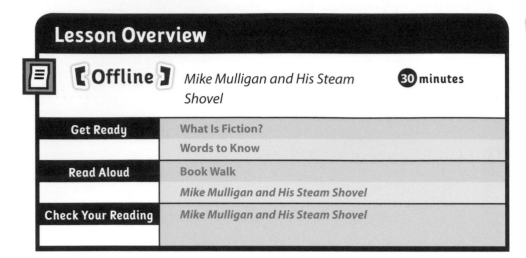

Lesson Overview		
〔 Offline 〕	*Mike Mulligan and His Steam Shovel*	**30** minutes
Get Ready	What Is Fiction?	
	Words to Know	
Read Aloud	Book Walk	
	Mike Mulligan and His Steam Shovel	
Check Your Reading	*Mike Mulligan and His Steam Shovel*	

Advance Preparation

Read *Mike Mulligan and His Steam Shovel* before beginning the Read Aloud activity, to locate Words to Know within the text.

〔 Materials 〕

Supplied
- *Mike Mulligan and His Steam Shovel* by Virginia Lee Burton

Story Synopsis

Mike and his trusty steam shovel, Mary Anne, have worked together happily for many years. Now Mike fears they might be replaced by new and modern shovels. What will become of Mike and Mary Anne?

Keywords

fiction – make-believe stories

 **30** minutes

Mike Mulligan and His Steam Shovel

Work **together** with students to complete offline Get Ready, Read Aloud, and Check Your Reading activities.

Get Ready

What Is Fiction?

Tell students that today they will read a picture book story called *Mike Mulligan and His Steam Shovel*. Explain that many picture book stories are make-believe. This kind of writing is called **fiction**. Fiction stories are made-up stories about people and things that are not real.

Explain to students that good readers can tell that a story is fiction, or make-believe, if things in the story couldn't happen in real life. Things like talking animals, machines with faces, or people who can fly are all make-believe. Good readers look for hints in the pictures and the words of a story to find out if the story is fiction.

Objectives
- Identify different types of text.
- Build vocabulary through listening, reading, and discussion.
- Use new vocabulary in written and spoken sentences.

Words to Know

Before reading *Mike Mulligan and His Steam Shovel*,

1. Have students say each word and phrase aloud.

2. Ask students if they know what each word and phrase means.

   ► If students know a word or phrase's meaning, have them define it and use it in a sentence.
   ► If students don't know a word or phrase's meaning, read them the definition and discuss the word or phrase with them.

cellar – a basement; a room under a building
furnace – something like a big oven, but it is used to heat a building
steam – the hot mist that is formed when water boils
steam shovel – a big, steam-driven machine used for digging
town hall – a building that has local government offices, like the mayor's office

Read Aloud

Book Walk

Prepare students by taking them on a Book Walk of *Mike Mulligan and His Steam Shovel*. Scan the book together, and ask students to make predictions about the story.

1. Have students look at the pictures on the **front cover**. Point to and read aloud the **book title**.

   ▶ What do you think the book is about? Answers will vary.

2. Have students point to the name of the **author and illustrator**. Read the name of the author and illustrator. Explain that sometimes the author of a book is also the illustrator.

3. Have students locate the **title page**. Explain that the title page repeats the book title, author's name, and illustrator's name.

4. Look through the book. Have students describe what they see in the **pictures**. All answers will vary.

   ▶ Where do you think the story takes place?
   ▶ What do you think might happen in the story?
   ▶ Have you ever pretended that one of your toys was real, or alive?

Objectives

- Make predictions based on title, illustrations, and/or context clues.
- Read and listen to a variety of texts for information and pleasure independently or as part of a group.

Mike Mulligan and His Steam Shovel

Now it's time to read the story. Have students sit next to you so that they can see the pictures and words while you read the story aloud.

Read aloud the entire story. Tell students to listen carefully for parts of the story that aren't real. Tell them also to look for things in the pictures that might be make-believe. Emphasize Words to Know as you come to them. If appropriate, use the pictures to help show what a word or phrase means.

Check Your Reading ....

Mike Mulligan and His Steam Shovel

Have students retell the story in their own words to develop grammar, vocabulary, comprehension, and fluency skills.

Objectives
- Identify different types of text.
- Answer questions requiring literal recall of details.

1. When students are finished retelling the story, **ask them the following questions** to check comprehension and encourage discussion.

   ▸ Is *Mike Mulligan and His Steam Shovel* a real story or a made-up story? made-up

   ▸ How can you tell? Answers will vary. Example: the steam shovel smiles.

   ▸ Name something that Mike and Mary Anne help build at beginning of the story. Answers will vary. Possible answers: *canals; highways; landing fields; cellars for skyscrapers*

   ▸ What color is Mary Anne? red

2. Turn to page 15, and have students look at the picture.

   ▸ What is make-believe in this picture? The steam shovel is crying.

   ▸ What does this tell you about the story? The story is make-believe, or made up; the story is fiction.

Explore *Mike Mulligan and His Steam Shovel*

Lesson Overview

[Offline]	*Mike Mulligan and His Steam Shovel*	**30** minutes

Get Ready	**Pictures Help Tell a Story**	
	Words to Know	
Read Aloud	**Book Walk**	
	Mike Mulligan and His Steam Shovel	
Check Your Reading	*Mike Mulligan and His Steam Shovel*	
Reading for Meaning	**Clues Found in Pictures**	

[Materials]

Supplied

- *Mike Mulligan and His Steam Shovel* by Virginia Lee Burton

Keywords

author – a writer
illustrator – the person who draws the pictures that go with a story

Advance Preparation

Before working with students, spend a few minutes reviewing Words to Know. Then review the Check Your Reading and Reading for Meaning activities to familiarize yourself with the questions and answers.

Big Ideas

► The author writes a story.
► An illustrator draws pictures that accompany a story.

[Offline] (30) minutes

Mike Mulligan and His Steam Shovel

Work **together** with students to complete offline Get Ready, Read Aloud, Check Your Reading, and Reading for Meaning activities.

Get Ready ....

Pictures Help Tell a Story

Tell students that the **pictures in a book help readers better understand the story.** Sometimes readers will find information in the pictures that's not written in the words of the story. Good readers look at the pictures while listening to a story to discover that extra information.

Words to Know

Before reading *Mike Mulligan and His Steam Shovel,*

1. Have students say each word and phrase aloud.

2. Ask students if they know what each word and phrase means.

   ▸ If students know a word or phrase's meaning, have them define it and use it in a sentence.
   ▸ If students don't know a word or phrase's meaning, read them the definition and discuss the word or phrase with them.

cellar – a basement; a room under a building
furnace – something like a big oven, but it is used to heat a building
steam – the hot mist that is formed when water boils
steam shovel – a big, steam-driven machine used for digging
town hall – a building that has local government offices, like the mayor's office

> **Objectives**
> • Describe illustrations and their relationship to story events.
> • Build vocabulary through listening, reading, and discussion.
> • Use new vocabulary in written and spoken sentences.

Read Aloud

Book Walk

Prepare students by taking them on a Book Walk of *Mike Mulligan and His Steam Shovel*. Scan the book together. Answers to questions may vary.

1. Point to and read aloud the **book title**.

2. Have students locate the name of the **author and illustrator**.

   ▸ Who is the author and illustrator of this book? Virginia Lee Burton
   ▸ What does it mean to be an author?
   ▸ What does it mean to be an illustrator?

3. Have students locate the title page.

   ▸ What information is found on the title page?

4. Look through the book. Have students describe what they see in the **pictures.**

   ▸ Have you ever seen big machines working at a construction site?
   ▸ Have you ever seen a big machine that looks like Mary Anne?

Objectives
- Identify author.
- Identify illustrator.
- Describe the role of author and/or illustrator.
- Read and listen to a variety of texts for information and pleasure independently or as part of a group.

Mike Mulligan and His Steam Shovel

Now it's time to read the story. Have students sit next to you so that they can see the pictures and words while you read the story aloud.

   Read aloud the entire story. Have students look at the pictures carefully as you read aloud so they can see how each picture relates to the text.

Check Your Reading

Mike Mulligan and His Steam Shovel

Have students retell the story in their own words to develop grammar, vocabulary, comprehension, and fluency skills. When finished, **ask students the following questions** to check comprehension and encourage discussion.

1. Show the pictures on pages 4 and 5.

   ▸ What do you see in these pictures? What's happening in the story? Answers may vary; guide students to understand that the pictures show Mike and Mary Anne digging canals.

2. Show the pictures on pages 8 and 9.

   ▸ What do you see in these pictures? What's happening in the story? Answers may vary; guide students to understand that Mike and Mary Anne are lowering hills so highways can be built.

3. Show the picture on page 16.

   ▸ What do you see in this picture? other steam shovels that were thrown away in a junkyard   What does this picture tell you about Mary Anne? Guide students to understand that the picture shows what could possibly happen to Mary Anne.

Objectives
- Describe illustrations and their relationship to story events.

Reading for Meaning

Clues Found in Pictures

Tell students that the **pictures in a story can sometimes give readers clues to help figure out the meaning of words** they don't know. Pictures can also tell readers important information, such as where and when a story takes place.

Objectives

- Identify and use picture clues to define words.
- Describe illustrations and their relationship to story events.

1. Have students look at the pictures on pages 4 and 5 while you read aloud the paragraph on page 5. Explain that they can figure out what the word *canal* means by looking at the pictures. Point out how Mary Anne is digging in the picture on page 4. The next picture shows the same place, but now boats are moving through water that looks like a river. So a *canal* is probably a man-made river.

2. Have students look at the picture on the pages indicated while you **read aloud** each of the following sentences from the story:

   ▸ Pages 26–27: "They finished the first corner neat and square . . ."
   ▸ Page 29: "They finished the second corner neat and square . . ."
   ▸ Page 31: "They finished the third corner . . . neat and square."
   ▸ Page 35: "Four corners . . . neat and square."

3. Help students use the pictures to determine the meaning of *neat and square*.

   ▸ What do you think *neat and square* means? straight; with corners like those of a square   Why do you think this? Each picture shows a corner that is straight and perfect.

4. Have students look at the picture on the pages indicated while you **read aloud** the following sentence from the story:

   ▸ Pages 20–21: "When they got there they found that the selectmen were just deciding who should dig the cellar for the new town hall."

5. Help students use the picture to determine the meaning of *selectmen*.

   ▸ What is happening in the picture? Mike is talking to people and showing Mary Anne to them.
   ▸ After looking at the picture and hearing the word *deciding* in the sentence, what do you think the word *selectmen* probably means? the people in the town who make decisions, or choices

6. Point to the pictures on page 26 and page 36.

   ▸ Is this story happening now or in the past? in the past   How can you tell? old-fashioned car; milk truck pulled by a horse; people wearing old-fashioned clothes

Reading for Meaning

Sensory Language: Sounds

Ask students the following questions to check comprehension.

Objectives

- Identify author's use of sensory language.
- Make inferences based on text and/or prior knowledge.

1. **Read aloud** this sentence from the story:
   "Clang! Clang! Clang! The Fire Department arrived."

   ► Which words help you hear a sound in your head? *Clang! Clang! Clang!*
   ► What would make this sound? a loud bell
   ► What would have a loud bell? the Fire Department truck

2. **Read aloud**:
   "Dirt was flying everywhere, and the smoke and steam were so thick that the people could hardly see anything. But listen! Bing! Bang! Crash! Slam! Louder and louder. Faster and faster."

   ► Which words help you hear sounds in your head? *Bing! Bang! Crash! Slam!*
   ► What is making these sounds? Mary Anne; the steam shovel
   ► What do these sounds tell you about what Mary Anne is doing? Mary Anne is working hard and fast.

Making Connections

A Day with Mary Anne

Tell students that Mike is lending them Mary Anne for the day. Have them think about what they would do with a steam shovel. Turn to page LC 21 in *K¹² Language Arts Activity Book*.

Objectives

- Respond to text through art, writing, and/or drama.
- Create illustrations that represent personal connections to text.

1. Have students color and cut out Mary Anne.

2. Help students glue their steam shovel to a larger piece of paper or board, and then have them draw a scene that shows what they would do with it.

3. When done, have students describe their adventure with the steam shovel.

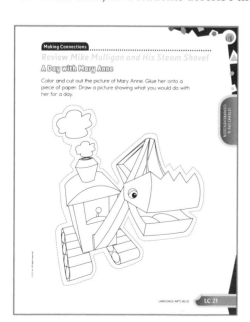

Beyond the Lesson

⊕ OPTIONAL: *I Stink!*

This activity is intended for students who have extra time and would benefit from hearing a book about a character similar to Mary Anne the steam shovel. Feel free to skip this activity.

1. Go to a library and look for a copy of *I Stink!* by Kate and Jim McMullen.

2. Lead a Book Walk, and then read the selection aloud.

3. Have students explain how Mary Anne and the garbage truck are alike and different.

4. Ask students which words help them hear what is happening in the story.

Objectives

- Compare and contrast two texts on the same topic.
- Identify author's use of sensory language.

Introduce "The Tale of Peter Rabbit"

Unit Overview

In this unit, students will explore the theme of *Peter Rabbit* through the following reading selections:

- ▶ "The Tale of Peter Rabbit"
- ▶ "The Tale of Benjamin Bunny"
- ▶ "The Tale of The Flopsy Bunnies"

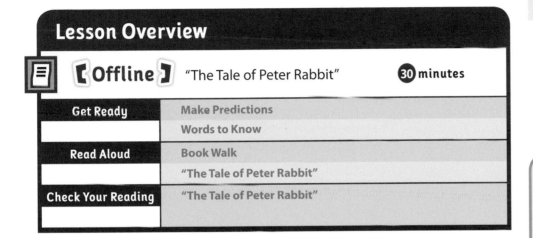

Lesson Overview		
Offline "The Tale of Peter Rabbit"		**30** minutes
Get Ready	Make Predictions	
	Words to Know	
Read Aloud	Book Walk	
	"The Tale of Peter Rabbit"	
Check Your Reading	"The Tale of Peter Rabbit"	

Materials

Supplied

- "The Tale of Peter Rabbit," *The Complete Adventures of Peter Rabbit* by Beatrix Potter, pp. 7–20

Story Synopsis

Peter, a mischievous rabbit, can't resist sneaking into Mr. McGregor's garden for a tasty meal. Is this his lucky day or will Peter get caught?

Keywords

prediction – a guess about what might happen that is based on information in a story and what you already know

Advance Preparation

Read "The Tale of Peter Rabbit" before beginning the Read Aloud activity, to locate Words to Know within the text.

Big Ideas

Comprehension entails actively thinking about what is being read.

[Offline] ⏱ 30 minutes

"The Tale of Peter Rabbit"

Work **together** with students to complete offline Get Ready, Read Aloud, and Check Your Reading activities.

Get Ready ●●

Make Predictions

Introduce students to making predictions by explaining that **a prediction is a guess** about what might happen in a story.

1. Tell students that sometimes we think we know what's going to happen in a story, and then we're surprised because something different occurs. Making predictions helps us to be active readers. It makes us want to keep reading a story to see if what we predict happens or not.

2. Have students practice making a prediction.
   Say: Paula woke up and looked outside the window. The ground was covered with a thick blanket of snow. "Oh, boy!" she shouted. Paula got dressed quickly and ran outside.

   ▸ What do you think, or predict, will happen next? Why? Answers will vary.

TIP Predictions are neither right nor wrong. We make the best prediction we can, based on the information we have. Do not to describe a prediction as "wrong" because this may discourage students from making predictions.

Words to Know

Before reading "The Tale of Peter Rabbit,"

1. Have students say each word aloud.

2. Ask students if they know what each word means.

   ▸ If students know a word's meaning, have them define it and use it in a sentence.
   ▸ If students don't know a word's meaning, read them the definition and discuss the word with them.

damp – a little wet
exert – when you work hard to do something
fortnight – two weeks
hoe – a gardening tool used for weeding, with a long handle and a small, square blade at the end
implore – beg
lane – a small road; a path
mischief – playful behavior that might cause trouble
wheelbarrow – a small cart with handles and one wheel in the front; it's used to carry things

Objectives

- Make predictions before and during reading.
- Build vocabulary through listening, reading, and discussion.
- Use new vocabulary in written and spoken sentences.

Read Aloud

Book Walk

Prepare students by taking them on a Book Walk of "The Tale of Peter Rabbit." Scan the story together, and ask students to make predictions.

1. Turn to the **table of contents**. Help students find today's selection, and turn to that page.

2. Point to and read aloud the **title of the story**.

3. Have students look at the **pictures** of the story. Answers to questions may vary.

    ▸ What do you think the story is about?

    ▸ Where do you think the story takes place?

    ▸ Have you ever seen a rabbit or other small, wild animal in your backyard or neighborhood?

"The Tale of Peter Rabbit"

Now it's time to read the story. Have students sit next to you so that they can see the pictures and words while you read the story aloud.

Read aloud the entire story. Pause at the following points in the story to ask students what they predict will happen next. Jot down their predictions for later reference.

▸ Page 11: Peter runs to Mr. McGregor's garden and squeezes under the gate.

▸ Page 12: Mr. McGregor runs after Peter.

▸ Page 14: Peter sneezes while hiding in the tool shed.

▸ Page 18: Peter runs toward the gate in front of Mr. McGregor.

Check Your Reading

"The Tale of Peter Rabbit"

Have students retell the story in their own words to develop grammar, vocabulary, comprehension, and fluency skills. When finished, **ask students the following questions** to check comprehension and encourage discussion. Answers to questions may vary.

▸ What did you predict would happen when Peter ran into Mr. McGregor's garden?

▸ Were you surprised that Mr. McGregor didn't catch Peter on page 12? Why or why not?

▸ Did you think Mr. McGregor would catch Peter when he sneezed in the tool shed? Why or why not?

▸ What did you predict would happen when Peter ran across the garden in front of Mr. McGregor? What really happened?

Explore "The Tale of Peter Rabbit"

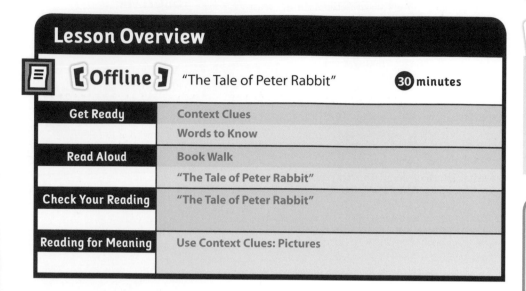

Lesson Overview

[Offline] "The Tale of Peter Rabbit" **30** minutes

Get Ready	Context Clues
	Words to Know
Read Aloud	Book Walk
	"The Tale of Peter Rabbit"
Check Your Reading	"The Tale of Peter Rabbit"
Reading for Meaning	Use Context Clues: Pictures

Materials

Supplied

- "The Tale of Peter Rabbit," *The Complete Adventures of Peter Rabbit* by Beatrix Potter, pp. 7–20

Keywords

context – the parts of a sentence or passage surrounding a word

context clues – a word or phrase in a text that helps you figure out the meaning of an unknown word

Advance Preparation

Before working with students, spend a few minutes reviewing Words to Know. Then review the Check Your Reading and Reading for Meaning activities to familiarize yourself with the questions and answers.

Big Ideas

Early readers acquire vocabulary through active exposure (by talking and listening, being read to, and receiving explicit instruction).

[Offline] ⏱ 30 minutes

"The Tale of Peter Rabbit"

Work **together** with students to complete offline Get Ready, Read Aloud, Check Your Reading, and Reading for Meaning activities.

Get Ready ··

Context Clues

Introduce students to the use of **context clues**. Explain that readers can sometimes use clues to figure out the meaning of a word. The words, phrases, and sentences around an unfamiliar word can give hints to its meaning.

1. Have students practice using context clues.
   Say: It was raining so hard that we had to postpone our game until tomorrow.

   ▸ What do you think the word *postpone* means? Answers will vary.

2. Tell students that the phrases *raining so hard* and *until tomorrow* are clues to the meaning of the word *postpone*. These clues help us figure out that *postpone* means "put off something until later." We can figure this out by thinking about the words that come before and after *postpone*.

3. Explain to students that looking at the pictures on a page can also help us figure out what an unfamiliar word means.

> **Objectives**
> - Identify and use context clues to define words.
> - Build vocabulary through listening, reading, and discussion.
> - Use new vocabulary in written and spoken sentences.

Words to Know

Before reading "The Tale of Peter Rabbit,"

1. Have students say each word aloud.

2. Ask students if they know what each word means.

   ▸ If students know a word's meaning, have them define it and use it in a sentence.
   ▸ If students don't know a word's meaning, read them the definition and discuss the word with them.

damp – a little wet
exert – when you work hard to do something
fortnight – two weeks
hoe – a gardening tool used for weeding, with a long handle and a small, square blade at the end
implore – beg
lane – a small road; a path
mischief – playful behavior that might cause trouble
wheelbarrow – a small cart with handles and one wheel in the front; it's used to carry things

Read Aloud

Book Walk

Prepare students by taking them on a Book Walk of "The Tale of Peter Rabbit."
Scan the story together to revisit the characters and events.

1. Turn to today's selection. Point to and read aloud the **title of the story**.

2. Have students look at the **pictures** of the story. Answers to questions will vary.

    ▸ What do you see Peter doing in the pictures that might get him in trouble?
    ▸ Did you ever get in trouble for going somewhere without permission?

Objectives

- Activate prior knowledge by previewing text and/or discussing topic.
- Read and listen to a variety of texts for information and pleasure independently or as part of a group.

"The Tale of Peter Rabbit"

Now it's time to read the story. Have students sit next to you so that they can see the pictures and words while you read the story aloud.

Read aloud the entire story. Tell students to listen to the words before and after an unknown word to help figure out what the word means. Remind them to look at the pictures for clues, too.

Check Your Reading

"The Tale of Peter Rabbit"

Have students retell the story in their own words. When finished, **ask students the questions** to check their ability to use context clues.

1. **Read aloud** the following sentence from the story:
    "Peter gave himself up for lost, and shed big tears . . . ."

    ▸ What does the word *shed* mean? cried
    ▸ What word or words give you a clue? Guide students to the clue word *tears*.

2. **Read aloud**:
    "He was so tired that he flopped down upon the nice soft sand . . . ."

    ▸ What does *flopped down* mean? fell down
    ▸ How do you know this is what it means? Guide students to the clue word *tired*.

3. **Ask students the following questions** to check comprehension and encourage discussion.

    ▸ Name something Peter eats in Mr. McGregor's garden. lettuce; French beans; radishes
    ▸ What does Mr. McGregor do with Peter's jacket and shoes, and why? He hangs them on a scarecrow to scare away the blackbirds.

Objectives

- Identify and use context clues to define words.
- Answer questions requiring literal recall of details.

Reading for Meaning ....

Use Context Clues: Pictures

Introduce students to using pictures clues. Explain that—in addition to the clues we get from reading the words around an unknown word—we can also look at nearby pictures for hints. That's because **a picture sometimes shows what is being described in the sentence with the unknown word.**

1. Point to the picture at the top of page 11, and **read aloud**:
   "Flopsy, Mopsy, and Cotton-tail, who were good little bunnies, went down the lane to gather blackberries . . . ."

   ▸ What does *gather* mean? Answers will vary.
   ▸ How does the picture help you figure it out? Answers will vary; guide students to recognize that the picture shows the bunnies picking, or collecting, the berries.

2. Point to the picture on page 15, and **read aloud**:
   "And [Mr. McGregor] tried to put his foot upon Peter, who jumped out of a window, upsetting three plants."

   ▸ What does *upset* mean in this sentence? Answers will vary.
   ▸ What is happening to the potted plants in the picture? Answers will vary; guide students to recognize that the picture shows Peter knocking over the plants, so if something has been *upset* it means that it's been knocked over.

3. Point to the picture at the top of page 18, and **read aloud**:
   "He slipped underneath the gate, and was safe at last in the wood outside the garden."

   ▸ What does *slip* mean? Answers will vary.
   ▸ What is Peter doing in the picture that helps you figure it out? Answers will vary; guide students to recognize that Peter is squeezing under the gate.

Review "The Tale of Peter Rabbit"

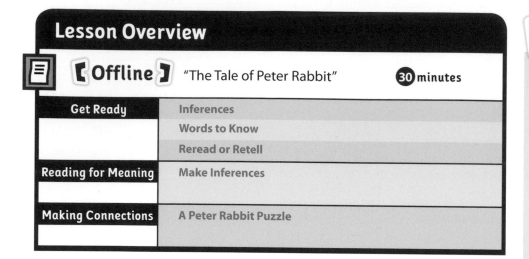

Lesson Overview

Offline · "The Tale of Peter Rabbit" · **30** minutes

Get Ready	Inferences
	Words to Know
	Reread or Retell
Reading for Meaning	Make Inferences
Making Connections	A Peter Rabbit Puzzle

Big Ideas

▸ Comprehension entails actively thinking about what is being read.
▸ Comprehension is facilitated when readers connect new information to information previously learned.

Materials

Supplied

- "The Tale of Peter Rabbit," *The Complete Adventures of Peter Rabbit* by Beatrix Potter, pp. 7–20
- *K¹² Language Arts Activity Book,* p. LC 23

Also Needed

- crayons
- scissors, round-end safety
- glue stick
- paper, drawing

Keywords

infer – to use clues and what you already know to make a guess

inference – a guess you make using the clues in a text and what you already know

 **30** minutes

"The Tale of Peter Rabbit"

Work **together** with students to complete offline Get Ready, Reading for Meaning, and Making Connections activities.

Get Ready ....

Inferences

Tell students that **when readers infer, they use clues to figure out what the author has not directly stated**. Good readers use clues in the pictures and the words of the story to figure things out, or make inferences. Good readers also use their own experiences to figure out things that the author has not directly stated. We can use clues and our own experiences to make inferences about things such as why a character does something or how a character feels.

Objectives

- Make inferences based on text and/or prior knowledge.
- Build vocabulary through listening, reading, and discussion.
- Use new vocabulary in written and spoken sentences.

Words to Know

Ask students to define the following words and use them in a sentence:

damp	fortnight	implore	mischief
exert	hoe	lane	wheelbarrow

Correct any incorrect or vague definitions.

Reread or Retell

If you'd like to, reread the story to students. Otherwise, have students retell the story using the pictures as a guide, or move on to the next activity.

Reading for Meaning

Make Inferences

Ask students the following questions to check their ability to infer.

1. Point to the picture at the top of page 12, and **read aloud** the sentence next to it.

   ► Why do you think Peter wants parsley? to feel better   What clues helped you figure this out? The word *sick* and the picture of Peter holding his stomach are clues that he feels bad.
   ► Have you ever eaten so much that it made you feel sick? What did you do to feel better? Answers will vary.

2. Point to the picture of the cat at the top of page 17, and **read aloud** the paragraph next to it.

   ► Why do you think Peter doesn't speak to the cat? He's afraid.
   ► What do you think Benjamin told Peter about cats? Answers will vary.
   ► What do you know about cats that helped you figure out that Peter is probably afraid of them? Answers will vary.

3. **Read aloud** the paragraph at the bottom of page 17.

   ► What does Peter do when he hears the hoe? He hides.
   ► Why do you think he does this? He's afraid of Mr. McGregor.   Why is he afraid? Mr. McGregor chased Peter and frightened him earlier in the story.

Objectives
- Make inferences based on text and/or prior knowledge.
- Support inferences with evidence from text and/or prior knowledge.

Making Connections

A Peter Rabbit Puzzle

Turn to page LC 23 in *K¹² Language Arts Activity Book*.

1. Have students color the picture puzzle of Peter Rabbit.

2. Help students cut out the puzzle pieces when done.

3. Mix up the puzzle pieces.

4. Have students put the puzzle back together. Tell them to look for color and shape clues on the puzzle pieces to figure out where each piece goes.

5. After the puzzle pieces are reassembled, help students glue them in the middle of a large sheet of paper.

6. Tell students to draw a scene from the story around the puzzle of Peter Rabbit.

7. Have students retell the part of the story their picture shows.

Objectives

- Respond to text through art, writing, and/or drama.
- Retell read aloud stories using various media.

Introduce "The Tale of Benjamin Bunny"

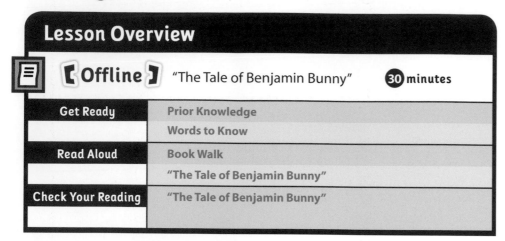

Lesson Overview

	[Offline] "The Tale of Benjamin Bunny"	30 minutes
Get Ready	Prior Knowledge	
	Words to Know	
Read Aloud	Book Walk	
	"The Tale of Benjamin Bunny"	
Check Your Reading	"The Tale of Benjamin Bunny"	

Advance Preparation

Read "The Tale of Benjamin Bunny" before beginning the Read Aloud activity, to locate Words to Know within the text.

Big Ideas

▸ Comprehension entails actively thinking about what is being read.
▸ Comprehension is facilitated when readers connect new information to information previously learned.

[Materials]

Supplied

● "The Tale of Benjamin Bunny," *The Complete Adventures of Peter Rabbit* by Beatrix Potter, pp. 21–34

Story Synopsis

Little Benjamin Bunny helps his reluctant cousin, Peter Rabbit, retrieve his coat and shoes that were left behind in Mr. McGregor's garden. All goes well until they have to hide from a cat.

This story includes a brief reference to a father spanking a misbehaving bunny with a little switch.

Keywords

prior knowledge – things you already know from past experience

 **Offline** (30) minutes

"The Tale of Benjamin Bunny"

Work **together** with students to complete offline Get Ready, Read Aloud, and Check Your Reading activities.

Get Ready

Prior Knowledge

Introduce students to the concept of prior knowledge.

1. Explain that good readers think about what they already know when reading a new story. We use **prior knowledge, or things we know from past experience**, to help us better understand a story. We do the same thing to help us understand the world around us.

   Say: Imagine that you are visiting a farm, and you see a small, white object on the ground. It's smooth and small enough to fit in your hand. What could it be? Answers will vary.

   Say: Now imagine that a hen walks up to the object and sits on it. What do you think the object is? an egg   Using what you already know about chickens, your prior knowledge, helps you figure out that the unknown item is an egg.

2. Explain that when we read, thinking about our **prior knowledge helps us connect new information in a story to things that we already know.** This helps us understand and remember what we've read.

3. Tell students that when they hear "The Tale of Benjamin Bunny," they should think about what they already know and how that might relate to the story.

Objectives

- Use prior knowledge to aid understanding of text.
- Build vocabulary through listening, reading, and discussion.
- Use new vocabulary in written and spoken sentences.

Words to Know

Before reading "The Tale of Benjamin Bunny,"

1. Have students say each word aloud.

2. Ask students if they know what each word or phrase means.

   ▶ If students know a word or phrase's meaning, have them define it and use it in a sentence.

   ▶ If students don't know a word or phrase's meaning, read them the definition and discuss it with them.

bed – a small bit of land where plants grow in a garden
bonnet – a woman's hat that ties under the chin
gig – a carriage with two wheels that's pulled by a horse
in the habit of – used to doing
pocket-handkerchief – a small piece of cloth used to wipe the nose
sow – to plant a seed
switch – a long, thin stick or twig
widow – a woman whose husband has died

Read Aloud

Book Walk

Prepare students by taking them on a Book Walk of "The Tale of Benjamin Bunny." Scan the story together.

1. Turn to the **table of contents.** Help students find today's selection, and turn to that page.

2. Point to and read aloud the **title of the story.**

3. Have students look at the **pictures** of the story. Answers to questions may vary.

   ▸ What do you think the story is about?
   ▸ Where do you think the story takes place?
   ▸ Do any of the characters in the pictures look familiar?
   ▸ Where might you have seen these characters before?

Objectives

- Make predictions based on title, illustrations, and/or context clues.
- Use prior knowledge to aid understanding of text.
- Read and listen to a variety of texts for information and pleasure independently or as part of a group.

"The Tale of Benjamin Bunny"

Now it's time to read the story. Have students sit next to you so that they can see the pictures and words while you read the story aloud.

Read aloud the entire story. Emphasize Words to Know as you come to them. If appropriate, use the pictures to help show what each word or phrase means.

TIP If students have questions about rabbit-tobacco (pages 24 and 32), tell them that this story was written long ago. We now know that smoking anything—even lavender—is not a healthy thing to do.

Check Your Reading

"The Tale of Benjamin Bunny"

Have students retell the story in their own words to develop grammar, vocabulary, comprehension, and fluency skills. When finished, **ask students the following questions** to check comprehension and encourage discussion. If students have trouble answering a question, **help them locate the answer in the story**.

▸ Why doesn't Peter have his coat and shoes? He dropped them when he was chased about the garden.
▸ Have you ever lost a coat or sweater? How did it happen? Answers will vary.
▸ What does Peter say when Benjamin asks where Peter's clothes are? He says they're on the scarecrow in Mr. McGregor's garden.
▸ Why is Peter's coat a bit shrunk? The rain caused the coat to shrink.
▸ Have any of your clothes ever shrunk? How did it happen? Answers will vary; if applicable, suggest that some clothing may have shrunk because it was dried in a dryer that was too hot.
▸ Why did Peter and Benjamin hide under a basket? They saw a cat.   How were they probably feeling? scared
▸ Have you ever hidden because you felt scared? Answers will vary.

Objectives

- Use prior knowledge to aid understanding of text.
- Answer questions requiring literal recall of details.

Explore "The Tale of Benjamin Bunny"

Lesson Overview

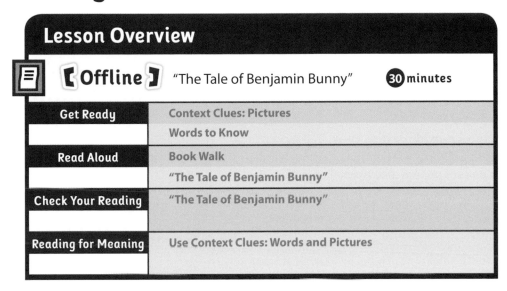

[Offline] "The Tale of Benjamin Bunny"	**30** minutes

Get Ready	Context Clues: Pictures
	Words to Know
Read Aloud	Book Walk
	"The Tale of Benjamin Bunny"
Check Your Reading	"The Tale of Benjamin Bunny"
Reading for Meaning	Use Context Clues: Words and Pictures

Materials

Supplied

• "The Tale of Benjamin Bunny," *The Complete Adventures of Peter Rabbit* by Beatrix Potter, pp. 21–34

Keywords

context – the parts of a sentence or passage surrounding a word

context clue – a word or phrase in a text that helps you figure out the meaning of an unknown word

Advance Preparation

Before working with students, spend a few minutes reviewing Words to Know. Then review the Check Your Reading and Reading for Meaning activities to familiarize yourself with the questions and answers.

Big Ideas

Early learners acquire vocabulary through active exposure (by talking and listening, being read to, and receiving explicit instruction).

 **30** minutes

"The Tale of Benjamin Bunny"

Work **together** with students to complete offline Get Ready, Read Aloud, Check Your Reading, and Reading for Meaning activities.

Get Ready

Context Clues: Pictures

Introduce students to the idea that **pictures provide context clues.** Tell them that—in addition to the clues we get from reading the words around an unknown word—we can also look at nearby pictures for hints. A picture sometimes shows what is being described in the sentence with the unknown word.

1. Turn to page 15 of *The Complete Adventures of Peter Rabbit*. Have students study the picture of Peter toppling the potted plants.

2. Review how students can figure out the meaning of *upset* by looking at what Peter is doing in the picture.

   Say: The story says that Peter upset three plants when he jumped out of the tool-shed.

   ▶ What clue in this picture can help you figure out what the word *upset* means in this sentence? It shows Peter knocking over the plants, so *upset* most likely means "to knock over."

Words to Know

Before reading "The Tale of Benjamin Bunny,"

1. Have students say each word aloud.

2. Ask students if they know what each word means.

   ▶ If students know a word's meaning, have them define it and use it in a sentence.

   ▶ If students don't know a word's meaning, read them the definition and discuss the word with them.

bed – a small bit of land where plants grow in a garden
bonnet – a woman's hat that ties under the chin
gig – a carriage with two wheels that's pulled by a horse
in the habit of – used to doing
pocket-handkerchief – a small piece of cloth used to wipe the nose
sow – to plant a seed
switch – a long, thin stick or twig
widow – a woman whose husband has died

> **Objectives**
> - Identify and use picture clues to define words.
> - Build vocabulary through listening, reading, and discussion.
> - Use new vocabulary in written and spoken sentences.

Read Aloud

Book Walk

Prepare students by taking them on a Book Walk of "The Tale of Benjamin Bunny."
Scan the story together to revisit the characters and events.

1. Turn to today's selection. Point to and read aloud the **title of the story**.

2. Have students look at the **pictures** of the story. Answers to questions will vary.

    ▶ What are some things you know about Mr. McGregor and his garden?
    ▶ What are some things you know about Benjamin Bunny and Peter Rabbit?

Objectives
- Activate prior knowledge by previewing text and/or discussing topic.
- Read and listen to a variety of texts for information and pleasure, independently or as part of a group.

"The Tale of Benjamin Bunny"

Now it's time to read the story. Have students sit next to you so that they can see the
pictures and words while you read the story aloud.

   Read aloud the entire story. Tell students to listen carefully to the words before
and after an unknown word to help figure out what it means. Remind them to follow
along and look for clues in the pictures, as well.

Check Your Reading

"The Tale of Benjamin Bunny"

Have students retell the story in their own words. When finished, **ask the
following questions** to check students' ability to use picture clues.

1. Point to the picture at the bottom of page 27, and **read aloud**:
   "Benjamin tried on the tam-o-shanter, but it was too big for him."

    ▶ What is a *tam-o-shanter*? a kind of hat
    ▶ What do you see in the picture that gives you a clue? Guide students to point to Benjamin wearing a flat hat.
    ▶ Are there also clues in the sentence? Guide students to recognize that the words *tried on* tell us it's something you can wear.

2. Point to the picture on page 29, and **read aloud**:
   "They went along a little walk on planks, under a sunny red-brick wall."

    ▶ What are *planks*? wooden boards
    ▶ What hint do you see in the picture? Guide students to point to the rabbits walking on wooden boards.
    ▶ Are there also clues in the sentence? ... *a little walk on planks* tells us they're something you can walk on.

Objectives
- Identify and use picture clues to define words.
- Identify and use context clues to define words.

Reading for Meaning

Use Context Clues: Words and Pictures

Introduce students to the idea of using words and pictures together. Tell them that sometimes we need to **do two things together to figure out the meaning of an unknown word.** We need to think about the **clues we get from reading the words around an unknown word.** We also need to think about the **hints in nearby pictures** because pictures sometimes show what is being described in the sentence with the unknown word.

1. Point to the pictures on pages 23–24, and **read aloud**:
   " . . . little Benjamin Bunny slid down into the road…to call upon his relations . . . Benjamin's aunt and his cousins—Flopsy, Mopsy, Cotton-tail and Peter."

   ▸ What does *relations* mean? people in your family
   ▸ What words give you a clue? *aunt and his cousins*
   ▸ How does the picture help you figure it out? Guide students to point to the family of bunnies.

2. Point to the picture at the top of page 34, and **read aloud**:
   "When Mr. McGregor returned about half an hour later, he observed several things which perplexed him. It looked as though some person had been walking all over the garden in a pair of clogs—only the foot-marks were too ridiculously little! Also he could not understand how the cat could have managed to shut herself up *inside* the greenhouse, locking the door upon the *outside*."

   ▸ What does the word *perplexed* mean? confused
   ▸ What words give you a clue? *...he could not understand* tells us that *perplexed* means "confused."
   ▸ How does the picture help you figure it out? Guide students to recognize that Mr. McGregor rubbing his chin shows that he's confused.

3. **Ask students the following questions** to check comprehension. Have them look at the picture at the bottom of page 30 while you **read aloud** the paragraphs next to it.

   ▸ What do Peter and Benjamin see around the corner? a cat
   ▸ The story does not tell us that they see a cat. How do you know that's what they see? The picture shows a cat.
   ▸ Why do the two rabbits immediately hide under a basket? They don't want the cat to see them.

Objectives
- Identify and use context clues to define words.
- Identify and use picture clues to define words.
- Make inferences based on text and/or prior knowledge.
- Support inferences with evidence from text and/or prior knowledge.

Review "The Tale of Benjamin Bunny"

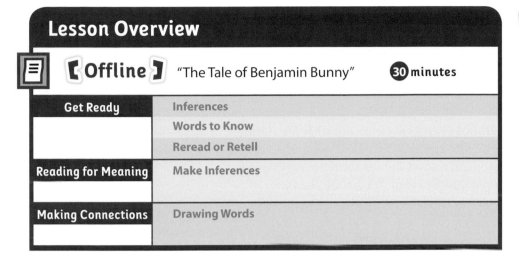

Lesson Overview

[Offline] "The Tale of Benjamin Bunny" **30** minutes

Get Ready	Inferences
	Words to Know
	Reread or Retell
Reading for Meaning	Make Inferences
Making Connections	Drawing Words

Big Ideas

▸ Comprehension entails actively thinking about what is being read.
▸ Comprehension is facilitated when readers connect new information to information previously learned.

[Materials]

Supplied

● "The Tale of Benjamin Bunny," *The Complete Adventures of Peter Rabbit* by Beatrix Potter, pp. 21–34
● *K¹² Language Arts Activity Book*, p. LC 25

Also Needed

● crayons

Keywords

infer – to use clues and what you already know to make a guess
inference – a guess you make using the clues in a text and what you already know

 **30** minutes

"The Tale of Benjamin Bunny"

Work **together** with students to complete offline Get Ready, Reading for Meaning, and Making Connections activities.

Get Ready

Inferences

Tell students that **when readers infer, they use clues to figure out what the author has not directly stated.** Good readers use clues in the pictures and words of a story to figure things out, or make inferences. Good readers also use their own experiences to figure out things that the author has not directly stated. We can use clues and our own experiences to make inferences about things, such as why a character does something or how a character feels.

Objectives
- Make inferences based on text and/or prior knowledge.
- Build vocabulary through listening, reading, and discussion.
- Use new vocabulary in written and spoken sentences.

Words to Know

Ask students to define the following words and use them in a sentence:

bed	gig	pocket-handkerchief	switch
bonnet	in the habit of	sow	widow

Correct any incorrect or vague definitions.

Reread or Retell

If you'd like to, reread the story to students. Otherwise, have students retell the story using the pictures as a guide, or move on to the next activity.

Reading for Meaning ··

Make Inferences

Ask students the following questions to check their ability to make inferences.

1. Point to the pictures of Peter at the top and bottom of page 28, and **read aloud**:
   "Peter did not seem to be enjoying himself; he kept hearing noises."
   "Peter did not eat anything; he said he should like to go home."

   ▸ How do you think Peter is feeling? nervous, scared   Why is he feeling this
     way? Guide students to recognize that Peter feels this way because he had
     a bad experience in the garden.
   ▸ What clues do the words and pictures give you? He keeps hearing noises.
     He wants to go home. He looks nervous.
   ▸ Have you ever been in a situation in which you thought you heard noises?
     How did that make you feel? Answers will vary.
   ▸ Do you think Peter might feel the same way? Guide students to recognize
     that their feelings in a similar situation can help them figure out how Peter
     feels.

2. **Read aloud**:
   "Peter heard noises worse than ever, his eyes were as big as lolly-pops!"

   ▸ What does "his eyes were as big as lolly-pops" mean? Answers will vary.
     What does it tell you about how Peter feels? Guide students to recognize
     that Peter is so scared that his eyes are wide with fear.
   ▸ Have you ever been so scared that your eyes got as big as lolly-pops?
     Answers will vary.

Objectives
- Make inferences based on
  text and/or prior knowledge.
- Support inferences with
  evidence from text and/or
  prior knowledge.

Making Connections

Drawing Words

Tell students they are going to draw a picture to show they know what a word means.

1. Turn to page LC 25 in *K¹² Language Arts Activity Book.*

2. Tell students to **choose one of the following words** from the story:
   - ► *relations*
   - ► *perplexed*
   - ► *planks*

3. After students choose a word, have them draw a picture that shows one of the following: who their relations are; a time when they were perplexed; or how they would use planks. (Choose the description that matches the word that students selected.)

4. If students have trouble using the word they choose, go back to the story and find the page with the word on it. Point to the related picture, and discuss how it shows what the word means.

5. When done, help students compose a sentence at the bottom of the page by writing the words they dictate. See possible sentence starters below. Use the sentence starter that matches the word that students chose to illustrate.
   - ► These are some of my relations. They are . . .
   - ► I was perplexed one time when . . .
   - ► I would use planks to . . .

Objectives
- Respond to text through art, writing, and/or drama.
- Demonstrate understanding through drawing, discussion, and/or writing.
- Make connections with text: text-to-text, text-to-self, text-to-world.

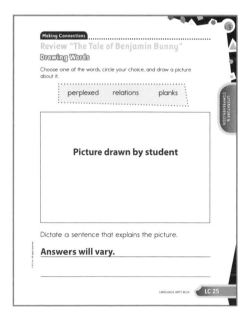

Making Connections
Review "The Tale of Benjamin Bunny"
Drawing Words

Choose one of the words, circle your choice, and draw a picture about it.

perplexed   relations   planks

Picture drawn by student

Dictate a sentence that explains the picture.
Answers will vary.

LANGUAGE ARTS BLUE   LC 25

Introduce "The Tale of The Flopsy Bunnies"

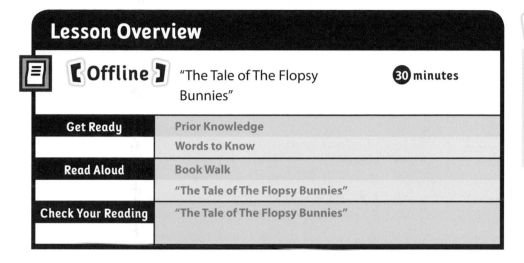

Lesson Overview

	[Offline]	"The Tale of The Flopsy Bunnies"	30 minutes
Get Ready		Prior Knowledge	
		Words to Know	
Read Aloud		Book Walk	
		"The Tale of The Flopsy Bunnies"	
Check Your Reading		**"The Tale of The Flopsy Bunnies"**	

Advance Preparation

Read "The Tale of The Flopsy Bunnies" before beginning the Read Aloud activity, to locate Words to Know within the text.

Big Ideas

▶ Comprehension entails actively thinking about what is being read.
▶ Comprehension is facilitated when readers connect new information to information previously learned.

[Materials]

Supplied

● "The Tale of The Flopsy Bunnies," *The Complete Adventures of Peter Rabbit* by Beatrix Potter, pp. 35–46

Story Synopsis

The Flopsy Bunnies have eaten too much lettuce and have fallen asleep. Now they're tied up in a sack, about to be taken away by Mr. McGregor. How will they make their escape?

Keywords

prior knowledge – things you already know from past experience

 **30** minutes

"The Tale of The Flopsy Bunnies"

Work **together** with students to complete offline Get Ready, Read Aloud, and Check Your Reading activities.

Get Ready

Prior Knowledge

Introduce students to the concept of prior knowledge.

1. Tell students that good readers think about what they already know when reading a new story. We use **prior knowledge, or things we know from past experience**, to help us better understand a story. We do the same thing to help us understand the world around us.

   Say: Imagine that you're visiting an aquarium where lots of fish live. You see a big, scary-looking fish in one of the tanks. It has a large fin on its back and many big, jagged teeth. What kind of fish could it be? Answers will vary.

   Say: Now imagine that you remember watching a TV show about ocean animals. You remember that a fish called a *shark* has a large fin and big teeth. What does this tell you about the fish in the tank? It's probably a shark.
   Your prior knowledge from the TV show helps you figure out that the unknown fish is a shark.

2. Explain to students that when we read, thinking about our **prior knowledge helps us connect new information in a story to things that we already know**, just like remembering what we saw in a TV show can help us understand what kind of fish we're looking at. This helps us better understand and remember what we've read.

3. Tell students that when they hear "The Tale of The Flopsy Bunnies," they should think about what they already know and how that might relate to the story.

> **Objectives**
> - Use prior knowledge to aid understanding of text.
> - Build vocabulary through listening, reading, and discussion.
> - Use new vocabulary in written and spoken sentences.

Words to Know

Before reading "The Tale of The Flopsy Bunnies,"

1. Have students say each word aloud.

2. Ask students if they know what each word means.

   ▸ If students know a word's meaning, have them define it and use it in a sentence.
   ▸ If students don't know a word's meaning, read them the definition and discuss the word with them.

cloak – a coat without sleeves; a cape
creep – to walk quietly on tiptoe
despair – a feeling that there is no hope at all; a deep sadness
rubbish – garbage; trash
tread – the sound of someone's footsteps
undo – untie

Read Aloud

Book Walk

Prepare students by taking them on a Book Walk of "The Tale of The Flopsy Bunnies." Scan the story together.

1. Turn to the **table of contents**. Help students find today's selection, and turn to that page.

2. Point to and read aloud the **title of the story**.

3. Have students look at the **pictures** of the story.

    ▸ What do you think the story is about? Answers to questions may vary.

    ▸ Where do you think the story takes place? Answers to questions may vary.

    ▸ Do any of the characters look familiar? Where might you have seen them before? If students have read "The Tale of Peter Rabbit" or "The Tale of Benjamin Bunny," they should be able to recount information from those stories.

Objectives

- Make predictions based on title, illustrations, and/or context clues.
- Use prior knowledge to aid understanding of text.
- Read and listen to a variety of texts for information and pleasure independently or as part of a group.

"The Tale of The Flopsy Bunnies"

Now it's time to read the story. Have students sit next to you so that they can see the pictures and words while you read the story aloud.

Read aloud the entire story. Emphasize Words to Know as you come to them. If appropriate, use the pictures to help show what each word means.

Check Your Reading

"The Tale of The Flopsy Bunnies"

Have students retell the story in their own words to develop grammar, vocabulary, comprehension, and fluency skills. When finished, **ask students the following questions** to check comprehension and encourage discussion.

- ▶ Who is Mr. McGregor? Have you heard any other stories with Mr. McGregor? Answers will vary; guide students to remember that Mr. McGregor owns the garden that rabbits like to get into.
- ▶ Who is Benjamin Bunny? Have you hear any other stories with Benjamin Bunny? If you have heard another story with Benjamin Bunny, what do you remember about it? Answers will vary. If students have heard "The Tale of Benjamin Bunny," guide them to remember that in that story, Benjamin helped Peter retrieve his clothes from Mr. McGregor's garden.
- ▶ Why does Benjamin put a paper bag over his head when he takes a nap? to keep off the flies
- ▶ What does Mr. McGregor do with the Flopsy Bunnies? He puts them in a sack.
- ▶ Why isn't this surprising? What did Mr. McGregor do to Peter in another story? Answers will vary; guide students to remember that Mr. McGregor tried to catch Peter in another story.

Explore "The Tale of The Flopsy Bunnies"

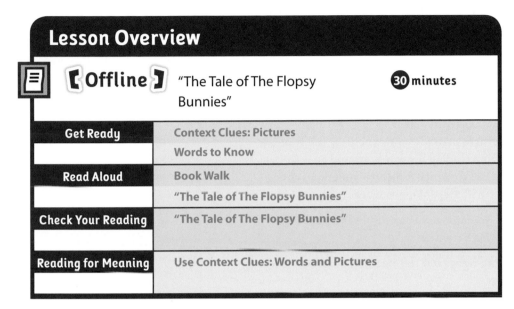

Lesson Overview

[Offline]	"The Tale of The Flopsy Bunnies"	**30** minutes
Get Ready	Context Clues: Pictures	
	Words to Know	
Read Aloud	Book Walk	
	"The Tale of The Flopsy Bunnies"	
Check Your Reading	"The Tale of The Flopsy Bunnies"	
Reading for Meaning	Use Context Clues: Words and Pictures	

[Materials]

Supplied

- "The Tale of The Flopsy Bunnies," *The Complete Adventures of Peter Rabbit* by Beatrix Potter, pp. 35–46

Keywords

context – the parts of a sentence or passage surrounding a word

context clue – a word or phrase in a text that helps you figure out the meaning of an unknown word

Advance Preparation

Before working with students, spend a few minutes reviewing Words to Know. Then review Check Your Reading and Reading for Meaning activities to familiarize yourself with the questions and answers.

Big Ideas

Early learners acquire vocabulary through active exposure (by talking and listening, being read to, and receiving explicit instruction).

[Offline] ⏱30 minutes

"The Tale of The Flopsy Bunnies"

Work **together** with students to complete offline Get Ready, Read Aloud, Check Your Reading, and Reading for Meaning activities.

Get Ready ....

Context Clues: Pictures

Introduce students to the idea that **pictures provide context clues.** Tell students that—in addition to the clues we get from reading the words around an unknown word—we can also look at nearby pictures for hints. A picture sometimes shows what is being described in the sentence with the unknown word.

1. Turn to page 27 of *The Complete Adventures of Peter Rabbit.* Have students study the picture of Benjamin with a hat on his head.

2. Review with students how they can figure out the meaning of *tam-o-shanter* by looking at Benjamin in the picture.

   Say: The story says that Benjamin took the tam-o-shanter off the scarecrow and tried it on.

   ► What clue in this picture helps you figure out what the word *tam-o-shanter* means? It shows Benjamin wearing a flat, round hat on his head, so *tam-o-shanter* most likely means "a flat, round hat."

> ⭐ **Objectives**
> - Identify and use picture clues to define words.
> - Build vocabulary through listening, reading, and discussion.
> - Use new vocabulary in written and spoken sentences.

Words to Know

Before reading "The Tale of The Flopsy Bunnies,"

1. Have students say each word aloud.

2. As students if they know what each word means.

   ► If students know a word's meaning, have them define it and use it in a sentence.
   ► If students don't know a word's meaning, read them the definition and discuss the word with them.

cloak – a coat without sleeves; a cape
creep – to walk quietly on tiptoe
despair – a feeling that there is no hope at all; a deep sadness
rubbish – garbage; trash
tread – the sound of someone's footsteps
undo – untie

Read Aloud

Book Walk

Prepare students by taking them on a Book Walk of "The Tale of The Flopsy Bunnies." Scan the story together to revisit the characters and events.

1. Turn to today's selection. Point to and read aloud the **title of the story.**

2. Have students look at the **pictures** of the story. Answers to questions may vary.

   ▶ Can you point to and name the characters you know from another story? How do you recognize them?

   ▶ Why do you think Mr. McGregor doesn't like rabbits in his garden?

Objectives

- Activate prior knowledge by previewing text and/or discussing topic.

- Read and listen to a variety of texts for information and pleasure independently or as part of a group.

"The Tale of The Flopsy Bunnies"

Now it's time to read the story. Have students sit next to you so that they can see the pictures and words while you read the story aloud.

Read aloud the entire story. Tell students to listen carefully to the words before and after an unknown word to help figure out what it means. Remind them to follow along and look for clues in the pictures, as well.

Check Your Reading

"The Tale of The Flopsy Bunnies"

Have students retell the story in their own words to develop grammar, vocabulary, comprehension, and fluency skills. When finished, **read each sentence from the story as directed, and then ask the questions** to check students' ability to use context and picture clues.

Objectives

- Identify and use picture clues to define words.

- Identify and use context clues to define words.

1. **Read aloud:**
   "It is said that the effect of eating too much lettuce is 'soporific.'
   I have never felt sleepy after eating lettuces; but then *I* am not a rabbit."

   ▶ What does *soporific* mean? makes you feel sleepy   What word clues help you know? *I have never felt sleepy after eating lettuces.*

2. **Read aloud:**
   "The youngest Flopsy Bunny got upon the window-sill."

   ▶ What does *window-sill* mean? the bottom ledge of a window   How do the pictures help you figure it out? Guide students to point to the bunny stepping onto the windowsill at the top of page 45, and then how she's sitting on it in the bottom picture.

Reading for Meaning

Use Context Clues: Words and Pictures

Introduce students to the idea of using words and pictures together. Tell them that sometimes we need to **do two things together to figure out the meaning of an unknown word.** We need to think about the **clues we get from reading the words around an unknown word.** We also need to think about the **hints in nearby pictures** because pictures sometimes show what is being described in the sentence with the unknown word.

Objectives

- Identify and use picture clues to define words.
- Identify and use context clues to define words.

1. Point to the pictures on page 38, and **read aloud**:
   "Mr. McGregor's rubbish heap was a mixture. There were jam pots and paper bags, and mountains of chopped grass . . . and some rotten vegetable marrows and an old boot or two."

   ‣ What does *mixture* mean? many things jumbled together
   ‣ What hints do you see in the picture? Guide students to point to all the mixed-up items.
   ‣ Are there also clues in the sentence? Help students recount all the things mentioned in the paragraph.

2. Point to the picture at the top of page 39, and **read aloud**:
   "The Flopsy Bunnies simply stuffed lettuces. By degrees, one after another, they were overcome with slumber, and lay down in the mown grass."

   ‣ What does the phrase *overcome with slumber* mean? falling asleep
   ‣ What word clues help you know? The words *lay down* tell us that the bunnies are very tired, so they are probably falling asleep.
   ‣ How does the picture help you figure it out? Guide students to point to the bunnies sleeping on the grass.

3. Point to the picture at the top of page 42, and **read aloud**:
   "But Mrs. Tittlemouse was a resourceful person. She nibbled a hole in the bottom corner of the sack."

   ‣ What does *nibbled* mean? chewed
   ‣ What words give you a clue? The words *a hole in the bottom corner* help us understand that *nibbled* probably means "chewed" because that's how a mouse would make a hole in the sack.
   ‣ How does the picture help you figure it out? Guide students to point to the mouse chewing a hole in the sack so the bunnies can escape.

TIP If students have trouble answering a question, reread the sentence or paragraph slowly, and pause to discuss what students see in the picture related to the text.

Review "The Tale of The Flopsy Bunnies"

Lesson Overview

[**Offline**]   "The Tale of The Flopsy Bunnies"   **30** minutes

Get Ready	Inferences
	Words to Know
	Reread or Retell
Reading for Meaning	Make Inferences
Making Connections	Who Am I?

Supplied

- "The Tale of The Flopsy Bunnies," *The Complete Adventures of Peter Rabbit* by Beatrix Potter, pp. 35–46
- *K¹² Language Arts Activity Book*, p. LC 26

Also Needed

- crayons

Big Ideas

▶ Comprehension entails actively thinking about what is being read.
▶ Comprehension is facilitated when readers connect new information to information previously learned.

Keywords

infer – to use clues and what you already know to make a guess

inference – a guess you make using the clues in a text and what you already know

〔 Offline 〕 30 minutes

"The Tale of The Flopsy Bunnies"

Work **together** with students to complete offline Get Ready, Reading for Meaning, and Making Connections activities.

Get Ready ••

Inferences

Tell students that **when readers infer, they use clues to fill in what is not written on the page**. Good readers are able to infer in different ways. They look for **clues in the pictures.** They think about the **words in the story.** And they use **prior knowledge from past experience** to help understand what they are reading. Good readers can figure out, or infer, things like why a character does something or how a character feels.

_____

Words to Know

Ask students to define the following words and use them in a sentence:

cloak	despair	tread
creep	rubbish	undo

Correct any incorrect or vague definitions.

_____

Reread or Retell

If you'd like to, reread the story to students. Otherwise, have students retell the story using the pictures as a guide, or move on to the next activity.

Objectives

- Make inferences based on text and/or prior knowledge.
- Build vocabulary through listening, reading, and discussion.
- Use new vocabulary in written and spoken sentences.

Reading for Meaning

Make Inferences

Ask students the following questions to check their ability to make inferences.

1. Point to the picture of Mr. McGregor's feet at the top of page 40, and **read aloud** the paragraph next to it.

   ▸ Whose tread do the mouse and Benjamin hear? Mr. McGregor's
   What clues help you know? Mr. McGregor empties the grass clippings right after they hear the tread; the picture shows Mr. McGregor's shoes.

2. Point to the picture at the top of page 46, and **read aloud** the paragraph next to it.

   ▸ Why does a rotten marrow fly through the window? Mr. McGregor threw it.
   ▸ What clue helps you understand? We know Mr. McGregor is very angry, so he probably threw the marrow out the window.

3. Point to the picture of the mouse at the bottom of page 46, and **read aloud** the paragraphs next to it.

   ▸ Who gave Mrs. Tittlemouse a present of rabbit wool? Why? Mrs. Tittlemouse helped the Flopsy Bunnies escape from the sack. We can infer that Mr. and Mrs. Flopsy Bunny gave Mrs. Tittlemouse the present to thank her.

Objectives

- Make inferences based on text and/or prior knowledge.
- Support inferences with evidence from text and/or prior knowledge.

Making Connections

Who Am I?

Have students complete page LC 26 in *K¹² Language Arts Activity Book*.

1. Choose one of the following characters from the story. Read aloud the clues that describe that character. **Do not read aloud the name of the character.**

(Mr. McGregor)	(Mrs. Flopsy Bunny)	(Mrs. Tittlemouse)
I wear a brown coat, hat, and boots.	I have a white, fluffy tail.	I am small and brown.
I have a white beard.	I wear a blue dress.	I have a long, skinny tail.
I use tools like a hoe and a rake.	I have many children.	I am resourceful.
I don't like rabbits in my garden.	My children were trapped in a sack.	I got a present of rabbit wool for helping my friends.

2. Have students draw a picture of the character.

3. Have them name the character.

4. Write the name of the character at the bottom of the activity page.

5. Ask students to explain how they **inferred** who the character was.

6. Have students point to pictures of the character in the story and describe the character to support their inference.

Objectives

- Demonstrate understanding through drawing, discussion, and/or writing.
- Make inferences based on text and/or prior knowledge.
- Support inferences with evidence from text and/or prior knowledge.

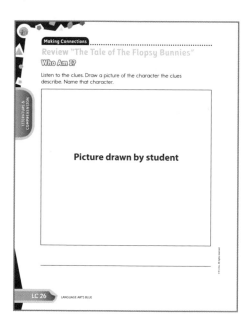

Making Connections
Review "The Tale of The Flopsy Bunnies"
Who Am I?

Listen to the clues. Draw a picture of the character the clues describe. Name that character.

Picture drawn by student

LC 26   LANGUAGE ARTS BLUE

Introduce "The Velveteen Rabbit"

Unit Overview

In this unit, students will explore the theme of *Animals Among Us* through the following selections:

- ▶ "The Velveteen Rabbit"
- ▶ "Rare and Wonderful Pandas"
- ▶ "The Lion and the Mouse"
- ▶ *Caps for Sale*
- ▶ "Emperors of the Ice"

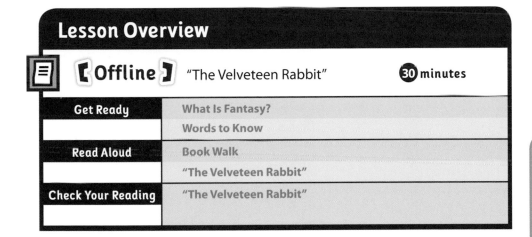

Lesson Overview

[Offline] "The Velveteen Rabbit"		**30** minutes
Get Ready	What Is Fantasy?	
	Words to Know	
Read Aloud	Book Walk	
	"The Velveteen Rabbit"	
Check Your Reading	"The Velveteen Rabbit"	

Advance Preparation

Read to the end of page 73 of "The Velveteen Rabbit" before beginning the Read Aloud activity, to locate Words to Know within the text.

Big Ideas

Comprehension requires an understanding of story structure.

[Materials]

Supplied

- "The Velveteen Rabbit," *K¹² Read Aloud Treasury*, pp. 64–80

Story Synopsis

In this classic children's story, a toy rabbit wants nothing more than to become "real." As the wise Skin Horse explains, "'Real isn't how you are made . . . but a thing that happens to you."

Keywords

fantasy – a story with characters, settings, or other elements that could not really exist

literal recall – the ability to describe information stated directly in a text

[Offline] 30 minutes

"The Velveteen Rabbit"

Work **together** with students to complete offline Get Ready, Read Aloud, and Check Your Reading activities.

Get Ready ···

What Is Fantasy?

Introduce students to the concept of fantasy by explaining that a **fantasy** is a story that has make-believe things in it.

1. **Say:** The parts of a story that are fantasy could never happen in the real world. For example, a toy rabbit is real, but a toy rabbit cannot think or move in the real world.

2. Tell students that good readers look for hints in the pictures and the words of a story to find out if the story is a fantasy.

   ▸ Is a fire-breathing dragon real or fantasy? fantasy   How do you know? It doesn't exist in the real world.

   ▸ Is a barking dog real or fantasy? real   How do you know? We hear dogs barking in the real world.

Words to Know

Before reading "The Velveteen Rabbit,"

1. Have students say each word aloud.

2. Ask students if they know what each word means.

   ▸ If students know a word's meaning, have them define it and use it in a sentence.

   ▸ If students don't know a word's meaning, read them the definition and discuss the word with them.

bracken – a kind of fern
burrow – a hole or tunnel dug in the ground; where rabbits live
clockwork – the machinery inside a toy that makes it move when it is wound up with a key
hind – found at the back; an animal's back legs are called its hind legs
insignificant – not important; small
nursery – a child's bedroom or playroom
velveteen – a smooth, soft fabric that feels like velvet

> **Objectives**
> - Identify and define fantasy.
> - Build vocabulary through listening, reading, and discussion.
> - Use new vocabulary in written and spoken sentences.

Read Aloud

Book Walk

Prepare students by taking them on a Book Walk of "The Velveteen Rabbit." Scan pages 64 through 73 together.

1. Turn to the **table of contents**. Help students find today's selection, and turn to that page.

2. Point to and read aloud the **title of the story.**

3. Have students look at the **pictures** of the story and answer the following questions. Answers to questions may vary.

   ▸ What do you think the story is about?
   ▸ Where do you think the story takes place?
   ▸ Do you ever pretend that any of your toys are real?

Objectives
- Make predictions based on title, illustrations, and/or context clues.
- Read and listen to a variety of texts for information and pleasure independently or as part of a group.

"The Velveteen Rabbit"

Now it's time to read the story. Have students sit next to you so that they can see the pictures and words while you read the story aloud.

Read aloud the first half of the story. Stop at the end of page 73. Emphasize Words to Know as you come to them. If appropriate, use the pictures to help show what each word means.

TIP The Skin Horse is a stuffed toy horse with a leather covering.

Check Your Reading

"The Velveteen Rabbit"

Have students retell pages 64 through 73 of the story in their own words to develop grammar, vocabulary, comprehension, and fluency skills. When finished, **ask students the following questions** to check comprehension and encourage discussion.

Objectives
- Identify and define fantasy.
- Compare and contrast experiences of characters in a text.
- Answer questions requiring literal recall of details.

▸ What does the Skin Horse tell the Velveteen Rabbit about becoming real? Use your own words. Answers will vary; guide students to understand that the horse says becoming real is something that happens to a toy when it is loved for a long time.

▸ How does the Velveteen Rabbit feel when the Boy says, "He isn't a toy. He's *Real*!"? happy   Why does he feel this way? because he thinks he is no longer a toy

▸ Are the rabbits in the wood real, or are they toys? real   How can you tell? Possible answers: they can move; they're furry; they twitch their noses; they have hind legs

▸ Can animals and toys actually talk? No   What does that tell us about the story? It's a fantasy.

▸ How does the real rabbit dance? He whirls around until he gets dizzy.

▸ Why doesn't the Velveteen Rabbit dance, even though he wants to? He's a toy; he doesn't have hind legs.

Explore "The Velveteen Rabbit"

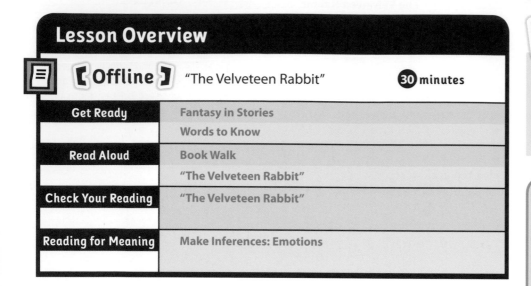

Lesson Overview

[Offline] "The Velveteen Rabbit"   **30** minutes

Get Ready	Fantasy in Stories
	Words to Know
Read Aloud	Book Walk
	"The Velveteen Rabbit"
Check Your Reading	"The Velveteen Rabbit"
Reading for Meaning	Make Inferences: Emotions

[Materials]

Supplied
- "The Velveteen Rabbit," *K¹² Read Aloud Treasury,* pp. 64–80

Keywords

fantasy – a story with characters, settings, or other elements that could not really exist

infer – to use clues and what you already know to make a guess

inference – a guess you make using the clues in a text and what you already know

Advance Preparation

Read pages 74–80 of "The Velveteen Rabbit" before beginning the Read Aloud activities, to locate Words to Know within the text. Then review Check Your Reading and Reading for Meaning activities to familiarize yourself with the questions and answers.

Big Ideas

▸ Comprehension entails actively thinking about what is being read.
▸ Comprehension is facilitated when readers connect new information to information previously learned.

 **30** minutes

"The Velveteen Rabbit"

Work **together** with students to complete offline Get Ready, Read Aloud, Check Your Reading, and Reading for Meaning activities.

Get Ready

Fantasy in Stories

Reinforce the concept of fantasy within a story.

1. Remind students that good readers can tell that a story is a **fantasy**, or make-believe, if parts of the story couldn't happen in real life. Things like machines with faces, talking animals, or a cloak that can make someone invisible are all fantasy.

2. Explain that good readers look for hints in the pictures and the words of a story to find out if the story is a fantasy.

   Say: Listen to this story: Miranda is a little girl. One day she flew up to a fluffy, white cloud. She sat on the cloud until it was time to fly back home for dinner.

   ▸ Which parts of the story are real? the girl; the cloud; dinner
   ▸ Which parts are fantasy? a girl flying; sitting on a cloud

> **Objectives**
> - Identify and define fantasy.
> - Build vocabulary through listening, reading, and discussion.
> - Use new vocabulary in written and spoken sentences.

Words to Know

Before reading "The Velveteen Rabbit,"

1. Have students say each word aloud.

2. Ask students if they know what each word means.

   ▸ If students know a word's meaning, have them define it and use it in a sentence.
   ▸ If students don't know a word's meaning, read them the definition and discuss the word with them.

bedclothes – sheets, blankets, pillowcases, and other coverings used on a bed
disinfect – to kill germs
germ – a very small living thing that can cause disease
rubbish – trash; garbage
scarlet fever – a disease you can catch that causes a rash, sore throat, and fever
shabby – worn out; in need of repair

Read Aloud

Book Walk

Prepare students by taking them on a Book Walk of "The Velveteen Rabbit." Scan pages 74 through 80 together.

1. Remind students that the Velveteen Rabbit is a toy that wants to be real.

2. Turn to today's selection. Point to and read aloud the **title of the story**.

3. Have students look at the **pictures** of the story. Answers to questions may vary.

   ▸ Which picture shows something that is fantasy, or make-believe? How do you know?

   ▸ Which picture shows something that can really happen? How can you tell?

Objectives
- Identify and define fantasy.
- Read and listen to a variety of texts for information and pleasure independently or as part of a group.

"The Velveteen Rabbit"

Now it's time to read the story. Have students sit next to you so that they can see the pictures and words while you read the story aloud. **Read aloud pages 64 through 80 of the story.**

TIP Scarlet fever used to be a common childhood disease. Thanks to vaccines and antibiotics, it is now rare for a child to come down with this disease.

Check Your Reading

"The Velveteen Rabbit"

Have students retell pages 64 through 80 of the story in their own words to develop grammar, vocabulary, comprehension, and fluency skills. When finished, **ask students the following questions** to check comprehension and encourage discussion.

Objectives
- Identify and define fantasy.
- Answer questions requiring literal recall of details.

▸ What does *fantasy* mean? Answers will vary; guide students to recall that it means "make-believe."

▸ The Velveteen Rabbit and the Skin Horse talk to each other in the story. Is this real or fantasy? fantasy   How can you tell? They're toys, and toys can't speak.

▸ The Velveteen Rabbit has feelings. Can a stuffed rabbit really have feelings? No Why not? It's a toy.

▸ Where does the Boy go when he gets better? the seaside

▸ What does the Fairy do to the Velveteen Rabbit? She turns him into a real rabbit.

Reading for Meaning

Make Inferences: Emotions

Tell students that good readers use clues to **infer**, or figure out, what is not written on the page. Good readers think about the **words in the story**, and they use **prior knowledge from past experience** to make inferences and better understand a story. Good readers can infer things such as why a character does something or how a character feels.

Ask students the following questions to check their ability to make inferences.

Objectives

- Make inferences based on text and/or prior knowledge.
- Support inferences with evidence from text and/or prior knowledge.

1. **Read aloud:**
   "'Hurrah!' thought the little Rabbit. 'Tomorrow we shall go to the seaside!'"

   ▸ How do you think the Velveteen Rabbit is feeling? excited; happy
   Why is he feeling this way? Guide students to understand that the
   Velveteen Rabbit feels this way because he thinks he is going on a trip
   with the Boy.

   ▸ Have you ever had plans to go on a trip? How did it make you feel?
   Answers will vary.   Do you think the Velveteen Rabbit felt the same way?
   Guide students to recognize that their feelings in a similar situation can
   help them figure out how the Velveteen Rabbit feels.

2. **Read aloud:**
   "And so the little Rabbit was put into a sack with the old picture-books and a lot of rubbish, and carried out to the end of the garden behind the fowl-house."

   ▸ How do you think the Velveteen Rabbit feels when he is put into a sack of
   trash? Possible answers: scared; sad; confused   Why do you think he is
   feeling this way? Answers will vary; guide students to understand that the
   Velveteen Rabbit doesn't understand why he's been thrown away and is
   probably feeling more than one emotion.

3. Remind students that when the Fairy made the Velveteen Rabbit real, he didn't realize it at first. Then **read aloud:**
   "'Run and play, little Rabbit!' she said. But the little Rabbit sat quite still for a moment and never moved. For when he saw all the wild rabbits dancing around him he suddenly remembered about his hind legs, and he didn't want them to see that he was made all in one piece."

   ▸ How do you think the Velveteen Rabbit feels when he sees the other
   rabbits dancing? Answers will vary; guide students to understand that the
   Velveteen Rabbit isn't aware he's a real rabbit yet, and he's embarrassed
   because he thinks he doesn't have hind legs like the other rabbits.

Review "The Velveteen Rabbit"

Lesson Overview

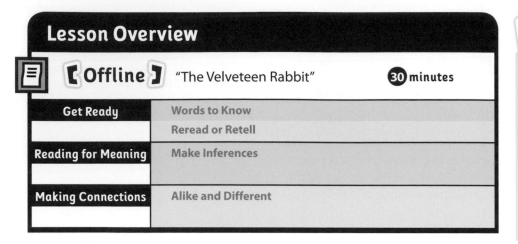

[Offline] "The Velveteen Rabbit"		30 minutes
Get Ready	Words to Know	
	Reread or Retell	
Reading for Meaning	Make Inferences	
Making Connections	Alike and Different	

Big Ideas

▸ Comprehension entails actively thinking about what is being read.
▸ Comprehension is facilitated when readers connect new information to information previously learned.

Materials

Supplied
- "The Velveteen Rabbit," *K¹² Read Aloud Treasury,* pp. 64–80
- *K¹² Language Arts Activity Book,* p. LC 27

Also Needed
- crayons

Keywords

compare – to explain how two or more things are alike

contrast – to explain how two or more things are different

graphic organizer – a visual tool used to show relationships between key concepts; formats include webs, diagrams, and charts

infer – to use clues and what you already know to make a guess

inference – a guess you make using the clues in a text and what you already know

 **30 minutes**

"The Velveteen Rabbit"
Work **together** with students to complete offline Get Ready, Reading for Meaning, and Making Connections activities.

Get Ready

Words to Know
Ask students to define the following words and use them in a sentence:

bedclothes	germ	scarlet fever
bracken	hind	shabby
burrow	insignificant	velveteen
clockwork	nursery	
disinfect	rubbish	

Correct any incorrect or vague definitions.

> **Objectives**
> - Build vocabulary through listening, reading, and discussion.
> - Use new vocabulary in written and spoken sentences.

Reread or Retell
If you'd like to, reread the story to students. Otherwise, have students retell the **entire** story using the pictures as a guide, or move on to the next activity.

Reading for Meaning

Make Inferences
Remind students that when readers **infer**, they use clues to fill in what is not written on the page. Good readers think about the **words in the story** and their **own experiences**. Doing so helps them figure out, or infer, things like what might be happening to a character, or what a character is doing.
   Ask students the following questions to check their ability to make inferences.

> **Objectives**
> - Make inferences based on text and/or prior knowledge.
> - Support inferences with evidence from text and/or prior knowledge.

1. **Read aloud:** ". . . Aunts and Uncles came to dinner, and there was a great rustling of tissue paper and unwrapping of parcels . . . "

   ▸ What do the words "great rustling of tissue paper and unwrapping of parcels" tell you? The Boy is opening presents.

2. **Read aloud:** "His face grew very flushed . . . and his little body was so hot that it burned the Rabbit when he held him close."

   ▸ Why is the Boy's body so hot that it burns the Velveteen Rabbit? The Boy has a fever.

3. **Read aloud:** "And while [the Boy] was playing, two rabbits crept out from the bracken and peeped at him. One of them was brown all over, but the other had strange markings under his fur, as though long ago he had been spotted, and the spots still showed through."

   ▸ Who is the rabbit with strange markings under his fur? the Velveteen Rabbit   How do you know this? The Velveteen Rabbit is now a real rabbit, but when he was a toy he had spots.

Making Connections

Alike and Different

Introduce students to a simple graphic organizer, which is used to organize information and demonstrate understanding in a visual way.

Objectives
- Demonstrate understanding through graphic organizers.
- Compare and contrast elements within a text.

1. On page LC 27 in *K¹² Language Arts Activity Book*, help students complete the Venn diagram.
   Say: This is called a Venn diagram. We use it to show how things are alike and how they are different. Let's use it to show how the Velveteen Rabbit is like a real rabbit in some ways, and how it is different from a real rabbit in other ways.

2. Ask students to name things that describe the Velveteen Rabbit, and write these attributes in the left circle of the Venn diagram. Possible answers: no hind legs; made out of velveteen; can't move; not alive

3. Ask students to name things that describe a real rabbit, and write these attributes in the right circle of the Venn diagram. Possible answers: has hind legs; furry; moves; alive

4. Ask students to name things that describe both the Velveteen Rabbit and a real rabbit, and write these attributes in the center of the Venn diagram, where the circles overlap. Possible answers: have eyes, ears, nose, paws, whiskers; feel soft

5. Discuss how reading the story helps students determine how the Velveteen Rabbit and a real rabbit are alike and different.

6. Have students color the pictures of the Velveteen Rabbit and real rabbit.

Introduce "Rare and Wonderful Pandas"

Lesson Overview

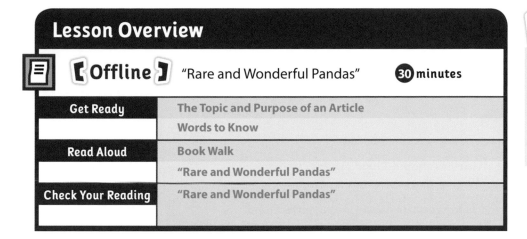

	Offline "Rare and Wonderful Pandas"	**30** minutes
Get Ready	The Topic and Purpose of an Article	
	Words to Know	
Read Aloud	Book Walk	
	"Rare and Wonderful Pandas"	
Check Your Reading	"Rare and Wonderful Pandas"	

Advance Preparation

Read "Rare and Wonderful Pandas" before beginning the Read Aloud activity, to locate Words to Know within the text.

Materials

Supplied

- "Rare and Wonderful Pandas," *K¹² World: Animals Around the World,* pp. 2–9

Story Synopsis

Who doesn't love pandas? These adorable animals are as interesting as they are rare.

Keywords

author's purpose – the reason the author wrote a text: to entertain, to inform, to express an opinion, or to persuade

nonfiction – writings about true things

topic – the subject of a text

 **30 minutes**

"Rare and Wonderful Pandas"

Work **together** with students to complete offline Get Ready, Read Aloud, and Check Your Reading activities.

Get Ready

The Topic and Purpose of an Article

Introduce students to some of the characteristics of nonfiction text.

1. Tell students that every magazine article has a **topic**. Good readers can figure out the topic by asking themselves, "What is this article mostly about?"

2. Explain that an author writes an article for a certain reason, or **purpose**. Good readers can figure out the purpose of an article by asking themselves, "Why did the author write this?"
   Say: Authors write articles for one of the following reasons: to teach us something, to entertain us, to convince us of something, or to tell us their opinion.

3. Have students practice naming the topic and purpose of an article.
   Say: Listen carefully as I read the title of an article and what it's about. In the article "Darling Dinosaurs," the author gives interesting facts about dinosaurs.

   ► What do you think is the topic of the article "Darling Dinosaurs"? dinosaurs
   ► Why do you think the author wrote the article? to teach us about dinosaurs

Objectives
- Identify topic.
- Identify the purpose of a text.
- Increase concept and content vocabulary.
- Use new vocabulary in written and spoken sentences.

Words to Know

Before reading "Rare and Wonderful Pandas,"

1. Have students say each word aloud.

2. Ask students if they know what each word means.

   ► If students know a word's meaning, have them define it and use it in a sentence.
   ► If students don't know a word's meaning, read them the definition and discuss the word with them.

bamboo – a tall, leafy plant with a hard, hollow stem
grind – to crush
jaw – the two bones that hold your teeth
law – a rule you must obey; a rule made by the government
lend – to let someone borrow something of yours
protect – to guard or keep safe
rare – not seen or done very often

Read Aloud

Book Walk

Prepare students by taking them on a Book Walk of "Rare and Wonderful Pandas." Scan the magazine article together and ask students to make predictions about the text.

1. Turn to the **table of contents**. Help students find today's selection, and turn to that page.

2. Point to and read aloud the **title of the article**.

3. Have students look at the **pictures** in the article. Answers to questions may vary.

   ▸ What do you think the article is about?
   ▸ What do you know about pandas?
   ▸ Have you ever seen a panda? What did it look like? How did it act?

4. Point to and read aloud any **headers, captions, or other features** that stand out. Answers to questions may vary.

   ▸ What do you think the article might tell us about pandas?

Objectives
- Make predictions based on title, illustrations, and/or context clues.
- Read and listen to a variety of texts for information and pleasure independently or as part of a group.

"Rare and Wonderful Pandas"

Now it's time to read the article. Have students sit next to you so that they can see the pictures and words while you read the article aloud.

Read aloud the entire article. Emphasize Words to Know as you come to them. If appropriate, use the pictures to help show what each word means.

Check Your Reading

"Rare and Wonderful Pandas"

Have students retell the article in their own words to develop grammar, vocabulary, comprehension, and fluency skills. When finished, **ask students the following questions** to check comprehension and encourage discussion.

▸ What is the topic of this article? pandas
▸ How do you know this is the topic? Most of the article is about pandas.
▸ Why do you think the author wrote this article? to teach about pandas
▸ How big is a newborn panda? about the size of a stick of butter
▸ What do pandas like to eat? bamboo

Objectives
- Identify topic.
- Identify the purpose of a text.
- Answer questions requiring literal recall of details.

Explore "Rare and Wonderful Pandas"

LITERATURE & COMPREHENSION

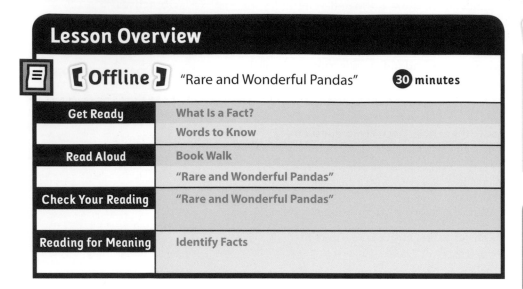

Lesson Overview

[Offline] "Rare and Wonderful Pandas"		30 minutes
Get Ready	What Is a Fact?	
	Words to Know	
Read Aloud	Book Walk	
	"Rare and Wonderful Pandas"	
Check Your Reading	"Rare and Wonderful Pandas"	
Reading for Meaning	Identify Facts	

Materials

Supplied

- "Rare and Wonderful Pandas," *K¹² World: Animals Around the World,* pp. 2–9

Keywords

fact – something that can be proven true

nonfiction – writings about true things

Advance Preparation

Before working with students, spend a few minutes reviewing Words to Know. Then review the Check Your Reading and Reading for Meaning activities to familiarize yourself with the questions and answers.

 **30** minutes

"Rare and Wonderful Pandas"

Work **together** with students to complete offline Get Ready, Read Aloud, Check Your Reading, and Reading for Meaning activities.

Get Ready ....

What Is a Fact?

Nonfiction text is writing about real things. Nonfiction articles are filled with **facts**. A fact is something that you can prove is true.

▶ What day is it? Answers will vary.
  Say: The day is a fact. You can prove what day it is.
▶ Is celery green? Yes
  Say: This is a fact. You can prove that celery is green.
▶ Does an elephant have a trunk? Yes
  Say: This is a fact. You can prove that an elephant has a trunk.

Remind students that they have read an article called "Rare and Wonderful Pandas." Ask them to tell you a fact about pandas. If they cannot name a fact, tell them that they will have a chance to hear facts about pandas when you reread the article.

Objectives

- Identify facts in informational text.
- Increase concept and content vocabulary.
- Use new vocabulary in written and spoken sentences.

Words to Know

Before reading "Rare and Wonderful Pandas,"

1. Have students say each word aloud.

2. Ask students if they know what each word means.

   ▶ If students know a word's meaning, have them define it and use it in a sentence.
   ▶ If students don't know a word's meaning, read them the definition and discuss the word with them.

bamboo – a tall, leafy plant with a hard, hollow stem
grind – to crush
jaw – the two bones that hold your teeth
law – a rule you must obey; a rule made by the government
lend – to let someone borrow something of yours
protect – to guard or keep safe
rare – not seen or done very often

Read Aloud

Book Walk

Prepare students by taking them on a Book Walk of "Rare and Wonderful Pandas." Scan the magazine article together to revisit the text.

1. Turn to today's selection.

2. Point to and read aloud the **title of the article**.

3. Have students look at the **pictures** in the article. Answers to questions may vary.

   ▶ What is something you learned about pandas that you didn't already know?

   ▶ Have you ever seen a panda at a zoo? If not, would you like to? Why or why not?

Objectives

- Activate prior knowledge by previewing text and/or discussing topic.
- Read and listen to a variety of texts for information and pleasure independently or as part of a group.

"Rare and Wonderful Pandas"

Now it's time to read the article. Have students sit next to you so that they can see the pictures and words while you read the article aloud.

Read aloud the entire article. Remind students to listen carefully for facts about pandas.

Check Your Reading

"Rare and Wonderful Pandas"

Have students retell the article in their own words to develop grammar, vocabulary, comprehension, and fluency skills. When finished, **ask students the following questions** to check comprehension and encourage discussion. If students have trouble responding to a question, **help them locate the answer in the article**.

Objectives

- Identify facts in informational text.
- Identify different types of text.

▶ The article says pandas like to walk on four legs when they grow up. What is this kind of information called? a fact

▶ What is special about a fact? It is true.

▶ Is everything in this article true? Yes   What is this kind of writing called? nonfiction

▶ The article says pandas live in the wild only in central China. Is this a fact? Yes   How do you know? You can prove it.

▶ What do pandas like to eat? bamboo

▶ What do pandas use to chew up tough bamboo? strong jaws; large, flat teeth

Reading for Meaning

Identify Facts

Ask students the following questions to further check their ability to identify, recall, and comprehend facts. If students have trouble responding to a question, **help them locate the answer in the article**.

Objectives

- Identify facts in informational text.

- What does a newborn panda look like? It's pink and covered with white fur. Is this a fact? Yes   How do you know? You can prove it.
- When does a panda learn to walk? when it's three months old
- How do pandas like to walk? on four legs
- How tall is a panda when it's walking on four legs? about three feet tall
- How tall is a panda when it stands on its two hind legs? about six feet tall
- How much bamboo does a panda eat in a day? about 40 pounds
- There are laws to protect pandas. What do the laws say? People can't hunt pandas or cut down the bamboo they eat.
- How do these laws help pandas? They keep pandas safe and healthy.
- Why do the people of China lend their pandas to zoos around the world? so other people can see them and enjoy them

Review "Rare and Wonderful Pandas"

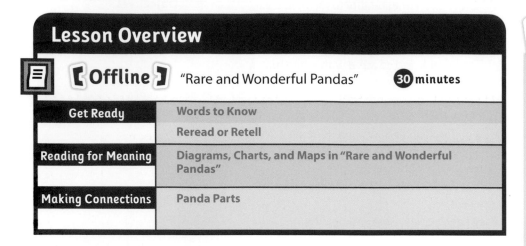

Lesson Overview

[Offline] "Rare and Wonderful Pandas" **30** minutes

Get Ready	Words to Know
	Reread or Retell
Reading for Meaning	Diagrams, Charts, and Maps in "Rare and Wonderful Pandas"
Making Connections	Panda Parts

Big Ideas

▸ Comprehension is the reason for reading.
▸ Comprehension is facilitated by an understanding of physical presentation (headings, subheads, graphics, and other features).

[Materials]

Supplied

- "Rare and Wonderful Pandas," *K¹² World: Animals Around the World,* pp. 2–9
- *K¹² Language Arts Activity Book,* p. LC 28

Also Needed

- crayons

Keywords

informational text – text written to explain and give information on a topic

visual text support – a graphic feature that helps a reader better understand text such as a picture, chart, or map

 **30 minutes**

"Rare and Wonderful Pandas"

Work **together** with students to complete offline Get Ready, Reading for Meaning, and Making Connections activities.

Get Ready ···

Words to Know
Ask students to define the following words and use them in a sentence:

bamboo	law	protect
grind	lend	rare
jaw		

Correct any incorrect or vague definitions.

 Objectives
- Increase concept and content vocabulary.
- Use new vocabulary in written and spoken sentences.

Reread or Retell
If you'd like to, reread the article to students. Otherwise, have students retell the article using the pictures as a guide, or move on to the next activity.

Reading for Meaning ·····································

Diagrams, Charts, and Maps in "Rare and Wonderful Pandas"
Tell students that sometimes the ideas in an article can be hard to understand. Seeing **pictures can make it easier to understand those ideas**. A map is a kind of picture that helps readers understand where a particular place is. Other pictures, such as charts and diagrams, have numbers or labels that give extra information. That extra information can help readers better comprehend the ideas in an article.

Ask students the following questions to check their understanding of text features.

 Objectives
- Identify the purpose of and information provided by illustrations, titles, charts, and graphs.

1. Point to the height chart on page 4.

   ▸ What does the chart show? how tall a panda is compared to a person when it's walking and when it's standing
   ▸ What does the chart show about a panda when it stands compared to when it walks? A panda is taller when it stands than when it walks.

2. Point to the diagram of the bamboo plant on page 7.

   ▸ What do readers learn by looking at the diagram, or picture, of the bamboo stalk? names of parts of a bamboo plant
   ▸ How many parts of a bamboo plant does this diagram name? three
   What are they? leaf; stalk; bamboo shoot

3. Point to the map on page 8.

   ▶ What is this kind of picture called? a map
   ▶ What does this map show? where pandas live in the wild
   ▶ According to the map, where do pandas live in the wild? central China;
     the middle of China

TIP Diagrams, charts, and maps are types of visual **text supports**.

Making Connections

Panda Parts

Have students complete a simple diagram to reinforce their understanding of visual text supports.

1. On page LC 28 in *K¹² Language Arts Activity Book*, have students color the picture of the panda. They should look at pictures of pandas in the article to help them recall the black-and-white coloring pattern.

2. Ask students to name what each line points to.

3. Write the name of each part in the corresponding blue box.

4. Have students describe what information the diagram is meant to teach.

5. Have them tell a fact they have learned about pandas.

6. Write the fact that students dictate on the line at the bottom of the page.

Objectives

- Build vocabulary through listening, reading, and discussion.
- Identify facts in informational text.
- Identify the purpose of and information provided by illustrations, titles, charts, and graphs.

Introduce "The Lion and the Mouse"

Lesson Overview

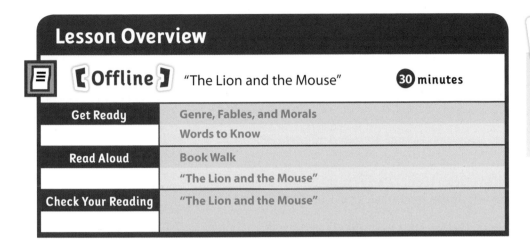

[Offline] "The Lion and the Mouse"	30 minutes
Get Ready	Genre, Fables, and Morals
	Words to Know
Read Aloud	Book Walk
	"The Lion and the Mouse"
Check Your Reading	"The Lion and the Mouse"

Advance Preparation

Read "The Lion and the Mouse" before beginning the Read Aloud activities, to locate Words to Know within the text.

Big Ideas

Comprehension requires an understanding of story structure.

[Materials]

Supplied

- "The Lion and the Mouse," *K¹² Read Aloud Treasury,* pp. 82–86

Story Synopsis

Over the years, adults have read Aesop's fables to children in an effort to teach morals in a lively and entertaining fashion. In this selection, the mighty lion learns that even the lowliest of creatures can literally save his life.

Keywords

fable – a story that teaches a lesson and may contain animal characters

genre – a category for classifying literary works

literal recall – the ability to describe information stated directly in a text

moral – the lesson of a story, particularly a fable

[Offline] 30 minutes

"The Lion and the Mouse"

Work **together** with students to complete offline Get Ready, Read Aloud, and Check Your Reading activities.

Get Ready

Genre, Fables, and Morals

Tell students that they will read a kind of story called a fable. Introduce the concept of a fable and its moral.

1. Explain that a story can be written to teach a lesson. This kind of story is called a **fable**. A fable often has characters who are animals that act like people.

2. Tell students that the lesson that a fable teaches is called a **moral**. Some well-known morals are look before you leap; treat others the way you would like to be treated; and you can't judge a book by its cover.

3. Have students practice figuring out the moral of a fable.
   Say: Listen to this fable. One day a tortoise and a hare had a race. The hare sped off and ran far ahead of the tortoise, who was slow by nature. The hare got so far ahead of the tortoise that he decided to take a nap. When the hare woke up from his nap, he saw that the tortoise was about to cross the finish line. No matter how fast he ran, the hare could not catch up, and the tortoise won the race.

   ► Does this story teach a lesson? Yes
   ► What do you think is the lesson, or moral, of this fable? Answers will vary; guide students to recognize that the moral is "Slow and steady wins the race."
   ► What do we call a story that teaches a lesson? a fable

TIP Although an objective for this lesson is to identify genre, there is no need to introduce that term to students.

Words to Know

Before reading "The Lion and the Mouse,"

1. Have students say each word aloud.

2. Ask students if they know what each word means.

   ► If students know a word's meaning, have them define it and use it in a sentence.
   ► If students don't know a word's meaning, read them the definition and discuss the word with them.

> **Objectives**
> - Identify genre.
> - Identify the moral or lesson of a text.
> - Build vocabulary through listening, reading, and discussion.
> - Use new vocabulary in written and spoken sentences.

ashamed – feeling embarrassed or guilty
beast – a wild animal
gnaw – to chew on something over and over
roam – to wander; to travel around without a purpose
scamper – to run quickly with small, light steps
snatch – to take or grab something quickly

Read Aloud ···

Book Walk

Prepare students by taking them on a Book Walk of "The Lion and the Mouse." Scan the story together.

1. Turn to the **table of contents**. Help students find today's selection, and turn to that page.

2. Point to and read aloud the **title of the story**.

3. Have students look at the **pictures** of the story. Answers to questions may vary.

   ▸ What do you think the story is about?
   ▸ Where do you think the story takes place?
   ▸ Have you ever done a favor for someone? If you have, what was the favor?

Objectives
- Make predictions based on title, illustrations, and/or context clues.
- Listen and respond to texts representing a variety of cultures, time periods, and traditions.

"The Lion and the Mouse"

Now it's time to read the story. Have students sit next to you so that they can see the pictures and words while you read the story aloud.

   Read aloud the entire story. Emphasize Words to Know as you come to them. If appropriate, use the pictures to help show what each word means.

TIP *Aesop is pronounced "EE-sahp."*

Check Your Reading ···

"The Lion and the Mouse"

Have students retell the story in their own words to develop grammar, vocabulary, comprehension, and fluency skills. When finished, **ask students the following questions** to check comprehension and encourage discussion.

Objectives
- Identify genre.
- Identify the moral or lesson of a text.
- Answer questions requiring literal recall of details.

   ▸ What kind of story is "The Lion and the Mouse"? a fable   How can you tell? It teaches a lesson; animals act like people in the story.
   ▸ What is the moral of this fable? Answers will vary; guide students to understand that the moral is "No matter how small you are, you can always help others."
   ▸ What is the lion doing when the mouse first comes by? sleeping
   ▸ What does the lion want to do to the mouse? He wants to eat the mouse for breakfast.
   ▸ How does the mouse feel when the lion says he's going to eat him? frightened

Explore "The Lion and the Mouse"

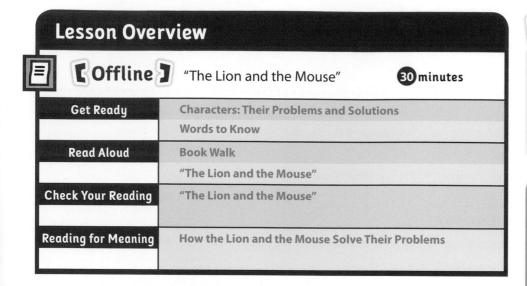

Lesson Overview

[Offline]	"The Lion and the Mouse"	30 minutes
Get Ready	Characters: Their Problems and Solutions	
	Words to Know	
Read Aloud	Book Walk	
	"The Lion and the Mouse"	
Check Your Reading	"The Lion and the Mouse"	
Reading for Meaning	How the Lion and the Mouse Solve Their Problems	

[Materials]

Supplied
- "The Lion and the Mouse," *K¹² Read Aloud Treasury,* pp. 82–86

Keywords

character – a person or animal in a story

problem – an issue a character must solve in a story

solution – how a character solves a problem in a story

Advance Preparation

Before working with students, spend a few minutes reviewing Words to Know. Then review the Check Your Reading and Reading for Meaning activities to familiarize yourself with the questions and answers.

Big Ideas

Comprehension requires an understanding of story structure.

[Offline] 30 minutes

"The Lion and the Mouse"

Work **together** with students to complete offline Get Ready, Read Aloud, Check Your Reading, and Reading for Meaning activities.

Get Ready

Characters: Their Problems and Solutions
Introduce the story structure elements of character, problem, and solution.

1. Tell students that the people in a story are called characters. **In a fable, the characters are often animals that act like people.**

2. Explain that a character usually needs to solve a problem. There can be more than one character that needs to solve a problem in a story.

3. Remind students of the fable "The Tortoise and the Hare."
   Say: A tortoise and a hare had a race. The hare sped off and got so far ahead of the slow tortoise that he decided to take a nap. While the hare slept, the tortoise slowly and steadily made his way to the finish line. The hare ran as fast as he could, but he could not catch up, and the tortoise won the race.

   ▸ Who are the characters in this fable? the tortoise; the hare
   ▸ What is the tortoise's problem? how to win the race when he walks so slowly
   ▸ How does the tortoise try to solve his problem? He walks slowly and steadily, and he never gives up.
   ▸ What is the hare's problem? how to win the race after he wakes up from a nap
   ▸ How does the hare try to solve his problem? He runs as fast as he can to catch up to the tortoise.
   ▸ Does the hare solve his problem? No, he loses the race.
   ▸ Does the tortoise solve his problem? Yes, he wins the race.

> **Objectives**
> - Identify character(s).
> - Identify story structure elements—problem and solution.
> - Build vocabulary through listening, reading, and discussion.
> - Use new vocabulary in written and spoken sentences.

Words to Know
Before reading "The Lion and the Mouse,"

1. Have students say each word aloud.

2. Ask students if they know what each word means.

   ▸ If students know a word's meaning, have them define it and use it in a sentence.
   ▸ If students don't know a word's meaning, read them the definition and discuss the word with them.

ashamed – feeling embarrassed or guilty
beast – a wild animal
gnaw – to chew on something over and over
roam – to wander; to travel around without a purpose
scamper – to run quickly with small, light steps
snatch – to take or grab something quickly

Read Aloud

Book Walk

Prepare students by taking them on a Book Walk of "The Lion and the Mouse." Scan the story together to revisit the characters and events.

1. Turn to today's selection. Point to and read aloud the **title of the story**.

2. Have students look at the **pictures** of the story.

   ► Which picture shows a character in the fable? Answers will vary.
   ► What is the name of the character in the picture? Answers will vary.
   ► What is this character's problem? Possible answers: the mouse is caught by the lion; the lion is caught by hunters and put in a net.

Objectives
- Identify story structure elements—problem and solution.
- Listen and respond to texts representing a variety of cultures, time periods, and traditions.

"The Lion and the Mouse"

Now it's time to read the story. Have students sit next to you so that they can see the pictures and words while you read the story aloud.

Read aloud the entire story. Tell students to listen for problems the characters need to solve in the story.

Check Your Reading

"The Lion and the Mouse"

Have students retell the fable in their own words to develop grammar, vocabulary, comprehension, and fluency skills. When finished, **ask students the following questions** to check comprehension and encourage discussion.

Objectives
- Identify character(s).
- Describe character(s).
- Answer questions requiring literal recall of details.

   ► Name the two characters in this fable. the lion; the mouse
   ► How would you describe the lion at the beginning of the story? What is he like? Possible answers: big; proud; hungry; angry; good sense of humor; fair
   ► How would you describe the mouse? What is he like? Possible answers: small; scared; thankful; smart; clever; helpful
   ► How does the lion get caught? He falls into a hole.
   ► How does the lion feel when he can't escape? Possible answers: angry; scared; sad
   ► How would you describe the lion at the end of the story? How has he changed from the beginning? Possible answers: thankful; happy; surprised; have students give examples from the fable to support their answers.

Reading for Meaning

How the Lion and the Mouse Solve Their Problems

Ask students the following questions to **check their understanding of problems and solutions**. If students have trouble identifying a character's problem, **have them look at the pictures to refresh their memory**.

Objectives

- Identify story structure elements—problem and solution.

- ▸ What is the mouse's problem at the beginning of the fable? The lion catches the mouse and wants to eat him.
- ▸ How does the mouse solve his problem? He convinces the lion to let him go.
- ▸ How does the mouse convince the lion to let him go? The mouse tells the lion that he might be able to help him one day.
- ▸ What is the lion's problem? He is tied to a tree and needs to escape.
- ▸ What does the lion do to try to solve his problem? He tugs and tears at the rope.   Does this solve the lion's problem? No
- ▸ What does the lion do when he believes he can't escape? He gives up; he cries; he feels sad.
- ▸ Who finally solves the lion's problem? the mouse
- ▸ How does the mouse solve the lion's problem? He gnaws and chews on the rope until it breaks.

Review "The Lion and the Mouse"

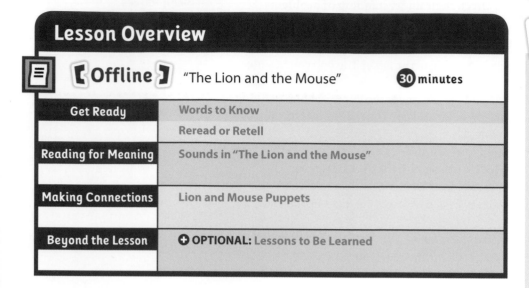

Lesson Overview

[Offline] "The Lion and the Mouse" **30** minutes

Get Ready	Words to Know
	Reread or Retell
Reading for Meaning	Sounds in "The Lion and the Mouse"
Making Connections	Lion and Mouse Puppets
Beyond the Lesson	⊕ OPTIONAL: Lessons to Be Learned

Big Ideas

Comprehension entails actively thinking about what is being read.

[Materials]

Supplied

- "The Lion and the Mouse,"
  K¹² Read Aloud Treasury,
  pp. 82–86
- *K¹² Language Arts Activity
  Book,* p. LC 29

Also Needed

- crayons
- scissors, round-end safety
- craft sticks (2)
- glue stick

Keywords

infer – to use clues and what
you already know to make a
guess

inference – a guess you make
using the clues in a text and
what you already know

sensory language –
language that appeals to the
five senses

 **30** minutes

"The Lion and the Mouse"

Work **together** with students to complete offline Get Ready, Reading for Meaning, Making Connections, and Beyond the Lesson activities.

Get Ready

Words to Know

Ask students to define the following words and use them in a sentence:

ashamed	gnaw	scamper
beast	roam	snatch

Correct any incorrect or vague definitions.

Objectives
- Build vocabulary through listening, reading, and discussion.
- Use new vocabulary in written and spoken sentences.

Reread or Retell

If you'd like to, reread the story to students. Otherwise, have students retell the story using the pictures as a guide, or move on to the next activity.

Reading for Meaning

Sounds in "The Lion and the Mouse"

Tell students that authors sometimes use words to help readers imagine the sounds of a story. Geese *honk*, lightning *cracks*, and bees *buzz*.

Objectives
- Identify author's use of sensory language.
- Make inferences based on text and/or prior knowledge.

▸ Which words in the following sentences help you imagine that you can hear sounds?

> *Crunch, crunch, crunch!* The boy ate a bag of crispy potato chips. *crunch, crunch, crunch*
> *Creak!* The old, heavy door opened slowly. *creak*

Read aloud from "The Lion and the Mouse," and then ask students the questions to check their understanding of sensory language.

1. **Read aloud:** "'Grrr!' growled the lion."

   ▸ Which word helps you imagine the sound the lion is making? *Grrr!*
   ▸ What does the sound "Grrr!" tell you? The lion is mad.

2. **Read aloud:** "But the lion opened his great big mouth and began to smack his lips."

   ▸ Which word helps you imagine the sound the lion is making? *smack*
   ▸ Can you smack your lips? Encourage students to make a smacking sound to better understand the concept.

3. **Read aloud:** "…the mouse chewed until all at once, *snip, snap*, he had gnawed through the very last strand.

   ▸ Which words help you imagine a sound? *snip, snap*
   ▸ What makes the *snip, snap* sound? the rope breaking

Making Connections

Lion and Mouse Puppets

Reinforce retelling skills by having students act out "The Lion and the Mouse" with puppets.

1. Have students color and cut out the pictures of the lion and the mouse on page LC 29 in *K¹² Language Arts Activity Book*.

2. Help them glue the pictures to craft sticks to create puppets.

3. Have students use the puppets to retell the fable.

4. Discuss the moral of the fable.

5. Ask students to think of a time when they helped someone who was much bigger than they are. Answers to questions may vary.

   ▸ How did it make you feel to be helpful?
   ▸ Was the person you helped surprised you could help him or her, even though you were smaller?
   ▸ Did the person you helped say "thank you"?

> **Objectives**
> - Reenact a story in correct sequence.
> - Retell read aloud stories using various media.
> - Make connections with text: text-to-text, text-to-self, text-to-world.

Beyond the Lesson

✚ OPTIONAL: Lessons to Be Learned

This activity is intended for students who have extra time and would benefit from hearing additional fables. Feel free to skip this activity.

1. Go to a library, and look for an age-appropriate book of Aesop's fables.

2. Lead a Book Walk, and then read aloud some or all of the fables.

3. Have students tell how their favorite fable in the book and "The Lion and the Mouse" are alike and different.

4. Have students explain the moral of their favorite fable in their own words.

> **Objectives**
> - Compare and contrast two texts on the same topic.

Introduce *Caps for Sale*

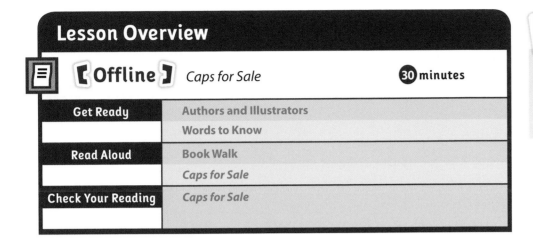

Lesson Overview

[Offline] *Caps for Sale*   **30** minutes

Get Ready	Authors and Illustrators
	Words to Know
Read Aloud	Book Walk
	Caps for Sale
Check Your Reading	*Caps for Sale*

Advance Preparation

Read *Caps for Sale* before beginning the Read Aloud activities, to locate Words to Know within the text.

Select a children's book from your personal library for Authors and Illustrators in the Get Ready. The book should have the names of the author and the illustrator printed on the cover or an inside page.

[Materials]

Supplied
- *Caps for Sale* by Esphyr Slobodkina

Story Synopsis
An unusual peddler walks up and down the streets in an attempt to sell his caps of many colors. What makes the peddler unusual? He wears all of his caps on top of his head! After he falls asleep under a tree, the peddler awakens to find his many caps are missing. Where can they be? Monkey business ensues.

Keywords
author – a writer
illustrator – the person who draws the pictures that go with a story

 **Offline** **30** minutes

Caps for Sale

Work **together** with students to complete offline Get Ready, Read Aloud, and Check Your Reading activities.

Get Ready ....

Authors and Illustrators

Introduce the concepts of author and illustrator.

 Objectives
- Describe role of author and/or illustrator.
- Build vocabulary through listening, reading, and discussion.
- Use new vocabulary in written and spoken sentences.

1. **Say:** Every book is written by someone. The person who writes a book is called an **author**.

2. **Say:** Many books have pictures in them. The person who makes the pictures is called an **illustrator**. The pictures an illustrator creates help readers better understand what the book is about. The pictures, or **illustrations**, can also be just for fun to make the book more enjoyable to read.

3. Explain that sometimes the author of a book is also the illustrator. That means the person who wrote the book also made all the pictures.

4. Show students a book from your personal library. Point to and read aloud the name of the author. Next point to and read aloud the name of the illustrator.

   ▶ What does an author do? write a book
   ▶ What does an illustrator do? make pictures for a book
   ▶ Can the author of a book and the illustrator of a book be the same person? Yes

Words to Know

Before reading *Caps for Sale*,

1. Have students say each word aloud.

2. Ask students if they know what each word means.

   ▶ If students know a word's meaning, have them define it and use it in a sentence.
   ▶ If students don't know a word's meaning, read them the definition and discuss the word with them.

country – places such as farms, open fields, and villages that are outside of towns and cities
disturb – to change the position of something
ordinary – normal; not special
peddler – a person who travels around, selling things
refresh – to make someone or something feel fresh and more energetic
upset – to tip or knock something over
wares – things that are for sale

TIP In this story, the words *disturb* and *upset* have similar meanings.

Read Aloud

Book Walk

Prepare students by taking them on a Book Walk of *Caps for Sale*. Scan the book together and ask students to make predictions about the story.

1. Have students look at the pictures on the cover. Point to and read aloud the **book title**.

   ▶ What do you think the book is about? Answers will vary.

2. Have students point to the name of the **author and illustrator**. Read aloud the name of the author and illustrator.

3. Have students locate the **title page**.

   ▶ What information is found on the title page? the book title; the name of the author and illustrator

4. Look through the book. Have students describe what they see in the **pictures**. Answers to questions may vary.

   ▶ Where do you think the story takes place?
   ▶ What do you think might happen in the story?
   ▶ Do you have a favorite cap or hat? What does it look like?

 TIP *Esphyr Slobodkina* is pronounced "es-FEER sloh-BAHD-keen-ah."

Objectives
- Identify author.
- Identify illustrator.
- Make predictions based on title, illustrations, and/or context clues.
- Listen and respond to texts representing a variety of cultures, time periods, and traditions.

Caps for Sale

Now it's time to read the story. Have students sit next to you so that they can see the pictures and words while you read the story aloud.

Read aloud the entire story. Emphasize Words to Know as you come to them. If appropriate, use the pictures to help show what each word means.

Check Your Reading

Caps for Sale

Have students retell the story in their own words to develop grammar, vocabulary, comprehension, and fluency skills. When finished, **ask students the following questions** to check understanding of the role of the author and illustrator and general comprehension of the story.

   ▶ The author of the book is named Esphyr Slobodkina. What does it mean to be an author? It means you are the writer.
   ▶ Esphyr Slobodkina is also the illustrator of the book. What does this mean? It means she drew the pictures.
   ▶ How does the peddler carry his caps? He wears them all on his head.
   ▶ Why does the peddler decide to take a walk in the country? No one wanted to buy any of his caps; he had no money for lunch.
   ▶ Where does the peddler rest? under a tree
   ▶ What does the peddler do under the tree? He falls asleep.

 TIP The name *Esphyr Slobodkina* might sound a bit unusual because it's Russian.

Objectives
- Describe role of author and/or illustrator.
- Answer questions requiring literal recall of details.

Explore *Caps for Sale*

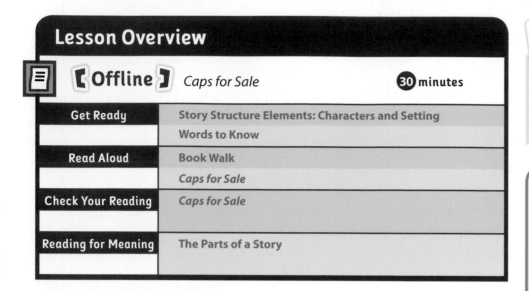

Lesson Overview

【Offline】 *Caps for Sale*	30 minutes
Get Ready	**Story Structure Elements: Characters and Setting**
	Words to Know
Read Aloud	**Book Walk**
	Caps for Sale
Check Your Reading	*Caps for Sale*
Reading for Meaning	**The Parts of a Story**

Advance Preparation

Before working with students, spend a few minutes reviewing Words to Know.
Then review the Check Your Reading and Reading for Meaning activities to familiarize
yourself with the questions and answers.

Big Ideas

▸ Comprehension requires an understanding of story structure.
▸ Comprehension is the reason for reading.
▸ Comprehension requires the reader to self-monitor understanding.

【Materials】

Supplied

- *Caps for Sale* by Esphyr
  Slobodkina

Keywords

character – a person or
animal in a story

retelling – using your own
words to tell a story that you
have listened to or read

self-monitor – to notice if
you do or do not understand
what you are reading

setting – when and where a
story takes place

story structure elements –
components of a story; they
include character, setting,
plot, problem, and solution

 **30 minutes**

Caps for Sale

Work **together** with students to complete offline Get Ready, Read Aloud, Check Your Reading, and Reading for Meaning activities.

Get Ready

Story Structure Elements: Characters and Setting
Good readers listen carefully to stories to learn the characters and setting of a story.

1. Tell students that the people or animals in a story are still characters, even if we never hear their names.

2. Tell students that where and when a story takes place is called the **setting**.

3. Point out that the author doesn't always directly state where and when a story happens. Good readers listen to the story and look at the pictures to figure out the setting.

   Say: Listen to this story: Chuck got up early Saturday morning. He cooked some jumbo Martian eggs and poured a glass of blue milk. After eating breakfast, he went outside to watch the sun rise above the Mountains of Mars.

   ▶ Where does the story take place? on Mars
   ▶ When does the story take place? Saturday morning
   ▶ Who is a character in the story? Chuck

Objectives
- Identify setting.
- Identify character(s).
- Build vocabulary through listening, reading, and discussion.
- Use new vocabulary in written and spoken sentences.

Words to Know
Before reading *Caps for Sale*,

1. Have students say each word aloud.

2. Ask students if they know what each word means.

   ▶ If students know a word's meaning, have them define it and use it in a sentence.
   ▶ If students don't know a word's meaning, read them the definition and discuss the word with them.

country – places such as farms, open fields, and villages that are outside of towns and cities
disturb – to change the position of something
ordinary – normal; not special
peddler – a person who travels around, selling things
refresh – to make someone or something feel fresh and more energetic
upset – to tip or knock something over
wares – things that are for sale

 In this story, the words *disturb* and *upset* have similar meanings.

Read Aloud

Book Walk

Prepare students by taking them on a Book Walk of *Caps for Sale*. Scan the book together.

1. Read aloud the **book title**.

2. Have students locate the name of the **author**. Read the name of the author.

3. Turn to the **dedication page**. Tell students that the author listed the names of people who are special to her on this page. Read aloud the dedication.

   ► Who would you put on the dedication page if you wrote a book? Answers will vary.

4. Look through the book. Have students describe what they see in the **pictures**.

   ► Where does the peddler walk? Possible answers: up and down the streets; in the town; in the country
   ► What do you see in the tree? monkeys; monkeys wearing caps

Caps for Sale

Now it's time to read the story. Have students sit next to you so that they can see the pictures and words while you read the story aloud.

Read aloud the story. Tell students to listen carefully so they can retell the beginning, middle, and end of the story later.

Check Your Reading

Caps for Sale

Ask students the following questions to check understanding of characters and setting, and general comprehension of the story.

► Who are the characters in the story? the peddler; the monkeys
► Where does the story begin? in a small town   How can you tell? from the pictures in the book and from the story
► Where does the middle of the story take place? in the country; under a tree   How can you tell? from the pictures in the book and from the story
► What do the monkeys do when the peddler shakes his finger at them and tells them to give back his caps? They shake their fingers back at him and say, "Tsz, tsz, tsz."
► How does this make the peddler feel? angry

Reading for Meaning

The Parts of a Story

Reinforce the concept of retelling a story in three parts. We retell stories so we can check our understanding of a story.

Objectives
- Retell the beginning, middle, and end of a story.
- Identify setting.

1. Remind students that a story has three main parts: **the beginning, the middle, and the end**.

   ▶ The **beginning** of a story introduces us to the characters. We might find out things like who the characters are, where they live, or what kind of job they have.
   ▶ In the **middle** of the story, readers usually learn that one of the characters has a problem, and he or she tries to solve the problem.
   ▶ The **end** of the story tells us how the problem is solved and how everything turns out.

2. **Have students retell the beginning, middle, and end of the story in their own words.** If students have trouble recalling parts of the story, **have them look at the pictures** to guide their retelling. **Ask students the following questions** when they have finished retelling the story.

   ▶ What happens at the beginning of *Caps for Sale*? The peddler walks up and down the streets of a town, trying to sell his caps.
   ▶ What does the peddler shout while he walks up and down the streets? "Caps! Caps for sale! Fifty cents a cap!"
   ▶ What happens in the middle of *Caps for Sale*? Possible answers: the peddler walks to the country and takes a nap under a tree; monkeys take the peddler's caps; the peddler tries to get his caps back from the monkeys.
   ▶ Where does the middle of the story take place? in the country; under a tree
   ▶ What happens every time the peddler tells the monkeys to give him back his caps? The monkeys copy the peddler; they do the same thing as the peddler.
   ▶ How does the peddler finally get all his caps back? He throws his own cap on the ground, and then the monkeys do the same thing.
   ▶ What happens at the end of *Caps for Sale*? The peddler gets his caps back, and then he walks back to town.

TIP Retelling a story is one way that good readers can self-monitor their comprehension.

Review *Caps for Sale*

Lesson Overview

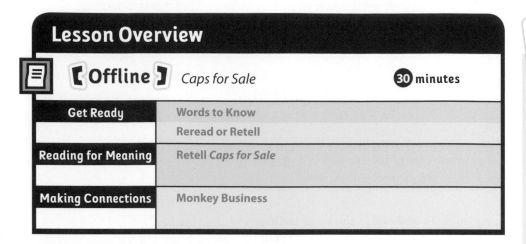

[Offline] *Caps for Sale*   **30** minutes

Get Ready	Words to Know
	Reread or Retell
Reading for Meaning	Retell *Caps for Sale*
Making Connections	Monkey Business

Advance Preparation

Gather caps for Making Connections.

Big Ideas

- ▶ Comprehension requires an understanding of story structure.
- ▶ Comprehension is the reason for reading.
- ▶ Comprehension requires the reader to self-monitor understanding.

Materials

Supplied

- *Caps for Sale* by Esphyr Slobodkina
- *K¹² Language Arts Activity Book,* p. LC 31

Also Needed

- scissors, round-end safety
- yarn
- tape, clear
- household objects – hole punch, caps (4–5)

Keywords

retelling – using your own words to tell a story that you have listened to or read

self-monitor – to notice if you do or do not understand what you are reading

30 minutes

Caps for Sale

Work **together** with students to complete offline Get Ready, Reading for Meaning, and Making Connections activities.

Get Ready

Words to Know

Ask students to define the following words and use them in a sentence:

country	peddler	upset
disturb	refresh	wares
ordinary		

Correct any incorrect or vague definitions.

Objectives

- Build vocabulary through listening, reading, and discussion.
- Use new vocabulary in written and spoken sentences.

Reread or Retell

If you'd like to, reread the story to students. Otherwise, have students retell the story using the pictures as a guide, or move on to the next activity.

Reading for Meaning

Retell *Caps for Sale*

Remind students that **retelling means using your own words to tell a story** you have heard or read. When good readers retell a story, they tell the most important things that happen in the beginning, middle, and end of the story. They mention the characters and the problems they have to solve. Good readers retell stories so they can check their understanding of a story.

Verify that students understand the concept of retelling and the idea of a beginning, middle, and end of a story.

Objectives

- Retell the beginning, middle, and end of a story.

- In what part of the story does the author tell us that no one wants to buy a cap from the peddler? the beginning   Retell that part of the story.
- In what part of the story does the author tell us that the peddler can't find the caps he wears on his head? the middle   Retell that part of the story.
- In what part of the story does the author tell us that the peddler picks up his caps and puts them back on his head? the end   Retell that part of the story.

TIP Retelling a story is one way that good readers can self-monitor their comprehension.

Making Connections

Monkey Business

Have students reenact a portion of the story as a response to the text and to reinforce the story's sequence. Gather scissors, yarn, tape, and a hole punch.

1. Have students cut out the mask on page LC 31 in *K¹² Language Arts Activity Book.*

2. Help them cut out the eye holes.

3. Use a hole punch to cut out the holes on the tabs so you can thread yarn through each tab.

4. Reinforce the holes with tape so the paper won't rip. Fold back the tabs.

5. Cut two lengths of yarn for each mask. Loop the yarn through the holes, and tie in a knot close to the end of each strand of yarn. Have students put on the mask, and tie the yarn behind their head.

6. Put a cap on your head, and have students put on the other caps you have gathered.

7. Stand up, and have students stand facing you. Reenact the actions of the peddler in the story, and have the students mimic you.

   ▸ Shake your finger and shout, "Give me back my caps!" (Students should shake their fingers and make the "tsz, tsz, tsz" sound.)
   ▸ Shake both hands and shout again.
   ▸ Stamp your foot and shout again.
   ▸ Stamp both feet and shout again.
   ▸ Throw your cap on the ground.

8. Gather all the caps. Play the Monkey Business game again, this time switching roles.

Objectives
- Reenact a story in the correct sequence.
- Respond to text through art, writing, and/or drama.

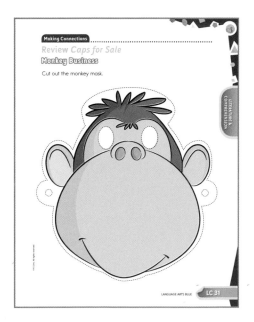

Introduce "Emperors of the Ice"

Lesson Overview

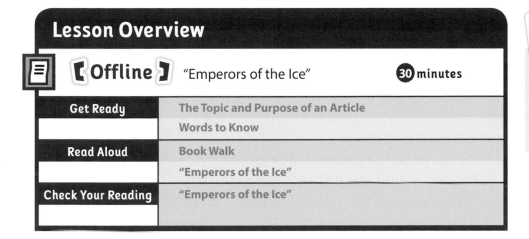

Offline — "Emperors of the Ice" — **30** minutes

Get Ready	The Topic and Purpose of an Article
	Words to Know
Read Aloud	Book Walk
	"Emperors of the Ice"
Check Your Reading	"Emperors of the Ice"

Advance Preparation

Read "Emperors of the Ice" before beginning the Read Aloud activity, to locate Words to Know within the text.

Materials

Supplied
- "Emperors of the Ice," *K¹² World: Animals Around the World,* pp. 10–17

Story Synopsis

Making the bottom of the world their home, emperor penguins fly through the water instead of the air. These amazing creatures make an annual trek across snow and ice that would tax most humans.

Keywords

author's purpose – the reason the author wrote a text: to entertain, to inform, to express an opinion, or to persuade

nonfiction – writings about true things

topic – the subject of a text

 **30** minutes

"Emperors of the Ice"
Work **together** with students to complete offline Get Ready, Read Aloud, and Check Your Reading activities.

Get Ready ....

The Topic and Purpose of an Article
Introduce students to some of the characteristics of nonfiction text.

1. Tell students that every magazine article has a **topic**. Good readers can figure out the topic by asking themselves, "What is this article mostly about?"

2. Explain that an author writes an article for a certain reason, or **purpose**. Good readers can figure out the purpose of an article by asking themselves, "Why did the author write this?" Authors write articles for one of the following reasons: to teach us something, to entertain us, to convince us of something, or to tell us their opinion.

3. Have students practice naming the topic and purpose of an article.
   Say: Listen carefully as I read the title of an article and what it's about. In the article "Lady Liberty," the author tells interesting facts about the Statue of Liberty.

   ▸ What do you think is the topic of the article "Lady Liberty"? the Statue of Liberty
   ▸ Why do you think the author wrote the article? to teach us things about the Statue of Liberty

Objectives
- Identify topic.
- Identify the purpose of a text.
- Increase concept and content vocabulary.
- Use new vocabulary in written and spoken sentences.

Words to Know
Before reading "Emperors of the Ice,"

1. Have students say each word aloud.

2. Ask students if they know what each word means.

   ▸ If students know a word's meaning, have them define it and use it in a sentence.
   ▸ If students don't know a word's meaning, read them the definition and discuss the word with them.

chick – a baby bird
continent – one of seven large land masses on the earth
flippers – the flat limbs of a sea animal, such as a penguin or seal, which are used for swimming
journey – a long trip
krill – very tiny shrimplike animals that live in the sea

Read Aloud

Book Walk

Prepare students by taking them on a Book Walk of "Emperors of the Ice." Scan the magazine article together and ask students to make predictions about the text.

1. Have students turn to the **table of contents**. Ask them what information is found on this page. Help students find today's selection, and turn to that page.

2. Point to and read aloud the **title of the article**.

3. Have students look at the **pictures** in the article. Answers to questions may vary.

   ▸ What do you think the article is about?
   ▸ What do you know about penguins?
   ▸ Where do you think penguins live?

4. Point to and read aloud any **headers, captions, or other features** that stand out.

   ▸ What do you think the article might tell us about penguins? Answers will vary.

Objectives

- Identify table of contents
- Make predictions based on title, illustrations, and/or context clues.
- Read and listen to a variety of texts for information and pleasure independently or as part of a group.

"Emperors of the Ice"

Now it's time to read the article. Have students sit next to you so that they can see the pictures and words while you read the article aloud.

   Read aloud the entire article. Emphasize Words to Know as you come to them. If appropriate, use the pictures to help show what each word means.

 Pay attention to the pronunciation of the word *Antarctica* (ant-AHRK-tih-kuh).

Check Your Reading

"Emperors of the Ice"

Have students retell the article in their own words to develop grammar, vocabulary, comprehension, and fluency skills. When finished, **ask students the following questions** to check comprehension and encourage discussion.

- ▸ What is the topic of this article? penguins
- ▸ What question did you ask yourself to figure out the topic? What is this article mostly about?
- ▸ Why do you think the author wrote this article? to inform, or to teach us about penguins
- ▸ Why does a father penguin cover an egg with his belly? to keep the egg warm
- ▸ What is an emperor penguin's favorite thing to eat? krill

Objectives

- Identify topic.
- Identify the purpose of a text.
- Answer questions requiring literal recall of details.

Explore "Emperors of the Ice"

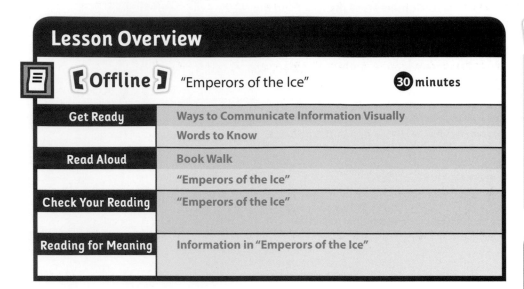

Lesson Overview

[Offline] "Emperors of the Ice" **30** minutes

Get Ready	Ways to Communicate Information Visually
	Words to Know
Read Aloud	Book Walk
	"Emperors of the Ice"
Check Your Reading	"Emperors of the Ice"
Reading for Meaning	Information in "Emperors of the Ice"

Materials

Supplied

- "Emperors of the Ice,"
  *K¹² World: Animals Around
  the World,* pp. 10–17

Also Needed

- yardstick

Keywords

literal recall – the ability to
describe information stated
directly in a text

visual text support –
a graphic feature that helps
a reader better understand
text, such as a picture, chart,
or map

Advance Preparation

Before working with students, spend a few minutes reviewing Words to Know.
Then review the Check Your Reading and Reading for Meaning activities to familiarize
yourself with the questions and answers.

Big Ideas

▸ Comprehension is enhanced when information is presented through more
than one learning modality; learning modalities are visual (seeing), auditory
(hearing), and kinesthetic (touching).
▸ Comprehension is facilitated by an understanding of physical presentation
(headings, subheads, graphics, and other features).

 **30 minutes**

"Emperors of the Ice"

Work **together** with students to complete offline Get Ready, Read Aloud, Check Your Reading, and Reading for Meaning activities.

Get Ready

Ways to Communicate Information Visually

Some readers learn and remember information more easily if they see it as well as hear it. Visual text supports such as **illustrations, maps, and charts provide information that readers can see**. These features can also provide information that goes beyond what is written in the text. **Seeing and hearing information together** helps readers gain a deeper understanding of ideas in an article than just hearing the information would.

1. Open the *K¹² World: Animals Around the World* magazine, and turn to page 10 of the "Emperors of the Ice" article. Point to the landscape photograph at the top of the page.

   Say: This is a picture of what Antarctica looks like. It's included in the article so we can get a better idea of what it's like where emperor penguins live.

   ► What does Antarctica look like? It's covered with snow and ice.
   ► Do you think it's cold in Antarctica? Yes

2. Point to the drawings of icicles at the top of page 10.

   ► Why do you think there are icicles at the top of the page? to show it's cold where emperor penguins live

3. Turn to page 14 and point to the photograph of the emperor penguins walking in a line.

   Say: The article tells us that every year, the emperor penguins take a long walk, or journey.

   ► Why do you think this picture is here? to show how they walk

---

Words to Know

Before reading "Emperors of the Ice,"

1. Have students say each word aloud.

2. Ask students if they know what each word means.

   ► If students know a word's meaning, have them define it and use it in a sentence.
   ► If students don't know a word's meaning, read them the definition and discuss the word with them.

chick – a baby bird
continent – one of seven large land masses on the earth
flippers – the flat limbs of a sea animal, such as a penguin or seal, which are used for swimming
journey – a long trip
krill – very tiny shrimplike animals that live in the sea

Objectives

- Identify the purpose of and information provided by illustrations, titles, charts, and graphs.
- Increase concept and content vocabulary.
- Use new vocabulary in written and spoken sentences.

Read Aloud

Book Walk

Prepare students by taking them on a Book Walk of "Emperors of the Ice." Scan the magazine article together to revisit the text.

1. Turn to today's selection.

2. Point to and read aloud the **title of the article**.

3. Have students look at the **pictures** in the article. Answers to questions may vary.

   ▶ What have you learned about emperor penguins by looking at the pictures?

   ▶ What is your favorite picture in the article, and why?

Objectives
- Activate prior knowledge by previewing text and/or discussing topic.
- Read and listen to a variety of texts for information and pleasure independently or as part of a group.

"Emperors of the Ice"

Now it's time to read the article. Have students sit next to you so that they can see the pictures and words while you read the article aloud.

Read aloud the entire article. Tell students to look closely at the pictures and other visual supports while you read to see if they can discover more information than what they hear in the article.

Check Your Reading

"Emperors of the Ice"

Have students retell the article in their own words to develop grammar, vocabulary, comprehension, and fluency skills. When finished, **ask students the following questions** to check comprehension and encourage discussion. If students have trouble responding to a question, **help them locate the answer in the article**.

Objectives
- Answer questions requiring literal recall of details.

- An emperor penguin is a bird with wings. Does that mean it can fly? No How do emperor penguins use their wings? They use them like flippers to swim.
- Why do emperor penguins march for days and days over snow and ice? to go to a place where they can have babies
- Why does a mother penguin leave her egg with the father penguin? She needs to go back to the sea to eat.
- How does a father penguin keep the egg warm? He covers it with his belly; he puts the egg on his feet to keep it off the cold ice.
- How big is a newborn emperor penguin chick? about the size of a banana

Reading for Meaning

Information in "Emperors of the Ice"

Ask students the following questions to check their understanding of text features.

Objectives
- Identify the purpose of and information provided by illustrations, titles, charts, and graphs.

1. Point to the map on page 10.

    ▶ Why is there a map on this page? to show where emperor penguins live
    ▶ Where is Antarctica? the bottom of the world; the South Pole

2. Point to the yardstick on page 11.

    ▶ Why is there a yardstick next to the penguin? to show how tall an emperor penguin is
    ▶ How tall is an emperor penguin? three feet
    ▶ Would you say that an emperor penguin is a big bird or a small bird? big; If students have trouble answering this question, stand a yardstick on end and tell students that an emperor penguin is as tall as the stick; have students stand next to the yardstick to better comprehend the height.

3. Point to the picture of the emperor penguin wearing a hat on page 12.

    ▶ Why is there a picture of an emperor penguin wearing a top hat and a bow tie? because the article says some people think a penguin looks like it's wearing a fancy dress suit

4. Point to the picture of the emperor penguins swimming underwater on page 12.

    ▶ Why is it important to include this picture in the article? to show that penguins are good swimmers; to show how penguins use their wings like flippers to swim through water

5. Point to the picture of krill at the top of page 13.

    ▶ What does this picture show? krill
    ▶ Why is this picture included in the article? to show what emperor penguins eat and what krill look like
    ▶ What are krill? tiny shrimplike sea animals

6. Point to the picture of the penguin eating krill at the bottom of page 13.

    ▶ What does this a picture show? an emperor penguin eating krill
    ▶ Why does the picture show an emperor penguin holding a bowl of krill and tossing some in its mouth? to show that emperor penguins enjoy eating krill the same way we enjoy eating a favorite snack

Review "Emperors of the Ice"

Lesson Overview

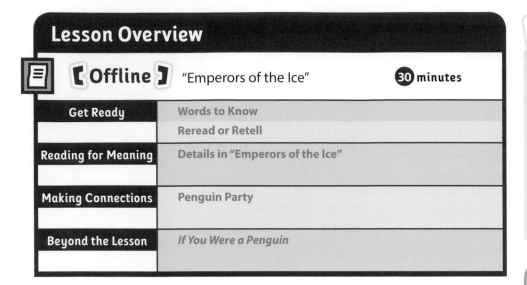

Get Ready	Words to Know
	Reread or Retell
Reading for Meaning	Details in "Emperors of the Ice"
Making Connections	Penguin Party
Beyond the Lesson	*If You Were a Penguin*

Offline — "Emperors of the Ice" — **30** minutes

Big Ideas

Comprehension entails an understanding of the organizational patterns of text.

Materials

Supplied
- "Emperors of the Ice," *K¹² World: Animals Around the World*, pp. 10–17
- *K¹² Language Arts Activity Book*, p. LC 33

Also Needed
- crayons

Keywords

detail – a piece of information in a text

informational text – text written to explain and give information on a topic

 **30** minutes

"Emperors of the Ice"

Work **together** with students to complete offline Get Ready, Reading for Meaning, Making Connections, and Beyond the Lesson activities.

Get Ready •••

Words to Know

Ask students to define the following words and use them in a sentence:

chick   flippers   krill
continent   journey

Correct any incorrect or vague definitions.

Objectives
- Increase concept and content vocabulary.
- Use new vocabulary in written and spoken sentences.

Reread or Retell

If you'd like to, reread the article to students. Otherwise, have students retell the article using the pictures as a guide, or move on to the next activity.

Reading for Meaning ••

Details in "Emperors of the Ice"

Tell students that nonfiction articles are filled with details about the topic. However, one detail isn't automatically as important as another. **Details that help readers better understand the topic of an article are important.** Other details might be interesting, but they aren't essential to remember. For example, it's important to know that pandas are an endangered species; it's interesting to know that a panda cub born at the National Zoo is named Tai Shan, but it doesn't help us know more about pandas. Learning to recognize the most important details helps good readers sort through information and make decisions about what they should remember.

Objectives
- Identify facts in informational text.
- Distinguish the most important details from less important details in text.

1. Ask students the following questions to check understanding of facts and details.

   ▸ How do penguins use their wings? to swim underwater   Is this an important detail about penguins? Yes
   ▸ How does a penguin chick stay warm? It stays under its father's belly; it sits on its father's feet.

2. **Read aloud** these two statements:

   Penguins have special feathers that keep them warm and dry. Black and white feathers make penguins look like they're wearing a fancy suit.

   ▸ Which detail is more important? the first one

3. **Read aloud** these two statements:

> Some people call Antarctica the "bottom of the world." Penguins have to find food in the water because they can't find much on the land.

   ▸ Which detail is more important? the second one

4. **Read aloud** these two statements:

> Penguins march from their homes by the sea to a place where they can have babies. Penguins march even when the wind blows.

   ▸ Which detail is more important? the first one

Making Connections

Penguin Party

Have students dictate an important detail about emperor penguins to reinforce the difference between important details and less important details.

1. Have students color the pictures of emperor penguins on page LC 33 in *K¹² Language Arts Activity Book*. They should look at pictures of emperor penguins in the article to help them recall the black-and-white coloring pattern.

2. Have students tell an **important detail** about emperor penguins. Possibilities include the following:

   ▸ Emperor penguins live in Antarctica.
   ▸ Emperor penguins like to eat krill.
   ▸ Emperor penguins use their flat wings like flippers to swim underwater.

3. Write the fact that students dictate on the Activity Book page.

Objectives

• Distinguish the most important details from less important details in text.

Beyond the Lesson ....

⊕ OPTIONAL: *If You Were a Penguin*

This activity is for students who have extra time and would benefit from hearing another book on the same topic. Feel free to skip this activity.

Objectives

- Compare and contrast two texts on the same topic.

1. Go to a library and look for a copy of *If You Were a Penguin* by Wendell and Florence Minor.

2. Lead a Book Walk, and then read aloud the book.

3. Ask students to tell new facts they've learned about penguins.

4. Have students describe how *If You Were a Penguin* and "Emperors of the Ice" are alike and different.

5. Have them tell which text they like best, and why.

Introduce *Make Way for Ducklings*

Unit Overview

In this unit, students will explore the theme of *Helping Hands* through the following reading selections:
▶ *Make Way for Ducklings*
▶ "The Elves and the Shoemaker"

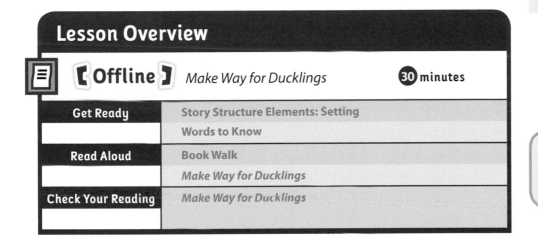

Lesson Overview

[Offline] *Make Way for Ducklings*		**30** minutes
Get Ready	Story Structure Elements: Setting	
	Words to Know	
Read Aloud	Book Walk	
	Make Way for Ducklings	
Check Your Reading	*Make Way for Ducklings*	

Advance Preparation

Read *Make Way for Ducklings* before beginning the Read Aloud activities, to locate Words to Know within the text.

Big Ideas

▶ Comprehension requires an understanding of story structure.
▶ Books have a front cover, a back cover, and a spine.
▶ The front cover displays the title of the book.

[Materials]

Supplied
● *Make Way for Ducklings* by Robert McCloskey

Story Synopsis
A mother and her ducklings are helped by a friendly policeman as they walk from one part of Boston to another.

Keywords
setting – when and where a story takes pace

[Offline] 🔟 minutes

Make Way for Ducklings

Work **together** with students to complete offline Get Ready, Read Aloud, and Check Your Reading activities.

Get Ready ··

Story Structure Elements: Setting
Explore the story structure element of setting.

1. Tell students that the **setting is where and when a story takes place**. Some stories have only one setting, while others have several. Good readers listen to the story and look at the pictures to figure out where and when a story takes place. They also look and listen carefully to find out if and when the setting changes.

2. Have students practice listening for a story's setting.

   Say: Listen to this story: Marco and his grandpa had fun playing at the park on Tuesday morning. Then they had lunch at a fancy restaurant. Next Grandpa took Marco to the movies. Marco was very tired and took a nap when he got home late in the afternoon.

   ▸ **Where** does the beginning of the story take place? at the park
   ▸ **When** does the beginning of the story take place? Tuesday morning
   ▸ Other than the park, **where else** does the story take place? a fancy restaurant; the movies; Marco's home
   ▸ **When** does the end of the story take place? late in the afternoon

> **Objectives**
> - Identify setting.
> - Build vocabulary through listening, reading, and discussion.
> - Use new vocabulary in written and spoken sentences.

Words to Know
Before reading *Make Way for Ducklings,*

1. Have students say each word aloud.

2. Ask students if they know what each word means.

   ▸ If students know a word's meaning, have them define it and use it in a sentence.
   ▸ If students don't know a word's meaning, read them the definition and discuss the word with them.

bank – the raised area at the edge of a river, pond, or canal
beckon – to signal someone to come to you
headquarters – the main police station
molt – to lose feathers so new ones can grow
pond – a body of water that is smaller than a lake
responsibility –a duty or job that you must do
traffic – cars moving on a street

TIP If students are familiar with the word *bank* meaning "a place to keep money," explain that some words can have more than one meaning.

Read Aloud

Book Walk

Prepare students by taking them on a Book Walk of *Make Way for Ducklings*. Scan the book together, and ask students to make predictions about the story.

1. Ask students to point to the front cover of the book, and then have them point to the back cover.

2. Have students look at the pictures on the cover.

3. Have them point to the **title**, and then read aloud the title.

   ► What do you think the book is about? Answers will vary.

4. Have students point to the name of the **author**. Read aloud the name of the author.

5. Have students locate the **title page** (in this book, it's the page with the book title, author's name, and a drawing of a duck).

   ► What information is found on the title page? the book title; the name of the author

6. Look through the book. Have students describe what they see in the **pictures**. Answers to questions may vary.

   ► Where do you think the story takes place?
   ► What do you think might happen in the story?

Objectives

- Identify front cover, back cover, title page, and title of book.
- Make predictions based on title, illustrations, and/or context clues.
- Read and listen to a variety of texts for information and pleasure independently or as part of a group.

Make Way for Ducklings

Now it's time to read the story. Have students sit next to you so that they can see the pictures and words while you read the story aloud.

Read aloud the entire story. Emphasize Words to Know as you come to them. If appropriate, use the pictures to help show what each word means.

Check Your Reading

Make Way for Ducklings

Have students retell the story in their own words to develop grammar, vocabulary, comprehension, and fluency skills. When finished, **ask students the following questions** to check understanding of setting and general comprehension of the story.

- ► Does this story have more than one setting? Yes
- ► What are Mr. and Mrs. Mallard doing at the beginning of the story? looking for a place to live
- ► Where do Mr. and Mrs. Mallard first land when they get too tired to fly anymore? Possible answers: Boston; a pond; the Public Garden
- ► Where does the middle of the story take place? on an island in the river
- ► How many eggs does Mrs. Mallard lay? eight
- ► Where does the end of the story take place? the Public Garden; the pond; an island in the pond

Objectives

- Identify setting.
- Answer questions requiring literal recall of details.

Explore *Make Way for Ducklings*

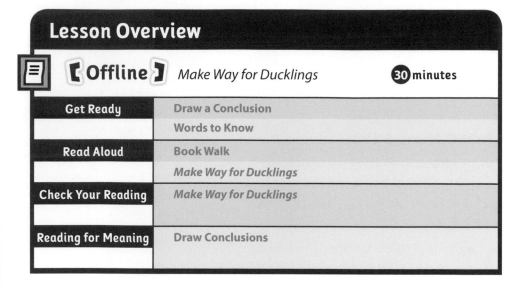

Lesson Overview

	[Offline] *Make Way for Ducklings*	**30** minutes
Get Ready	Draw a Conclusion	
	Words to Know	
Read Aloud	Book Walk	
	Make Way for Ducklings	
Check Your Reading	*Make Way for Ducklings*	
Reading for Meaning	Draw Conclusions	

[Materials]

Supplied
- *Make Way for Ducklings* by Robert McCloskey

Keywords

draw a conclusion – to make a decision about something not stated directly in a text by considering information provided and what you know from past experience

Advance Preparation

Before working with students, spend a few minutes reviewing Words to Know. Then review the Check Your Reading and Reading for Meaning activities to familiarize yourself with the questions and answers.

Big Ideas

▶ Comprehension entails actively thinking about what is being read.
▶ Comprehension is facilitated when readers connect new information to information previously learned.

[Offline] 30 minutes

Make Way for Ducklings

Work **together** with students to complete offline Get Ready, Read Aloud, Check Your Reading, and Reading for Meaning activities.

Get Ready

Draw a Conclusion

Explain to students that sometimes an author doesn't tell readers all they need to understand a story. Good readers look for clues in the words and pictures to help them figure out what the author has not directly stated. Good readers also think about what they know from personal experience. When readers do this, they **draw a conclusion**. A conclusion is based on what they read and see, together with their knowledge learned from personal experience.

1. Model how to draw a conclusion.

   Say: I will read a sentence, and then I will draw a conclusion: Every time Sandy wants a sandwich, she asks her mother to make peanut butter and jelly. I can draw a conclusion that peanut butter and jelly is Sandy's favorite sandwich. I think this because she always asks for this type of sandwich, and I know that if I choose the same type of food over and over, it's because it's one of my favorites.

2. **Read aloud** the following paragraph, and then help students draw a conclusion:

   Christy snacked on popcorn, peanuts, cotton candy, and fudge at the fair. That night, Christy had a bad stomachache.

   ► Why do you think Christy had a bad stomachache? She ate too many snacks at the fair.
   ► How do you know this? Guide students to think about a time when they may have eaten too much and, as a result, gotten a stomachache.

3. Tell students that they should look for clues in *Make Way for Ducklings* as they listen to the story and look at the pictures.

Words to Know

Before reading *Make Way for Ducklings*,

1. Have students say each word aloud.

2. Ask students if they know what each word means.

   ► If students know a word's meaning, have them define it and use it in a sentence.
   ► If students don't know a word's meaning, read them the definition and discuss the word with them.

> **Objectives**
> - Draw conclusions using text, illustrations, and/or prior knowledge.
> - Support conclusions using text, illustrations, and/or prior knowledge.
> - Build vocabulary through listening, reading, and discussion.
> - Use new vocabulary in written and spoken sentences.

bank – the raised area at the edge of a river, pond, or canal
beckon – to signal someone to come to you
headquarters – the main police station
molt – to lose feathers so new ones can grow
pond – a body of water that is smaller than a lake
responsibility –a duty or job that you must do
traffic – cars moving on a street

Read Aloud

Book Walk

Prepare students by taking them on a Book Walk of *Make Way for Ducklings*. Scan the book together.

1. Read aloud the **book title**.

2. Have students locate the name of the **author**. Read the name of the author.

3. Look through the book. Have students describe what they see in the **pictures**.

   ▸ Why might the ducks be looking for a new place to live at the beginning of the story? **Answers will vary.**
   ▸ After looking at the pictures, do you think this story is happening now or in the past? Point to the pictures of cars to help students draw the conclusion that the story happens in the past.

Objectives
- Draw conclusions using text, illustrations, and/or prior knowledge.
- Read and listen to a variety of texts for information and pleasure independently or as part of a group.

Make Way for Ducklings

Now it's time to read the story. Have students sit next to you so that they can see the pictures and words while you read the story aloud.

    Read aloud the entire story. Remind students that both the words and the pictures give clues to help them understand parts of the story that aren't directly stated by the author.

Check Your Reading

Make Way for Ducklings

Have students retell the story in their own words to develop grammar, vocabulary, comprehension, and fluency skills. When finished, **ask students the following questions** to check comprehension and encourage discussion.

▸ What do the people on the swan boat feed the ducks? **peanuts**
▸ Why do Mr. and Mrs. Mallard think the island in the river is a good place to make a nest? **because it's quiet; because it's close to the Public Garden**
▸ Why can't Mrs. Mallard visit Michael after she lays her eggs? **She has to sit on the eggs to keep them warm.**

Objectives
- Answer questions requiring literal recall of details.

- What is something Mrs. Mallard teaches the ducklings? Possible answers: how to swim; how to dive; how to walk in a line; to come when they are called
- Who is the first one to help Mrs. Mallard and her ducklings get across the street? Michael; the policeman   Who helps next? the four policemen sent from headquarters

Reading for Meaning

Draw Conclusions

Remind students that sometimes they can figure out something that the author doesn't state directly by using clues in the words and the pictures, and by thinking about their own experiences. Ask the following questions to check their understanding of how to draw and support a conclusion.

1. Point to the picture of the swan boat, and **read aloud**:

   "... a strange enormous bird came by. It was pushing a boat full of people, and there was a man sitting on its back."

   - What do the ducks think they see? a big bird
   - How do you know? Mr. Mallard says "good morning" to it.
   - What is it really? a boat
   - How do you know? The picture shows that it's a boat; also, guide students to recognize that they already know that a real swan would not be so large.

2. Point to the pictures of the kids riding their bikes, and **read aloud**:

   "This is no place for babies, with all those horrid things rushing about."

   - What are the horrid things? children on bikes
   - How do you know? The picture shows a boy on his bike knocking over one of the ducks.

3. Point to the picture of the policeman feeding peanuts to the ducks, and **read aloud**:

   "... they met a policeman called Michael. Michael fed them peanuts, and after that the Mallards called on Michael every day."

   - How does Michael feel about the ducks? He likes the ducks; he wants to help the ducks.
   - How do you know? He feeds them every day; he helps the mother duck and her babies cross the street safely later in the story.
   - What does it tell you about the ducks? They like peanuts.
   - How do you know? They come back every day for more.

TIP If students have trouble answering a question, reread the sentence or paragraph slowly, and pause to discuss what students see in the picture(s) related to the text.

Objectives

- Draw conclusions using text, illustrations, and/or prior knowledge.
- Support conclusions using text, illustrations, and/or prior knowledge.

Review *Make Way for Ducklings*

Lesson Overview

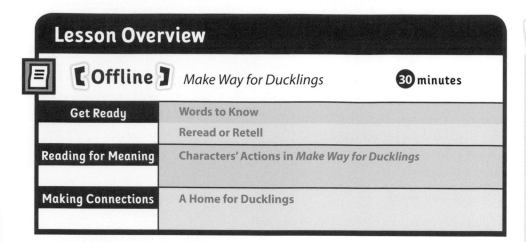

[Offline] *Make Way for Ducklings*   **30** minutes

Get Ready	Words to Know
	Reread or Retell
Reading for Meaning	Characters' Actions in *Make Way for Ducklings*
Making Connections	A Home for Ducklings

Big Ideas

Comprehension is facilitated when readers connect new information to information previously learned.

Materials

Supplied

- *Make Way for Ducklings* by Robert McCloskey
- *K¹² Language Arts Activity Book*, p. LC 35

Also Needed

- crayons
- scissors, round-end safety
- glue stick
- paper, drawing

Keywords

character – a person or animal in a story

draw a conclusion – to make a decision about something not stated directly in a text by considering information provided and what you know from past experience

 **30 minutes**

Make Way for Ducklings

Work **together** with students to complete offline Get Ready, Reading for Meaning, and Making Connections activities.

Get Ready

Words to Know

Ask students to define the following words and use them in a sentence:

bank	**molt**	**responsibility**
beckon	**pond**	**traffic**
headquarters		

Correct any incorrect or vague definitions.

Reread or Retell

If you'd like to, reread the story to students. Otherwise, have students retell the story using the pictures as a guide, or move on to the next activity.

> **Objectives**
> - Identify details that explain characters' actions.
> - Build vocabulary through listening, reading, and discussion.
> - Use new vocabulary in written and spoken sentences.

Reading for Meaning

Characters' Actions in Make Way for Ducklings

Remind students that a **character** is a person or animal in a story. Tell students that you will be discussing the characters in *Make Way for Ducklings*, and how they act. To better understand characters' actions, it's helpful to think about our own actions in different situations.

> **Objectives**
> - Identify details that explain characters' actions.

- ► Did you ever feed an animal in the wild or at the zoo? Why? Answers will vary.
- ► Did you ever stop to help someone? Why or why not? Answers will vary.

Verify that students understand why characters do things in the story by asking the following questions:

- ► Why do Mr. and Mrs. Mallard stop at the Public Garden at the beginning of the story? They are too tired to fly any farther; they're looking for a place to live.
- ► Why do Mr. and Mrs. Mallard follow the swan boat around the pond? to get the peanuts people throw to them
- ► Why do Mr. and Mrs. Mallard decide not to build their nest in the Public Garden? It's too dangerous.
- ► Why does Mr. Mallard decide to take a trip? to see what the rest of the river is like
- ► Why does Michael the policeman stop traffic? to help Mrs. Mallard and the ducklings cross the street safely   How does he know they need help? They stand by the side of the road and keep quacking loudly.
- ► Why does Michael call Clancy at headquarters? He knows the ducks will need more help crossing the street later on.

Making Connections

A Home for Ducklings

Help students draw conclusions about why the ducks choose a particular location to raise their family, and then illustrate the ducks' home to include items that meet their needs.

1. Have students color and cut out the ducks on page LC 35 in *K¹² Language Arts Activity Book*.

2. Have them think about why Mr. and Mrs. Mallard chose to build a nest on the island in the river.

3. Have students look at the pictures that show Mr. and Mrs. Mallard on the island with their nest. Ask the following question, and discuss what students see in the pictures.

   ▸ What did the island have that the ducks needed to raise their family?
   a place for a nest; water; food

4. Have students arrange and glue the cut-out ducks on the drawing paper. Then have them draw a home for the ducks. Suggestions for items to draw include

   ▸ A nest
   ▸ A place for the nest, such as the island
   ▸ Water for drinking and learning to swim and dive
   ▸ Plants to eat and to protect the nest
   ▸ Peanuts that people feed to the ducks

Objectives

- Respond to text through art, writing, and/or drama.
- Draw conclusions using text, illustrations, and/or prior knowledge.

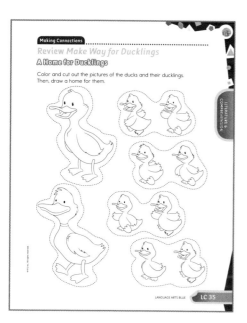

Introduce "The Elves and the Shoemaker"

Lesson Overview

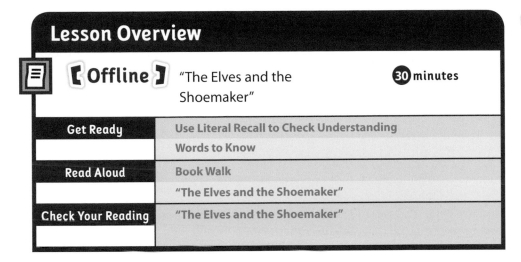

	Offline	"The Elves and the Shoemaker"	30 minutes
Get Ready		Use Literal Recall to Check Understanding	
		Words to Know	
Read Aloud		Book Walk	
		"The Elves and the Shoemaker"	
Check Your Reading		"The Elves and the Shoemaker"	

Advance Preparation

Read "The Elves and the Shoemaker" before beginning the Read Aloud activities, to locate Words to Know within the text.

Big Ideas

▸ Comprehension requires the reader to self-monitor understanding.
▸ Comprehension entails asking and answering questions about the text.

Materials

Supplied

- "The Elves and the Shoemaker," *K¹² Read Aloud Treasury*, pp. 88–92

Story Synopsis

A poor, tired shoemaker gets some unexpected and anonymous help with his work. Who could be behind it?

Keywords

literal recall – the ability to describe information stated directly in a text

self-monitor – to notice if you do or do not understand what you are reading

table of contents – a list at the start of a book that gives the titles of the book's stories, poems, articles, chapters, or nonfiction pieces and the pages where they can be found

[Offline] 30 minutes

"The Elves and the Shoemaker"

Work **together** with students to complete offline Get Ready, Read Aloud, and Check Your Reading activities.

Get Ready

Use Literal Recall to Check Understanding

Introduce the concept of **literal recall**, the ability to recall what has been stated directly in a text.

1. Tell students that it's important for readers to remember information stated directly in a story they have heard or read. One way to check this is by asking questions whose answers can be found right in the story. These types of questions are sometimes called "right there" questions because we can find the answers "right there" in the words of the story.

2. **Read aloud**:

   Kiki learned how to ice skate today. Her mother took her out to the frozen pond behind their house. Then her mother showed her what to do. Kiki was nervous at first. But before she knew it, Kiki was gliding across the ice like a swan.

3. Model answering "right there" questions based on the story.

   Say: If someone asked me what Kiki learned today, I would say she learned how to ice skate. I know this because it says so right there in the story. I can put my finger right on the answer.

4. Demonstrate how you can put your finger right on answers in the story. Read aloud the story again, and then ask the following questions:

   ▸ Where is the pond? behind Kiki's house   How do you know this? It says so right there in the story.

   ▸ Who shows Kiki how to ice skate? her mother

 Literal recall is a stepping stone for thinking more deeply about text.

Objectives
- Answer questions requiring literal recall of details.
- Build vocabulary through listening, reading, and discussion.
- Use new vocabulary in written and spoken sentences.

Words to Know

Before reading "The Elves and the Shoemaker,"

1. Have students say each word aloud.

2. Ask students if they know what each word means.

   ▸ If students know a word's meaning, have them define it and use it in a sentence.

   ▸ If students don't know a word's meaning, read them the definition and discuss the word with them.

bench –a table in a workshop
customer – people who buy things from a seller
fine – very good or excellent
leather – animal skin that is used to make things, like shoes
price – the amount of money you must pay to buy something
ragged – old and torn

Read Aloud

Book Walk

Prepare students by taking them on a Book Walk of "The Elves and the Shoemaker." Scan the story together.

1. Have students turn to the **table of contents**. Ask them to explain what is found in the table of contents.

2. Help students find today's selection, and turn to that page.

3. Point to and read aloud the **title of the story**.

4. Have students look at the **pictures** of the story. Answers to questions may vary.

   ▸ What do you think the story is about?
   ▸ Where do you think the story takes place?
   ▸ Did anyone ever secretly do you a favor? What was it?
   ▸ Did *you* ever secretly do someone a favor? What did you do?

Objectives
- Identify table of contents.
- Make predictions based on title, illustrations, and/or context clues.
- Listen and respond to texts representing a variety of cultures, time periods, and traditions.

"The Elves and the Shoemaker"

Now it's time to read the story. Have students sit next to you so that they can see the pictures and words while you read the story aloud.

   Read aloud the entire story. Emphasize Words to Know as you come to them. If appropriate, use the pictures to help show what each word means.

Check Your Reading

"The Elves and the Shoemaker"

Have students retell the story in their own words to develop grammar, vocabulary, comprehension, and fluency skills. When finished, **ask students the following literal recall questions** to check understanding and encourage discussion.

Objectives
- Answer questions requiring literal recall of details.

   ▸ Where does the shoemaker live? in a little town   How do you know this? It says so right in the story.
   ▸ Where does the shoemaker put the pieces of leather that he cuts out before he goes to bed? on his bench
   ▸ How does the shoemaker react when he finds the finished shoes in the morning? He's surprised; his eyes get big.
   ▸ What does the shoemaker do with the shoes he finds in the morning? He sells them to a customer.
   ▸ At first, does the shoemaker know who finishes his shoes for him? No

Explore "The Elves and the Shoemaker"

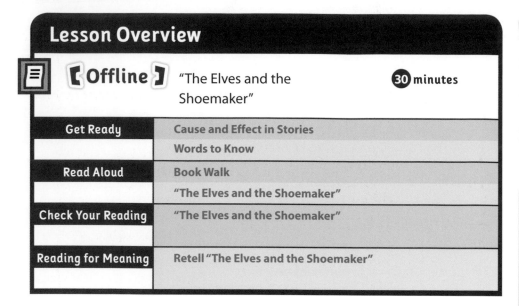

Lesson Overview

| **Offline** | "The Elves and the Shoemaker" | **30** minutes |

Get Ready	Cause and Effect in Stories
	Words to Know
Read Aloud	Book Walk
	"The Elves and the Shoemaker"
Check Your Reading	"The Elves and the Shoemaker"
Reading for Meaning	Retell "The Elves and the Shoemaker"

Materials

Supplied
- "The Elves and the Shoemaker," *K¹² Read Aloud Treasury,* pp. 88–92

Keywords

cause – the reason something happens

effect – the result of a cause

retelling – using your own words to tell a story that you have listened to or read

self-monitor – to notice if you do or do not understand what you are reading

Advance Preparation

Before working with students, spend a few minutes reviewing Words to Know. Then review the Check Your Reading and Reading for Meaning activities to familiarize yourself with the questions and answers.

Big Ideas

- Comprehension requires an understanding of story structure.
- Comprehension requires the reader to self-monitor understanding.

【 Offline 】 ⏱ 30 minutes

"The Elves and the Shoemaker"

Work **together** with students to complete offline Get Ready, Read Aloud,
Check Your Reading, and Reading for Meaning activities.

Get Ready

Cause and Effect in Stories

Introduce the concept of cause and effect in stories.

1. Tell students that doing one thing can make another thing happen. The thing
   that someone does is called the **cause**, and the thing that happens is called the
   effect.

2. Explain that sometimes the cause and effect happen to things you can see and
   touch. Other times, they are things you say or do. Examples of cause and effect
   are all around us.

   ▶ **Cause:** You drop a glass.
      Effect: The glass breaks.
   ▶ **Cause:** You are hungry.
      Effect: You eat a sandwich.
   ▶ **Cause:** You say "thank you" to a clerk.
      Effect: The clerk says "you're welcome" back to you.

3. Have students practice figuring out cause and effect relationships.
   Say: There's a dent in the roof of Martin's toy car. What might have caused this?
   Possible answers: He dropped it; he stepped on it; it fell off a shelf.
   Say: Alicia won the race. What might happen next? Possible answers: She might
   jump for joy; she might get a medal.

4. Tell students that they will hear more examples of cause and effect in the story
   "The Elves and the Shoemaker."

Objectives
- Describe cause-and-effect relationships in text.
- Build vocabulary through listening, reading, and discussion.
- Use new vocabulary in written and spoken sentences.

Words to Know

Before reading "The Elves and the Shoemaker,"

1. Have students say each word aloud.

2. Ask students if they know what each word means.

   ▶ If students know a word's meaning, have them define it and use it in a
     sentence.
   ▶ If students don't know a word's meaning, read them the definition and
     discuss the word with them.

bench – a table in a workshop
customer – a person who buys things from a seller
fine – very good or excellent
leather – animal skin that is used to make things, like shoes
price – the amount of money you must pay to buy something
ragged – old and torn

Read Aloud

Book Walk

Prepare students by taking them on a Book Walk of "The Elves and the Shoemaker." Scan the story together to revisit the characters and events.

1. Turn to today's selection. Point to and read aloud the **title of the story**.

2. Have students look at the **pictures** of the story. Answers to questions may vary.

   ▸ Which picture shows the shoemaker?
   ▸ Which picture shows the elves?
   ▸ Which picture shows someone making shoes?

Objectives
- Identify character(s).
- Listen and respond to texts representing a variety of cultures, time periods, and traditions.

"The Elves and the Shoemaker"

Now it's time to read the story. Have students sit next to you so that they can see the pictures and words while you read the story aloud.

Read aloud the entire story. Tell students to listen carefully to hear how things that characters in the story do cause other things to happen. **Remember: The thing that someone does is the *cause*, and the thing that happens because of it is the *effect*.**

Check Your Reading

"The Elves and the Shoemaker"

Ask students the following questions to check their understanding of cause-and-effect relationships.

Objectives
- Describe cause-and-effect relationships in text.

▸ Why does the shoemaker leave the cut-out leather on the bench on the first night? It's too late to finish making the shoes; he's tired.
▸ What happens because of this? The elves come and finish the shoes for him.
▸ Do you think the elves would have helped the shoemaker if he had finished making the shoes before he went to bed? Why or why not? Answers will vary.
▸ How does the poor shoemaker get the money to buy more leather? A customer buys the shoes that the elves made.
▸ Why do the shoemaker and his wife hide behind a door? They want to see who is making the shoes.
▸ What happens after the elves do a dance? The shoemaker has good luck from that day on; the shoemaker is never sad again; the shoemaker always has money for leather.

Reading for Meaning

Retell "The Elves and the Shoemaker"
Revisit how and why good readers retell stories.

1. Remind students that retelling means using your own words to tell a story that you have listened to or read. **When good readers retell a story, they tell the most important things that happen in the beginning, middle, and end of the story.** They mention the characters and the things that the characters do and cause to happen.

2. Explain that good readers retell stories so they can check their understanding of a story.

3. Verify that students understand the concept of retelling and the idea of a beginning, middle, and end of a story.

   ▸ In what part of the story does the shoemaker first find a pair of new, finished shoes on his bench in the morning? the beginning   Retell that part of the story.
   ▸ In what part of the story does the shoemaker start to become rich? the middle   Retell that part of the story.
   ▸ In what part of the story do the shoemaker and his wife find out who is making the shoes? the end   Retell that part of the story.

 TIP Retelling a story is one way that good readers can self-monitor their comprehension.

Objectives
• Retell familiar stories.
• Retell the beginning, middle, and end of a story.

Review "The Elves and the Shoemaker"

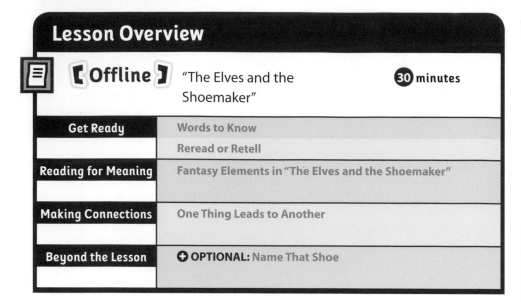

Lesson Overview

[Offline] "The Elves and the Shoemaker"   **30** minutes

Get Ready	Words to Know
	Reread or Retell
Reading for Meaning	Fantasy Elements in "The Elves and the Shoemaker"
Making Connections	One Thing Leads to Another
Beyond the Lesson	⊕ OPTIONAL: Name That Shoe

Big Ideas

Comprehension requires an understanding of story structure.

[Materials]

Supplied

- "The Elves and the Shoemaker," *K¹² Read Aloud Treasury,* pp. 88–92
- *K¹² Language Arts Activity Book,* p. LC 37

Keywords

cause – the reason something happens
effect – the result of a cause
fantasy – a story with characters, settings, or other elements that could not really exist

[Offline] 🕐 **30** minutes

"The Elves and the Shoemaker"

Work **together** with students to complete offline Get Ready, Reading for Meaning, Making Connections, and Beyond the Lesson activities.

Get Ready ....

Words to Know

Ask students to define the following words and use them in a sentence:

bench	fine	price
customer	leather	ragged

Correct any incorrect or vague definitions.

Objectives
- Build vocabulary through listening, reading, and discussion.
- Use new vocabulary in written and spoken sentences.

Reread or Retell

If you'd like to, reread the story to students. Otherwise, have students retell the story using the pictures as a guide, or move on to the next activity.

Reading for Meaning ....

Fantasy Elements in "The Elves and the Shoemaker"

Tell students that some stories have elements of fantasy. When something is **fantasy**, it isn't real. A story with fantasy elements has make-believe things in it. The parts of a story that are fantasy could never happen in the real world. For example, a pig is real, but a pig does not have wings and it cannot fly. Characters such as witches, fairies, elves, and giants are fantasy.

Objectives
- Distinguish fantasy from realistic text.

Ask students the following questions to check their understanding of fantasy and realistic text.

- ▶ Every day, the shoemaker cuts out leather to make shoes. Is this real or fantasy? real   How do you know? This is what shoemakers do in the real world.
- ▶ At night, the elves finish making the shoes for the shoemaker. Is this real or fantasy? fantasy   How can you tell? There are no elves in the real world.
- ▶ The shoemaker sells all the shoes he finds on his bench every morning. Eventually it makes him rich. Can this really happen? Yes, people can sell shoes and they can get rich.
- ▶ The shoemaker and his wife hide behind a door and peep through a crack. Is this real or fantasy? real   How can you tell? People can really do this.
- ▶ At the end of the story, the elves sing a little song. Is this real? Why or why not? No, it's not real because elves are fantasy.

Making Connections

One Thing Leads to Another

Guide students to demonstrate understanding of cause-and-effect relationships by matching each cause with its resulting effect.

1. Have students study the pictures on page LC 37 of *K¹² Language Arts Activity Book*.

2. Have students match a cause on the left with its effect on the right by drawing a line to connect the events.

3. When done, have them describe each cause-and-effect relationship.

Objectives
- Describe cause-and-effect relationships in text.

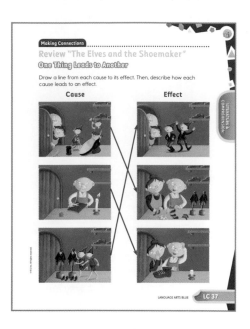

Beyond the Lesson

⊕ OPTIONAL: Name That Shoe

This activity is intended for students who have extra time and would benefit from making a personal connection to the story. Feel free to skip this activity.

1. Tell students that they get to be shoemakers and design a pair of shoes. Have them draw a pair of shoes they would like to own.

2. Have students describe their shoes.

   ▸ What are they made of? Where would you wear the shoes?

3. Turn to a page in "The Elves and the Shoemaker" that shows a pair of shoes made by the elves. Have students describe how their shoes are the same as the elves' and how they are different.

Objectives
- Make connections with text: text-to-text, text-to-self, text-to-world.